❀ ❀ ❀ ❀ ❀ ❀ ❀ ❀ ❀

The Big Book of Skits

❀ ❀ ❀ ❀ ❀ ❀ ❀ ❀ ❀

Other titles in the "Big Book" series

The Big Book of Skits

*36 short plays
for young actors*

Edited by
Sylvia E. Kamerman

Publishers   PLAYS, INC.   *Boston*

Library of Congress Cataloging-in-Publication Data

The big book of skits / edited by Sylvia E. Kamerman.
   p.   cm.
 Summary: A collection of thirty-five plays by various authors. Includes full production notes.
 ISBN 0-8238-0304-X
 1. Amateur plays. 2. Children's plays. [1. Plays—Collections.]
I. Kamerman, Sylvia E.
PN6119.9.B54   1996
812'.041—dc20   95-48020
                                                          CIP
                                                          AC

Manufactured in Canada

Contents

❋ ❋ ❋ ❋ ❋ ❋ ❋ ❋ ❋

The Big Book
of Skits

❋ ❋ ❋ ❋ ❋ ❋ ❋ ❋ ❋

A Flutter of Lace

by Bill Majeski

Heroes win damsels in this sentimental trio of romances. . . .

Characters

NARRATOR, *male*
HERB BIFFENBAFF, *a baseball star*
MARY ANN DREW
JACK DRIPPNER, *a poor but honest lad*
MR. PINCE-NEZ
JEAN, *his secretary*
LARRY SHAW, *airplane mechanic*
NORMA FENSTER
YOUNG WOMAN
SPECTATORS, *offstage voices*

SETTING: *Bare stage. A desk or table is at one side.*
AT RISE: NARRATOR *enters, carrying two books and a magazine, which he puts on table.*
NARRATOR (*To audience*): Most readers of romance novels are aware of the changes in them over the years. Change is inevitable. But looking back (*Picking up book*), the most common item once used to bring boy and girl together was (*Reaches into his pocket and pulls out a handkerchief*) a handkerchief. (*Pauses*) Yes, this simple object (*Holds it up*) brought about countless romances in the novels of years gone by. Novels like *All-Wool Morrison* or *Herb Biffenbaff Goes to College* always seemed to have a handkerchief as a catalyst to inspire a meeting of a boy and girl. For example . . . (*Opens book and begins to read*) "The roar of the crowd swelled in his ears as Herb Biffenbaff took a bat from the rack and stepped to the plate."

3

(HERB BIFFENBAFF *enters, bat in hand, and assumes batting stance at an imaginary home plate, center.*) "Seven thousand strong, spectators jammed the stands to see Fairmont play its arch-rival, Topper University."

SPECTATORS (*Calling from offstage*): Biffenbaff! Biffenbaff of Fairmont. Come on! You can do it!

NARRATOR (*Reading*): "The score was tied. It was the bottom of the ninth. The bases were loaded. Two men were out. The first pitch. A strike. Then he saw Mary Ann Drew, the dean's lovely daughter." (MARY ANN DREW, *holding lacy handkerchief, enters from opposite side of stage. HERB looks over at her, then resumes stance.*) "Mary Ann smiled shyly. The second pitch. Strike two. Herb looked at Mary Ann. She smiled at him again. Slowly a handkerchief fluttered to earth." (MARY ANN *lets her handkerchief flutter to the ground.*) "Herb turned to call her attention to it. As he did so, the pitcher released the spheroid." (HERB *turns his back to the imaginary pitcher and points to* MARY ANN's *handkerchief. Sound of a thud is heard.* HERB *stops still, then falls to floor.*) "The sound of ball on head reverberated around the stadium. Herb was down." (MARY ANN *crosses to* HERB, *kneels at his side.*) "And the cheers from the stands reached a roaring crescendo as the winning run was forced in from third."

SPECTATORS (*Calling from offstage*): Biffenbaff! Biffenbaff! Biffenbaff of Fairmont. You've done it again! (HERB *gets up and he and* MARY ANN *walk off, arm in arm.*)

NARRATOR (*Holding up handkerchief*): See what I mean? A handkerchief. It brought Herb and Mary Ann together, and I'm sure they lived happily ever after. . . . There was another type of story called the Horatio Alger tale. It's about a very poor lad, who worked his way up the ladder of success. They were books like *Paul the Peddler*. (*He picks up other book, opens it and begins to read.*) "Jack Drippner, tired from lifting 300-pound boxes of raisins onto freight cars, smiled in satisfaction at a job well done." (JACK *enters left and pantomimes lifting cartons.*) "Forty 300-pound boxes of raisins, and he hadn't dropped one. He had been on the job 24 hours without sleep, without water, without pay, to make sure the raisins went out on schedule. It was important they did because the boss, Mr. Pince-Nez, told him . . . (PINCE-NEZ *enters and addresses* JACK.)

PINCE-NEZ: Jack, son of Mr. and Mrs. Drippner, from a background of poverty, if we get the raisins out on time, I'll remember it. And someday, when I pass away . . .

JACK (*Eagerly*): Yes? Yes? What, Mr. Pince-Nez? (*By this time,* PINCE-NEZ *has turned and exited without replying.* JACK *goes back to work.*)

NARRATOR (*Reading*): "Mr. Pince-Nez *never* finished that sentence, but Jack worked harder and harder, anyway. He had saved his money, so someday he could go to college and study lock-making . . . a trade! (JEAN *enters right. She carries handkerchief.* JACK *notices her, smiles, and works even faster.*) "Hello, what's this? Jean, Mr. Pince-Nez's secretary, was smiling at Jack. Jack lifted more raisins than he had ever lifted before. Jack looked at her again. Slowly, a handkerchief fluttered to the floor." (JEAN *drops her handkerchief to the floor.* JACK *bends over to pick it up.*) "As he bent to retrieve the dainty linen, disaster struck." (*Sound of a crash is heard, and* JACK *falls, down and out.*) "Seven 300-pound boxes of raisins fell on him. Through the dim haze he heard voices . . ." (PINCE-NEZ *rushes on.* JEAN *looks down at* JACK.)

JEAN: He's cute.

PINCE-NEZ (*Angrily*): He's fired! (*Blackout.* JACK, JEAN, *and* PINCE-NEZ *exit. Lights come up.*)

NARRATOR (*Holding up handkerchief*): See what I mean? A handkerchief, again. . . . And then there was another type of romance. The slick-magazine love story. (*He picks up magazine, begins to read.*) "Larry Shaw looked carefully at the job he was working on." (LARRY SHAW *enters, in coveralls, carrying tools. He surveys what is meant to be an airplane motor. Then he bends down and pantomimes repairing it with tools.*) "He tinkered with the open-seat, one-wing monoplane. He uttered a tiny oath as a cranshaw bolt fell onto his foot." (LARRY *suits actions to words.*) "He had to get the plane fixed in time to win the Double Pylondo Handicap Race, for that meant $6,000, enough to start his own tiny unscheduled airline. And he had to do it by 8 o'clock, because Angela Harrison insisted he take her to the country club dance. Angela—rich, haughty, austere. As he slammed a flange tight, he heard a musical voice call cheerily. . . ." (NORMA FENSTER *enters from opposite side.*)

NORMA: Howdy, Flyboy, can you help me?

NARRATOR (*Reading*): "Larry gulped as he looked up into two of the loveliest eyes he had ever seen. He ran his hand through his wavy hair." (LARRY *runs hand through hair.*)

NORMA: You have grease in your hair.

NARRATOR (*Reading*): "Then she smiled again. And again."

NORMA: I hear you give flying lessons. I'd like you to teach me to fly, by nightfall, if possible.

NARRATOR (*Reading*): "Larry got angry. His twinkling, nay, laughing eyes became cold and hard."

LARRY (*Angrily*): Now, see here, young lady. I'm too busy to be talking with rich, spoiled playgirls. I suggest you leave.

NORMA (*Sadly*): I'm not a rich playgirl! (*Takes out handkerchief and dabs her eyes*) I'm but a mere dental assistant's assistant. Norma Fenster by name.

NARRATOR (*Reading*): "Larry felt ashamed. Slowly, a handkerchief fluttered to the earth." (NORMA *drops her handkerchief.* LARRY *sees the handkerchief and bends to pick it up.*) "Larry retrieved the handkerchief, but as he rose, he whacked his head against his three-tail, dove-tonsil carburetor, sending him sprawling." (LARRY *rises, then falls.*) "Norma rushed over to him, cradling his head in her arms." (NORMA *assists* LARRY.) "Slowly, Larry revived, and together the two walked off, their eyes meeting, their arms linked. (LARRY *and* NORMA *exit.* NARRATOR *closes the magazine, puts it back on table.*) Another handkerchief-inspired romance. But you see how things have changed. That never happens in today's romantic fiction. Lifestyles change. In today's society, the handkerchief is no longer a romance-inspiring device. (NARRATOR *puts his handkerchief into his pocket. As he removes his hand, he drops the handkerchief and it falls to the ground unnoticed. He turns and heads offstage.* YOUNG WOMAN *enters behind him.*)

YOUNG WOMAN (*Calling*): Pardon me, is this your handkerchief? (*She picks up handkerchief, as* NARRATOR *turns. She hands it to him. They smile at each other.*)

NARRATOR (*Slowly*): Why, yes. Yes, it is. I must have dropped it.

YOUNG WOMAN: Yes, I thought you did. (*They look at each other warmly. Then, arm in arm, they start to walk off slowly.* NARRATOR *turns to audience.*)

NARRATOR: Say, maybe times haven't changed as much as I thought! (*Curtain*)

THE END

Production Notes

A FLUTTER OF LACE

Characters: 5 male, 4 female. All parts, with the exception of Narrator and Pince-Nez, may be doubled and played by one boy and one girl. As many offstage voices as desired for Spectators.

Playing Time: 10 minutes.

Costumes: Herb, baseball uniform; Jack, work clothes; Mr. Pince-Nez, three-piece suit; Larry, mechanic's coveralls; women, outfits suitable to each period. Modern dress for others.

Properties: Two books; one magazine; four handkerchiefs; baseball bat; assorted boxes (if desired).

Setting: Bare stage, with desk or table at one side.

Lighting: No special effects.

Sound: Spectators calling encouragement from offstage; ball hitting batter in the head; sound of crash as indicated in text.

The Job Interview

by Robert Mauro

Confusion reigns at employment agency. . . .

Characters

MR. JOHNSON, *job counselor*
MS. PETERS, *job applicant*

TIME: *Monday morning.*
SETTING: *Sign hanging on backdrop reads,* ACME EMPLOYMENT AGENCY. IF THERE'S A JOB, WE'LL FIND IT. *Desk center is covered with papers and job applications. Phone and intercom are also on desk. Chair is at left of desk.*
AT RISE: MR. JOHNSON *enters carrying large pile of applications. He juggles them, then drops them all over the floor.*
MR. JOHNSON (*Picking up applications; discouraged*): Terrific. Just great. This is just what I need first thing on a Monday morning. And as usual, there are more applicants than there are jobs. (*Tries to put papers in order*) Look at this mess. They're all out of order. Where are the A's? (*He looks around helplessly, then throws applications on desk.*) We'll just have to start with (*Picks up application*) this one. Alice Peters. She wants to work in the Wild and Woolly Circus as a lion tamer. (*Sarcastically*) Good luck, lady. I hope you've had your tetanus shots. I hear those lions have sharp teeth. (*Sits behind desk and presses button on intercom*) Nancy, please send Ms. Peters in. (*After a moment,* MS. PETERS *enters, carrying briefcase.* MR. JOHNSON *stands and shakes her hand.*) Ms. Peters?
MS. PETERS: Yes. How do you do?
MR. JOHNSON: I'm Phil Johnson. Nice to meet you. (*Gestures to chair*) Please have a seat. (*They both sit.*) So—you actually want this sort of a job? (*He looks at application.*)

8

MS. PETERS (*Enthusiastically*): Oh, yes. I've loved playing with them ever since I was a little girl.

MR. JOHNSON (*Surprised*): You have? That must have been pretty scary.

MS. PETERS (*Puzzled*): Excuse me?

MR. JOHNSON: You like to work with animals?

MS. PETERS (*Confused*): Animals?

MR. JOHNSON: Yes. This place you'd like to work is a circus, you know.

MS. PETERS: A *circus?* (*Suddenly*) Oh, yes! I know what you mean. So was the last place I worked. At times, it was more like a zoo, especially at tax time.

MR. JOHNSON (*Puzzled*): At tax time?

MS. PETERS: Yes, sir. It was crazy. But I like working when the pressure is on. In fact, I do my best work under pressure.

MR. JOHNSON: Good. That's a point in your favor, because this sort of work involves a lot of pressure.

MS. PETERS: No problem. I knew that when I studied it at college.

MR. JOHNSON: You went to college to learn this?

MS. PETERS: Yes. (*Confidently*) I was a straight-A student. I also made Phi Beta Kappa.

MR. JOHNSON (*Shaking his head*): Amazing what they teach in college these days. Listen, Ms. Peters, you're way overqualified for this job.

MS. PETERS: I don't think so. (*Eagerly*) Look, Mr. Johnson, I really want this job. I'm a good worker. Give me a chance. You won't be sorry.

MR. JOHNSON (*Relenting*): O.K. It's up to you. You seem very eager to take the job, and we like that kind of enthusiasm.

MS. PETERS (*Pleased*): Great! Believe me, I'll make the Acme Employment Agency proud they selected me for the position.

MR. JOHNSON: Fine. That's what we like to hear. Now, I just have a few questions for you.

MS. PETERS: O.K. Ask away.

MR. JOHNSON: How do you feel about carrying water?

MS. PETERS (*Puzzled*): Excuse me?

MR. JOHNSON: Carrying water. As much as ten or twenty gallons at a time.

MS. PETERS (*Suddenly*): Oh! You mean for the water coolers! Aren't there custodial people who do that?

MR. JOHNSON: I'm not talking about water for the water coolers, Ms. Peters. It's for the animals.

MS. PETERS (*Offended*): Mr. Johnson, I really wish you wouldn't refer to my future coworkers as animals.

MR. JOHNSON: I'm sorry, but that's exactly what they are.

MS. PETERS (*Shaking her head; in disbelief*): This must be some place.

MR. JOHNSON (*Shrugging*): When you've seen one circus, you've seen them all. So I guess you don't mind carrying water or working with animals.

MS. PETERS: Mr. Johnson, all I know is that I need this job. If they're animals, they're animals. I'll work with them.

MR. JOHNSON: Good. Now, have you had all your shots?

MS. PETERS (*Puzzled*): Shots? I didn't think this job involved much travel.

MR. JOHNSON: On the contrary. You'll be traveling all over the United States, Canada, and Europe.

MS. PETERS (*Surprised*): I will?

MR. JOHNSON: Yes. Even Japan and China.

MS. PETERS (*Astounded*): Really? I thought I'd be working exclusively in Manhattan.

MR. JOHNSON: Only when you're at Madison Square Garden.

MS. PETERS: Oh, you mean when we put on a trade show?

MR. JOHNSON: Trade show? (*Shakes head*) Wait a minute. (*Looks at application*) You are Alice Peters, aren't you?

MS. PETERS: No. I'm Joan Peters.

MR. JOHNSON: Then you're not applying for the job of lion tamer in the Wild and Woolly Circus?

MS. PETERS: No. I'm applying for the job of computer systems analyst with Whitney, Whitney, and Shultz.

MR. JOHNSON: Oh, boy. I'm afraid there's been a little mix-up here.

MS. PETERS: Does this mean I won't be needing any shots?

MR. JOHNSON: No. (*Wryly*) Not unless you want to give me one. (*Apologetically*) I'm really sorry about this.

MS. PETERS (*In understanding tone*): That's all right. Accidents happen. So, what about the systems analyst position? I'm really interested in it.

MR. JOHNSON: Let me check on that for you. (*He looks through pile of applications, pulls one out.*) Ah, here's your application. (*Looks it over*) Yes. You're well qualified for that position. It pays quite well, and the benefits are excellent.

MS. PETERS (*Brightly*): That's great. When can I start?

MR. JOHNSON (*With nervous laugh*): Well, it seems that this high-paying systems analyst job . . .

MS. PETERS (*Interrupting; angrily*): Yeah? The one with all those excellent benefits?

MR. JOHNSON: Well . . . the systems analyst job was filled by the lion tamer. (MS. PETERS *screams and, shaking fist, approaches* MR. JOHNSON, *who rises and rushes toward exit, with* MS. PETERS *in angry pursuit. Quick curtain*)

THE END

Production Notes

THE JOB INTERVIEW

Characters: 1 male; 1 female.

Playing Time: 10 minutes.

Costumes: Mr. Johnson and Ms. Peters wear business suits. Ms. Peters carries a briefcase.

Setting: Acme Employment Agency. Sign reading ACME EMPLOYMENT AGENCY. IF THERE'S A JOB, WE'LL FIND IT is on backdrop. Desk center is covered with papers and job applications. Phone and intercom are also on desk. Chair is at left of desk.

Lighting and Sound: No special effects.

Murder on the Orient Express Subway

by Claire Boiko

Broad takeoff featuring three fictional sleuths . . .

Characters

REX RUMOR
AGATHA CRUSTY
HERCULES PEAROT
MISS MARBLES
INSPECTOR HAYSTACK
CONDUCTOR
VIOLINIST
PEG-LEGGED SAILOR
ZELDA, THE GYPSY
DIPLOMAT
MOTHER
CHILD WITH TEDDY BEAR
OFFICER MACDUFF
RUBBER-FACE O'HOULIHAN
WOMAN AGENT
INNOCENT BYSTANDER

SETTING: *Television studio, with two chairs down right.*
BEFORE RISE: REX RUMOR *enters, bows to audience.*
REX: Good afternoon. I am your host, Rex Rumor, and today we are privileged to meet England's most celebrated writer of detective fiction, Dame Agatha Crusty, who has written seven hundred thirty-nine mystery novels. (*White-haired, elderly* AGATHA CRUSTY *enters on the run, scribbling with*

12

feather pen on sheets of manuscript. She skids to a stop center, waving manuscript.)

AGATHA (*Triumphantly*): Seven hundred and *forty* mystery novels! (*She collapses onto chair, fanning herself with manuscript.*)

REX (*Applauding*): Isn't she *something?* She's ninety-nine years old—

AGATHA: And very bright for my age. (REX *sits next to* AGATHA.)

REX: Miss Crusty, I know everyone watching this interview is asking himself the same question: What is your most famous mystery?

AGATHA (*Absentmindedly*): My most famous mystery. I'll never forget that one. It was—now, let me think. It was the memorable—it's right on the tip of my tongue.

REX (*In a stage whisper*): *Murder on the Orient Avenue Express.*

AGATHA (*Delighted*): A little birdie whispered it into my ear— *Murder on the Orient Avenue Express.*

REX: Tell us, Miss Crusty. How did the story come about?

AGATHA: It all began in the Scottish Highlands.

REX: No, no, Miss Crusty. That was *The Case of the Grouchy Grouse.*

AGATHA: Then was it on top of a pyramid in Egypt?

REX: Ha, ha! You're joshing us, Miss Crusty. You know it all began when you decided to take your three popular detectives for a midnight subway ride on the Orient Avenue Express. Remember? You met at the turnstile. (*Stagehand enters, putting turnstile in front of curtain, then exits.*)

AGATHA: Ah, yes. The first of my detectives to arrive was— uh—

REX: Your favorite creation, the clever European, Hercules Pearot. (PEAROT *enters, drops coin into turnstile, exits through curtain.*)

AGATHA: Next came what's-her-name. Miss Who's-it. The one who sees all, knows all, and blabs all. (MISS MARBLES *enters, drops coin into turnstile, waves to* AGATHA, *and exits through curtain.*)

REX: That would be eagle-eyed Miss June Marbles, of course. (INSPECTOR HAYSTACK *enters and gets stuck in turnstile.*)
INSPECTOR HAYSTACK: Help! (AGATHA *marches to turnstile, drops in coin.* HAYSTACK *lifts his hat to her, then stumbles through curtain, getting tangled in it.*)
AGATHA (*Shaking head regretfully*): That was Detective Inspector Haystack of Scotland Yard. He is *such* a bumbler! I keep trying to knock him off in my books, but he bounces back like a ruddy rubber ball. (*To* REX) Then what happened?
REX: You went through the turnstile to join your detectives on the Orient Avenue Express. (AGATHA *drops coin in turnstile and goes through curtains, which open.* REX *exits.*)

* * *

SETTING: *Interior of a subway train. A long bench stands center, above which are subway windows facing out on dark tunnel. Above windows are advertisements for murder mysteries. There are sliding subway doors on both sides, and straps hang above bench.*
AT RISE: CONDUCTOR *stands beside doors.* PEAROT, MARBLES, *and* HAYSTACK *sit together on bench.* AGATHA *stands with arm upraised, hanging onto a strap.*
AGATHA (*To audience*): I held fast to the strap, waiting for the journey to begin. The subway door opened . . . (*Subway door opens.*)
CONDUCTOR: Stand aside, please. Make way for villains, felons, black-guards, and rascals. Now boarding. (VIOLINIST; PEG-LEGGED SAILOR; ZELDA, THE GYPSY; DIPLOMAT; MOTHER; CHILD WITH TEDDY BEAR; OFFICER MACDUFF; RUBBER-FACE O'HOULIHAN; WOMAN AGENT; *and* INNOCENT BYSTANDER *enter, sit on bench. Detectives peer at suspects, but they don't notice.*)
AGATHA: What a treat! Into the subway came a dozen marvelously sinister people. I suspected them all.
CONDUCTOR: Board! The Orient Avenue Express is about to leave. Please remain seated in case of emergency, which will happen at any moment. (*Train noises are heard. Blinking*

lights begin. All jiggle in place, as if train were in motion.
MARBLES *scribbles in notebook.*)
PEAROT (*Tapping head; with French accent*): *Eh bien,* Agatha
  Crusty. Already my leetle brain cells, they smell something.
  I ask myself—Pear*oh,* why are all these strange people aboard
  the Orient Avenue Express tonight, at midnight? Eh?
HAYSTACK: Good question, Pear-rot.
PEAROT (*Patiently*): S'il vous plaît. The name is Pear*oh.* I be-
  come enraged when people call me Pear-rot.
MARBLES (*Waving her pencil*): Aha! My vast experience in pry-
  ing, spying, and peeping through keyholes has led me to the
  conclusion that these persons are not what they appear to be.
AGATHA: Most interesting. Blab on, Miss Marbles.
MARBLES (*Pointing to* VIOLINIST): That violinist is one-time
  prodigy Yehudi Glinch, who carries a desperate grudge
  against *him* (*Thrusting pencil at* SAILOR), that fake peg-
  legged sailor, who is in reality—would you believe it—a *music
  critic!* (*Points to* ZELDA) The gypsy woman is none other than
  Zelda. Notice the diplomat (*Indicates* DIPLOMAT), who has
  turned a cold shoulder to Zelda. He is her runaway husband,
  who left her for a life in the glittering capitals of the world.
HAYSTACK: Hold on a minute, there. That alleged mother and
  her so-called child (*Points to* MOTHER *and* CHILD)—why,
  they are none other than the famous jewel thieves, Slippery
  Sam and his midget uncle, Slimy Stan. (*Points to* MACDUFF
  and O'HOULIHAN) And those two. I recognize them, to be
  sure. One is Detective MacDuff of Scotland Yard, and the
  other is his prisoner, Rubber-Face O'Houlihan. (*Subway
  sounds stop. All cease jiggling. Doors open.*)
CONDUCTOR: Clandestine Plaza. All those with secret codes
  and appointments at foggy lampposts, please exit here. (*All
  remain seated. Doors close, subway sounds begin, and those
  onstage jiggle.*)
PEAROT (*Suspiciously*): That conductor, he seems typical. Or—
  does he seem too typical, eh?
MARBLES (*Pointing to* WOMAN AGENT): The woman who
  seems to be a foreign agent is actually the famous actress
  Lulu De Lys.

HAYSTACK (*Pointing out* BYSTANDER): How about that fellow over there? I say he's your average innocent bystander.

MARBLES: Ha! That is Maxwell Fiasco, famous Broadway producer. He has never had a flop, but there's a broken heart for every light on his marquee. As a matter of fact, a new play of his opened this very night.

AGATHA: Most interesting. (*Lights, noises, jiggling stop. Doors open.*)

CONDUCTOR: Hawkshaw Junction. Change here for Gumshoe, Flatfoot, Sleuthhound, and Beagle. (*All remain seated. Doors close, all jiggle as flashing lights and noises resume.*)

AGATHA (*To audience*): As our journey continued, the suspects began to mutter. (*Suspects mutter.*) Inside the car, tension began to rise. Before we reached the next stop, *something happened!* (*All continue to jiggle.* BYSTANDER *takes newspaper from pocket, turns to back pages, begins to read. Lights go off. Subway noises stop. Sounds of shot, then thud, are heard. Doors open. Screams follow. Lights come up.* BYSTANDER, *newspaper over his face, is lying in doorway, knife in his chest, noose around neck.* PEAROT *and* MARBLES *run to* BYSTANDER. PEAROT *listens at chest,* MARBLES *feels pulse.*)

PEAROT: *Sacré bleu!* This man has been stabbed, shot, garrotted, drowned (*Lifting paper*), scalped, smothered—

MARBLES: Poisoned, hanged, exposed to black plague, and pushed from a moving object.

HAYSTACK (*Calmly*): Dead, no doubt. That'd be murder, wouldn't it? (*Drags body inside train*)

CONDUCTOR: Last stop. Orient Avenue.

HAYSTACK (*Running to doors*): Close those doors, Conductor. (CONDUCTOR *closes doors.*) Nobody gets off. Nobody gets on. Now then, Pear-rot. Who dunnit?

PEAROT: Pear*oh*, Pear*oh*, you imbecile! (*Calmly, rising*) Who dunnit? I, Pear*oh*, I and my leetle brain cells, will tell you who dunnit. (*Indicating suspects*) They *all* dunnit.

MARBLES: Arrest them, Haystack.

HAYSTACK (*Puzzled*): Where am I going to get twelve pairs of handcuffs?

PEAROT: Wait. First we must have confessions. (*To suspects*) Somebody confess. We know you all did the deed.

VIOLINIST (*Falling to his knees, opening case and waving bow*): I did it! I stabbed him with my bow. I meant to stab that make-believe sailor, there. (*Points to* SAILOR) He is a vile, unspeakable music critic, who sent me on the road to ruin by shouting rude things in the middle of my cadenza!

SAILOR (*Waving revolver*): Yes, Yehudi Glinch, and I'd do it again. Listen, everybody. *I* did it. I shot him by mistake. I thought he was that rotten violinist who played Mozart's E minor concerto in E major!

GYPSY (*Unwinding bandanna from head*): No, you are all wrong. I, Zelda, choked him with my kerchief. I was certain he was my miserable husband, a diplomat who abandoned me fifteen years ago to become the toast of the glittering capitals of the world, while I stayed behind—a stale cookie in the caravan of life.

DIPLOMAT (*Holding bottle above his head*): So, Zelda, we meet again. I thought it was *you* I had drowned in this bottle of vintage champagne. Yes, I wanted to be free at last. Free, (*Louder*) free, I tell you! Free of the incessant jangling of your golden earrings! (MOTHER *removes wig and takes knife, which was concealed under it.*)

MOTHER (*Unable to disguise male identity and voice*): Blimey! I scalped the poor beggar by mistake. I thought it was me midget Uncle Slimy Stan. (*Points to* CHILD) The blackguard was stealing me latest haul of diamonds, thinking I wasn't on to him.

CHILD (*Waving teddy bear; in adult voice*): Why, I meself smothered the unfortunate blighter with me teddy bear, thinking he was me crooked nephew Slippery Sam. (*Points to* MOTHER) He wasn't giving me a fair cut of his loot.

MACDUFF (*Holding out poison vial; in Irish accent*): Alas. I poisoned the poor wee man. I could not stand him anymore. I had to get rid of Rubber-Face O'Houlihan.

O'HOULIHAN (*Displaying subway strap*): I thought the mug was you, MacDuff. So I hanged him on the subway strap.

MARBLES: So far, so good. But who exposed him to the black plague?

WOMAN AGENT (*Waving giant test tube*): I did. I pretended to be an international agent so this man, the producer, Maxwell Fiasco, would not guess that in reality I am—(*She rips off coat, hat, and dark glasses, revealing gaudy dress.*)

OTHERS: Lulu De Lys. World-famous actress!

WOMAN AGENT (*Blowing kisses*): My public! Yes, I alone have the motive to kill Fiasco. Tonight a play was born on Broadway—it should have been *my* play. Instead, Fiasco gave my part to an *understudy*. He did me dirt. So, I did him in. (*She strikes a pose; all applaud.*)

HAYSTACK: Wait. Not so fast. Then who threw him off a moving object?

CONDUCTOR: I threw him off the subway. I thought he was a bundle of newspapers. Sorry about that.

PEAROT: Another case solved by my leetle brain cells.

MARBLES: Hah! You'd never have solved it without my super snooping.

HAYSTACK (*Ignoring her; to suspects*): Line up nicely. Have your thumbs ready for fingerprinting.

AGATHA: One moment, if you please. (*Crosses to corpse*) I'm surprised at all of you. You've missed the most important clue. (*Picks up newspaper*) The newspaper!

MARBLES: Fiasco was reading the newspaper. So?

AGATHA: Yes, the theater reviews. (*Reads*) "A Fiasco for Fiasco."

OTHERS: Fiasco?

AGATHA: Yes! His first flop. He was enraged. He was apoplectic.

PEAROT: Ah! Then Maxwell Fiasco died of apoplexy *before* he was stabbed, shot, garroted, drowned, scalped, smothered—

MARBLES: Poisoned, hanged, exposed to black plague, and pushed off a moving object. In other words—*nobody* dunnit.

HAYSTACK: Hold on there. This turn of events is disappointing, Agatha Crusty. There was no murder most foul. We *always* have a nice little murder, isn't that right, Pear-rot?

PEAROT (*Advancing on HAYSTACK*): Idiot! I warned you about my name. (*Grabs him around neck. HAYSTACK falls to floor.* AGATHA *crosses calmly to* HAYSTACK, *kneels, and feels for pulse.*)

AGATHA: Quite dead. (*Shouting at* HAYSTACK) Was that a nice enough little murder for you, Haystack? (*Curtains begin to close, slowly; to audience*) I never did like that character! (*Doors open slowly.*)

CONDUCTOR: Orient Avenue. Last stop on the Orient Avenue Express Subway. Everybody out, and mind the doors! (*Quick curtain*)

THE END

Production Notes

MURDER ON THE ORIENT
EXPRESS SUBWAY

Characters: 8 male; 4 female; 4 male or female for Conductor, Violinist, Officer MacDuff, Rubber-Face O'Houlihan.

Costumes: Rex Rumor wears smoking jacket, cravat; Agatha Crusty, white wig, Victorian traveling suit, high-button shoes; Hercules Pearot, black moustache, dark suit, bowler hat; Miss Marbles, gray wig, tweed suit, sensible shoes; Inspector Haystack, slouch hat, trench coat, dark trousers; Gypsy Woman, bright colored skirt and peasant blouse, hoop earrings, red bandanna; Violinist, tuxedo; Peg-legged Sailor, Navy uniform, patch over eye; Woman Agent, large, brimmed hat, dark glasses, coat over gaudy dress; Mother, house dress with apron; Child, Lord Fauntleroy suit with straw hat; Bystander, dark suit; Conductor, uniform; Officer MacDuff, police uniform; O'Houlihan, prison clothes and rubber mask; Diplomat, dark suit and tie.

Properties: Feather pen; paper; turnstile; coins; spectacles; notebook; violin bow; violin case; bandanna; champagne bottle; rubber knife; teddy bear; vial; subway strap; giant test tube; table; chair.

Setting: Interior of subway train. Center stage, across stage, is bench long enough to accommodate 16 characters. Sliding doors, right. Subway windows and advertisements above bench.

Lighting: Lights may flash as subway is in motion.

Sound: Sound of subway starting, in motion, stopping, doors opening and closing, as indicated in text.

Jeremy Whistler, Mad Scientist

by David LaBounty

Science kits experiments backfire. . . .

Characters

JEREMY WHISTLER, *10-year-old mad scientist*
SARAH WHISTLER, *his 7-year-old sister*
MRS. WHISTLER

SCENE 1

TIME: *The present.*
SETTING: *Jeremy's house. Up left is a bed, its side facing audience. At the head of the bed is a small gerbil cage on nightstand. At center stage is a small dining room table with three chairs, one facing audience, one on either end. The table is set with plates, silverware, and bowls. Up right, directly across from bed, is a black rollaway wall, which conceals a giant orange-and-white striped cat's tail.*
AT RISE: *Stage is dark, except for spotlight focusing on JEREMY, sitting on his bed. He is wearing a white lab coat, and is facing the audience with his head in his hands. After a moment he sighs heavily, addresses audience.*
JEREMY: What was I thinking? Some scientist I turned out to be! More like a mad scientist. (*Raises hands in helpless gesture*) I know scientists make mistakes, but I'll bet in the whole history of science no one has ever messed up like this. It all started a few weeks ago. My birthday was coming up and I just happened to mention to my mother that I might like a

20

science kit. Who would have guessed she'd actually take me seriously? (*Lights come up on center stage, illuminating dining room area. MRS. WHISTLER enters, wearing a robe and carrying large, brightly wrapped package, which she places in the middle of the dining room table.*)

MRS. WHISTLER (*Calling over her shoulder*): Sarah! Jeremy! Time for breakfast! (*Spotlight follows JEREMY as he crosses into dining room. At the same time, SARAH WHISTLER enters right. She wears pajamas and looks half asleep.*) Good morning, Sarah.

SARAH (*Mumbling as she sits down*): Morning, Mom.

MRS. WHISTLER (*Handing JEREMY the present*): Happy birthday, darling.

JEREMY (*Suddenly wide-eyed*): What is it, Mom?

MRS. WHISTLER: Open it and see. (*JEREMY tears through wrapping paper, pulls out large box.*)

JEREMY (*Excited*): Wow! Dr. Whizenbaum's Deluxe Science Kit! Thanks, Mom! (*MRS. WHISTLER is smiling proudly as the lights begin to fade. Spotlight on JEREMY reappears and follows him as he crosses stage. Once he's in his room, the spotlight grows to illuminate entire bedroom area. JEREMY addresses audience.*) Of course, at the time I was completely excited and grateful. My very own science kit! If only I'd known then what I know now. (*JEREMY pulls a small black box with a cord attached from science kit, and crosses to gerbil cage with it.*) That night I was in my room, working on Einstein's cage, minding my business, when all the lights in the house went out. (*JEREMY plugs cord into imaginary outlet. Spotlight flickers madly and then goes out, leaving the stage completely dark.*)

MRS. WHISTLER (*Offstage*): Jeremy! (*Tight spotlight appears on JEREMY, cringing.*)

JEREMY (*Scared*): How was I supposed to know plugging in Dr. Whizenbaum's Homemade Electric Gerbil Feeder would be dangerous? Boy, was Mom upset. (*MRS. WHISTLER enters room. Spotlight expands, showing her at the foot of Jeremy's bed. She is wearing jeans and shirt, and has a lit candle in one hand. She is tapping the floor expectantly. JEREMY looks apologetic. Spotlight holds this scene for a few seconds, then* MRS. WHISTLER *exits and spotlight focuses directly on JEREMY again, who looks back at gerbil cage.*) Einstein wasn't too happy, either, seeing as how it was his food I burned. (JEREMY *sits on bed.*) But that was only the beginning. There was the time I turned my sister another color.

SARAH (*Offstage*): Mommmyyy! (*Lights over dining room come up.* MRS. WHISTLER *is standing in front of dining room table.* SARAH *runs on; she's wearing regular clothes, but her face and arms are colored orange.*)

JEREMY (*Sheepishly*): You see, my sister hates her freckles. So I used Dr. Whizenbaum's kit to create Freckle-Free Lotion potion.

MRS. WHISTLER (*Shocked*): Sarah! What happened to you?

SARAH (*Sniffling, near tears*): J-Jeremy gave me a lotion for m-my freckles.

MRS. WHISTLER (*Yelling at the ceiling*): Jeremy!!

JEREMY (*Tentatively walking into dining room*): Yes, Mom?

MRS. WHISTLER (*Pointing at SARAH, who is now scratching her arms*): Did you do this to your sister?

JEREMY (*Nodding*): Yes.

MRS. WHISTLER: What were you thinking?

JEREMY: Mom, don't worry, it's perfectly harmless. Dr. Whizenbaum guarantees his lotions are safe.

MRS. WHISTLER (*Amazed*): Safe? Your sister is orange. (*Pointing*) Go to your room, young man. I'll deal with you later. (*Lights fade in dining room. Spotlight follows JEREMY, who has his head down, back to his room. He sits on bed and addresses audience.*)

JEREMY: That was bad. Sarah was furious, Mom was furious. I did try to point out that technically her freckles did disappear—at least until the rash cleared up—and she did get to stay home from school for three whole days. But did either one of them appreciate that? Did they appreciate me when Sarah returned to her normal color? Of course not. I was grounded for a week. (*Sighs heavily*) Then there was the pea incident. (*Lights come up in dining room.* SARAH *and* MRS. WHISTLER *are sitting at the table.* JEREMY, *still in his bed-*

room, pulls two beakers out of the science kit and pretends he is pouring liquid from one to the other.)

MRS. WHISTLER (*Dishing out food, including peas, on plates*): Jeremy! Dinner!

JEREMY: Coming! (*Still mixing beakers, JEREMY addresses audience.*) Do you like peas? Me, I hate them. I'd rather eat sandpaper. So I came up with this great idea. (*Holds up one of the beakers and smiles*) Dr. Whizenbaum's Pleasant Tasting Pea Formula.

MRS. WHISTLER (*Impatiently*): Jeremy! Now!

JEREMY (*Jumping up from his bed*): Coming! (JEREMY *runs into dining room and sits in chair facing audience. He places beaker next to his plate.*)

MRS. WHISTLER (*Suspiciously*): What's that?

JEREMY (*Proudly*): Dr. Whizenbaum's Pleasant Tasting Pea Formula!

MRS. WHISTLER (*Nodding skeptically*): And what do you plan to do with it?

JEREMY: Pour it on my peas. (*He "pours" beaker contents onto his plate. Suddenly, fizzing and popping sounds are heard. JEREMY, SARAH, and MRS. WHISTLER quickly scoot back from table. After a moment, fizzing and popping stop. JEREMY cautiously approaches his plate, gingerly picks up a pea and places it in his mouth.*)

SARAH (*Disgusted*): Eeuuww!

JEREMY (*Instantly screwing up his face*): Yecchh! (JEREMY *spits pea out onto plate and starts wiping his tongue with his napkin. SARAH starts giggling.*)

MRS. WHISTLER (*Trying to stifle laughter*): Tell me, Jeremy, how are your peas?

JEREMY (*Still wiping his mouth with napkin*): Aw-ho!

MRS. WHISTLER: What?

JEREMY (*Removing napkin*): Awful! (SARAH *and* MRS. WHISTLER *break into laughter.* JEREMY *gets up from table and walks back to his room. Laughter of* MRS. WHISTLER *and* SARAH *fades out, as do the lights over the dining room. Tight spotlight comes back up on* JEREMY, *who is sitting on bed. He shakes his head.*) Those peas tasted worse than sandpaper! At least Mom didn't make me eat them. Of course, she wouldn't let me get up from the table until I had eaten two helpings of regular peas! (*With head in hands*) But this time— this time I went too far. All my other experiments have been relatively harmless, until now. (*Shaking his head*) This one's a doozy. (*Sits up straight*) But I refuse to take the blame for this. It's Mom's fault for getting me that science kit in the first place. (*Slouches back down*) Yeah, right. When she sees this, I'm dead. (*Suddenly hopeful*) I don't know. Do you think she'll notice the five-hundred-pound cat in the basement? (*Spotlight up right. During* JEREMY's *last speech, rollaway wall has been quietly rolled back to reveal cat's tail. Offstage, a very loud, very ominous-sounding cat meowing is heard.* JEREMY *sits up very straight, eyes wide in shock. All lights out. Quick curtain*)

THE END

Production Notes

JEREMY WHISTLER, MAD SCIENTIST

Characters: 1 male; 2 female.
Playing Time: 10 minutes.
Costumes: Jeremy wears white lab coat. Mrs. Whistler is in robe, and Sarah in pajamas when they first enter; they later change to jeans, shirts.
Properties: Brightly wrapped science kit, containing black box with a cord attached, two beakers; lighted candle.
Setting: Jeremy's house. Up left is a bed, its side facing audience. At the head of the bed is a small gerbil cage on nightstand. At center stage is a small dining room table with three chairs, one facing audience, one on each end. The table is set with plates, silverware, and bowls. Up right, directly across from bed, is a black rollaway wall. The wall conceals a giant orange-and-white striped cat's tail.
Lighting: Spotlights, as indicated throughout.
Sound: Fizzing and popping, recording of cat meowing, as indicated.

All That Glitters . . .

by Virginia Miller McDonough

False suspicions, fool's gold . . .

Characters

JANE SARGENT
TARA SARGENT, *her younger sister*
MARISA SARGENT, *their mother*
CHARLIE SARGENT, *their father*
GRACE BENNETT, *a guest*

SETTING: *Living room of Sargent's Bed and Breakfast. Sofa is center stage. Door right leads outside. Door left leads to the rest of the house.*

AT RISE: JANE *is on sofa, reading.* TARA *enters left.*

TARA: I just went through her things, and I can't find it anywhere.

JANE (*Looking up*): What are you talking about?

TARA: Mom's wedding ring.

JANE (*Concerned*): Mom's wedding ring is missing?

TARA (*Smugly*): Yes, and I know what happened to it.

JANE: How would you know?

TARA: I'll bet Mrs. Bennett took it.

JANE (*Shocked*): She wouldn't have taken Mom's ring.

TARA: She's the only guest we've had all week. No one else could have taken it.

JANE (*Horrified*): Wait a minute. You don't mean you went through Mrs. Bennett's things.

TARA (*Self-righteously*): Yes, but I didn't find it. She must have hidden it.

JANE (*Angrily*): Tara, that's illegal! You have no right to search a guest's room!

1358-0913

TARA (*Shrugging*): Mrs. Bennett's out. She'll never know.

JANE: Mom never even wears her ring. How do you know it's missing?

TARA: Because she was looking for it. Saturday is Mom and Dad's anniversary, and she wanted to shine it up so she could wear it to dinner that night. (*Pauses*) You know, I think it hurts Dad's feelings that she never wears it.

JANE: But she'd just get paint in it.

TARA: Anyway, Mom went to get the ring, and it was gone.

JANE: I'm sure it's around somewhere. It's probably in the studio.

TARA (*Impatiently*): The box she always keeps it in was empty. (*Bluntly*) There's no question about it. Someone stole it.

JANE (*Laughing*): Remember when you decided Mr. Taylor had stolen your diary, and then it turned up in the cabinet with Mom's sketch books—right where you'd hidden it.

TARA: This is different. The ring is gold! And don't forget, Dad designed it, and his work is getting more and more valuable all the time. That ring could be priceless someday! (GRACE BENNETT *enters right, carrying shopping bags*.)

GRACE: Hello, girls. It's such a beautiful day. You should get outside and enjoy it!

TARA (*Suspiciously*): You mean you want us to leave?

GRACE (*Confused*): Leave? Oh, no, not at all. I only meant that these first days of spring are so invigorating! (*Opens her arms, dramatically*) All the buds starting to appear, the rich smell of earth after a long, snow-covered winter . . .

TARA (*Looking at her intently*): Where have you been, Mrs. Bennett?

GRACE: I was touring your town and, of course, picking up a few gifts for my grandchildren. I always like to take something back to them after . . . (*Catches* TARA's *eye and stops short. Then, to* JANE) Where are your parents?

JANE: Mom's in her studio, and Dad went down to the foundry.

GRACE: The foundry?

JANE: Where he has his sculptures cast in bronze.

GRACE: Oh, yes, of course. (*Looks uncomfortably at* TARA, *who is still staring at her*) I think I'll go put my things away. (*Exits left*)

TARA: Did you hear that?

JANE: What?

TARA: She wanted us to leave, and she made sure Mom and Dad were out. (MARISA SARGENT *enters right, wiping her hands on a cloth.*)

MARISA: I thought you were going to come help me stretch those canvases, Tara.

TARA (*Crossing her arms; decisively*): Mom, I know where your ring is.

MARISA (*Excitedly*): Oh, you do?

TARA: Yes, Mrs. Bennett stole it!

MARISA (*Taken aback*): Tara, don't be ridiculous! Grace wouldn't have taken my ring. (*Sternly*) If we're going to run a bed and breakfast, you're going to have to stop suspecting our guests of stealing things! I'm sure I just misplaced the ring.

JANE: When was the last time you wore it? Maybe you left it in one of your pockets.

MARISA: I've checked everywhere. (GRACE *enters left.*)

GRACE: Hello, Marisa. How is the painting going? I think it must be so *romantic* to be an artist.

MARISA: Actually, I've been preparing canvases all morning. Nothing very romantic, I'm afraid.

GRACE: Preparing them to become masterpieces! (*Clasps her hands over her heart*) Sounds romantic to me. (*Throws her head back in laughter.* MARISA *laughs, too.*)

TARA (*Pointing to* GRACE's *mouth*): There!

GRACE: What? What is it?

TARA (*Pointing to* GRACE; *excited*): Look, there in her mouth! Gold! She must have melted the ring down!

GRACE (*Confused*): What ring?

TARA: She was going to smuggle the gold out in her teeth!

GRACE: Smuggle gold in my teeth? What are you talking about?

MARISA (*Horrified*): Tara! What's gotten into you? (*Upset*) Grace, I'm sorry . . .

TARA (*To* GRACE): Open your mouth again.

MARISA (*Angrily*): Tara!

GRACE (*Angrily*): You impertinent brat! You've treated me with disrespect since I arrived—all those snippy questions. You must be the one who went through my things today.

MARISA (*Shocked*): What? Tara! (*To* GRACE) I am so sorry. She's got an overactive—

GRACE (*Interrupting*): If you suspect me, call my dentist. I've had this gold bridge for many years.

MARISA: Of course we don't suspect you!

GRACE (*Sternly*): I'm going for a walk, and when I return I'll pack my things. I will be taking the 4:10 train home. (*Exits*)

MARISA (*Angrily*): Tara! How could you? Your behavior was absolutely inexcusable!

CHARLIE (*Entering*): Hi! What's with Mrs. Bent-Out-Of-Shape? She almost knocked me down out front. (*All look at* TARA.)

TARA: I guess I made her mad. (*Quickly*) But, Dad, I just know she stole Mom's wedding ring, and—

MARISA (*Upset*): Charlie, I've misplaced the ring. Tara thought Grace stole it.

CHARLIE (*Shocked*): You accused one of our guests of stealing?

JANE: In the worst possible way!

CHARLIE: So much for my anniversary surprise. (*Pulls ring from pocket*) Here's your ring, Marisa. (*Hands it to her*)

MARISA: *You* had it?

CHARLIE (*Pulling box from pocket and handing it to her*): Happy anniversary.

MARISA (*Opening box*): Oh, honey! What a beautiful necklace. The same leaf pattern as my wedding ring! (*Hugs him*)

CHARLIE: Well, I know you don't like to wear rings, and I thought a necklace wouldn't get in your way as much. I took the ring to match the design. I didn't think you'd notice it was missing.

TARA (*Putting her hands to her head*): Poor Mrs. Bennett!

MARISA (*To* TARA): Yes, young lady, what are you going to do about poor Mrs. Bennett?

TARA: I guess I should apologize.

JANE: I'd like to see you get out of this one. (GRACE *enters carrying a paper bag.*)

TARA (*Sincerely*): Oh, Mrs. Bennett, I owe you a big apology. This is all my fault.

GRACE: Your parents are partly to blame.

MARISA: Oh, but we—

GRACE (*Interrupting*): Your parents are highly creative artists. It's no wonder you have a keen imagination. You just need to learn to channel it. Here. (*Pulls a spiral notebook out of bag, hands it to* TARA) I bought this for you.

TARA: A notebook?

GRACE: And these. (*Hands her pens from bag*)

TARA: A pack of pens?

GRACE: When I return next year I want you to be on your third or fourth book like this. Fill them with stories, Tara. Put that active imagination of yours to constructive use.

TARA (*Relieved*): Oh, thank you so much! I promise I will! Will you really come back next year?

GRACE: Presuming the rest of the week goes well.

MARISA (*Relieved*): So you will finish the week here. I'm so glad. (*Shakes her head*) This was a horrible misunderstanding.

GRACE: I thought so, too, at first, (*Starts to laugh*) but actually it's terribly funny! Imagine melting down a ring to smuggle it in my teeth! (*All laugh except* CHARLIE, *who looks at* TARA *in bemusement.* TARA *points to* GRACE's *mouth.*)

TARA: Look! Mom's pearl earring! (*All scowl at* TARA, *who giggles. Quick curtain*)

THE END

Production Notes

ALL THAT GLITTERS . . .

Characters: 4 female; 1 male.

Playing Time: 15 minutes.

Setting: Living room in Sargent's Bed and Breakfast. Sofa is center. Exit right leads outside; exit left to rest of house.

Costumes: Jane, Tara, and Charlie wear casual everyday clothes. Grace wears a colorful dress and jewelry. Marisa wears jeans and an oversized, paint-stained man's shirt.

Properties: Book, cloth, two shopping bags, ring, small box with necklace inside, notebook and pack of pens in a paper bag.

Lighting and Sound: No special effects.

The Return of Rip Van Winkle, Jr.

by Frank V. Priore

Rip has a rude awakening when confronted by the I.R.S.

Characters

FRANK VAN WINKLE
GLORIA VAN WINKLE
RIP VAN WINKLE, JR.
MR. MILTON
JOHN DIEDRICH
BILL PARKER

SCENE 1

TIME: *The present.*

SETTING: *Living room of Frank and Gloria Van Winkle, in a little town somewhere in the Catskill Mountains. Sofa and an armchair are left of center, TV down right, telephone on a small stand next to it. Small desk stands down left. Front door of house is up right. An open doorway in right wall leads to other rooms.*

AT RISE: *FRANK VAN WINKLE sits at desk. Various coins, coin folders and coin catalogues are spread out on desk. He holds up coins and examines them with a magnifying glass. There is a knock on the front door.*

FRANK (*Glancing over his shoulder at front door, then calling*): Gloria! Will you get that, please? (*Goes back to his work. GLORIA VAN WINKLE enters through open doorway.*)

GLORIA: Did you call me, Frank?

31

FRANK: Yes, dear. Would you see who's at the door? I'm trying to sort out this pile of coins.

GLORIA (*Annoyed*): Why can't you take a two-minute break to answer the door?

FRANK: Because after I finish this, I have to work on that article I'm writing for *Coin Collectors Weekly*. And then I have to prepare my notes for tonight's meeting of the Catskill Coin Club. (*Louder knocking is heard.*)

GLORIA (*Calling*): Coming! (*To* FRANK, *annoyed*) You and that coin collection! That's all you ever think about! (*She crosses to door, and opens it to* RIP VAN WINKLE, JR., *an old man with a long white beard, wearing a simple pullover shirt, pants belted with a large buckle, boots, the tops of which roll down, and a cloth cap. All his clothing is threadbare.*)

RIP: Please be pardoning me, madam, but is this the Van Winkle house?

GLORIA: Yes.

RIP: And would you be Dame Van Winkle?

GLORIA: I beg your pardon?

RIP: Er, that is, are you *Mrs.* Van Winkle?

GLORIA: I'm Gloria Van Winkle. Who are you?

FRANK (*Rising*): What's going on here?

RIP: Ah, you must be Mr. Van Winkle.

FRANK: That's right.

RIP (*Excitedly*): Glory be! I've finally found the right house! (*He takes a few steps into room*) Howdy, boy! (*He takes* FRANK's *hand and shakes it vigorously.*) I'm your great-grandfather!

FRANK (*Withdrawing his hand*): You are not! I've seen pictures of all my great grandparents, and you're not one of them.

RIP: Well, yes, that's true. But you see, it was easier to say great-grandfather than to say (*Counting off on his fingers*) great, great, great, great, great, great, great, great-grandfather; that's who I really am.

FRANK: Nonsense. My great, great, er . . . etc., etc. grandfather was the famous Rip Van Winkle.

RIP: You're right, and I'm his son, Rip Van Winkle, Jr.

GLORIA: But how can that be? That would make you almost 200 years old!

RIP (*Groaning and holding his lower back*): Don't remind me. I wish I'd had enough sense to heed my father's warning about the mysterious things that happen in those mountains—especially after what happened to him! (*Gives an ironic laugh*) No, not me! I had to go off and look for Hendrick Hudson and his crew.

GLORIA: I guess you found them.

RIP: That I did. I remember it as well as if it had happened yesterday. Of course, for me it *did* happen yesterday. There they were in a little clearing in the woods—Hendrick Hudson and his crew, exactly the way my father had described them. They were all playing nine-pins. Old Captain Hudson himself invited me to play along with them.

GLORIA: Did you?

RIP (*Frowning*): Yes, I did, and I lost. (*Quickly*) I would have beaten him, though, if he hadn't tricked me into spotting him twenty pins!

FRANK: Your story is quite remarkable . . . if it's true.

RIP: Oh, it's true, all right—all too true. I knew I shouldn't have sampled Hendrick Hudson's brew, but my curiosity got the better of me. (*Sighs*) When I woke up this morning, I found out that two centuries had passed. Instead of making me sleep twenty years the way my father did, I was out for almost 200 years.

FRANK: Why have you come to our house?

RIP: Well, I thought you might put me up for a few days.

FRANK (*Angrily*): So that's what you're up to!

RIP: I beg your pardon?

FRANK: I have to admit you had me going there for a while, but now I see through your little game.

RIP (*Puzzled*): Game? I don't understand.

GLORIA: Frank, what are you talking about?

FRANK (*To* GLORIA): This man is a fraud, dear. He made up this entire fantastic story just to save the cost of a hotel room! (*Turning to* RIP) What are you trying to do, see the Catskills on ten dollars a day?

RIP: But I assure you . . .

FRANK: I think you'd better leave right now, whoever you are.

RIP (*Indignantly*): Sir, I resent being viewed as a fraud by my own kinfolks! Every word I have spoken is the truth, and I am perfectly willing to pay for my lodgings. Unfortunately, your local establishments aren't willing to accept the money I offer them.

FRANK: I find that hard to believe.

RIP: It's true! (*Reaches into pocket and pulls out three coins*) I presented these to every innkeeper I came across, but they all laughed at me and told me to be off.

FRANK (*Staring at coins in* RIP's *hand*): May . . . may I look at those coins?

RIP (*Handing him coins*): Certainly. And every last one is genuine. (FRANK *quickly takes coins to his desk, examines them with a magnifying glass, looking back and forth between coins and catalogue.*)

FRANK (*Excitedly*): They are genuine! (*Pointing out features*) Look—there's a sundial and the word "fugio" on front and thirteen interlocked rings on the back. They stood for the original thirteen colonies.

RIP (*Surprised*): Do you mean there are more than thirteen?

FRANK (*Laughingly*): Quite a few more. You say the hotel managers wouldn't accept these coins?

RIP: That's right.

FRANK: Hah! They weren't coin collectors, that's for sure. These coins are priceless collectors' items—worth much more than a few nights' lodgings!

RIP: I don't understand. Brom Vanderwalde gave them to me yesterday for helping him shoe his horse . . . (*Realizing*) Oh, I keep forgetting, yesterday was a long time ago, wasn't it? (*Suddenly weary and downhearted, he goes to armchair*) May I sit a moment? These old bones aren't what they used to be.

FRANK (*Helping him into the chair*): Yes, please do, Grandfather Rip.

RIP (*Pleased*): You . . . you called me grandfather!

GLORIA (*Surprised*): Frank, does this mean you believe him?

FRANK: Yes. As incredible as his story is, he must be telling the truth. Nobody would give up these coins, just to avoid paying for a hotel.

RIP: Then, may I stay with you?

FRANK: Of course. I insist.

RIP: I'll help out wherever I can. I'm a whiz at shoeing horses.

FRANK: Don't worry about that, Grandfather Rip. We . . . ah . . . keep very few horses around here.

RIP: Oh, yes, I noticed that. All the vehicles I saw on your roads moved without the aid of horses. I must admit, the first one I saw gave me quite a start.

FRANK: Wait until I tell you about airplanes.

RIP: Airplanes? Do you mean to say . . . (*He gazes toward the ceiling, lifts one hand and moves it in a circle.*)

FRANK: That's right. We have machines that fly through the sky.

RIP: Astonishing! Don't they ever bump into the moon?

FRANK: Well, they don't fly *that* high.

RIP (*Shaking his head*): Heavens! There's so much I have to learn about this century.

GLORIA: We'll get you some books from the library.

RIP: Thank you. That should be very helpful.

GLORIA: I'll bet you could write a book about life in the eighteenth century.

RIP (*Laughingly*): I probably could.

FRANK: Say, that's a great idea! A book about life in the 1700's by someone who's actually lived then. It would be a bestseller!

GLORIA: Frank, what makes you think people would believe that Grandfather Rip is from the 18th century?

FRANK: Why wouldn't they?

GLORIA: Well, until you saw those coins, you were ready to show him to the door. And not everyone's a coin expert. Then there's another problem. Grandfather Rip is old, but he certainly doesn't look 200 years old.

RIP: That's more of Hendrick Hudson's mischief. His brew made me sleep for almost 200 years, but it aged me only about twenty years, the same as it did my father.

FRANK (*To* GLORIA): Let's worry about all those problems when we come to them, shall we? Right now, I think we should try to make Grandfather Rip comfortable. (*To* RIP) Would you like something to eat? You must be hungry.

RIP: That is surely the truth! I'm famished. I haven't had a bite to eat since lunch, and that was back in 1786!

GLORIA: I can pop a TV dinner into the microwave.

RIP: TV? I've never heard of that kind of meat before. Is it anything like venison?

GLORIA (*Laughing*): It tastes better than venison, Grandfather Rip.

FRANK (*As* RIP *starts to rise*): Here, let me help you. (*He does.*)

RIP: If you don't mind, I'll accompany your wife to the kitchen. I want to take a gander at one of those TV critters. (RIP *and* GLORIA *start for doorway.*)

FRANK: Before you do, Grandfather Rip . . .

RIP (*Looking back*): Yes?

FRANK (*Indicating coins in his hand*): May I have these for my collection?

RIP: Certainly. (*Snickers*) But don't try to pay for a hotel room with them! (RIP *and* GLORIA *exit.*)

FRANK (*To himself*): Well, now. I have quite a bit to do. (*He goes to desk, picks up pad of paper and pen, and crosses to sofa and sits.*) Whom should I write to first? A publisher! (*He starts to write, then stops.*) No, that will come later. I should start with the newspaper. (*Puts paper and pen on sofa, rises and moves to phone*) I'll call Dave Morton, down at the *Herald*. (*Dials a number, then speaks into phone*) Hello. Dave Morton, please . . . Dave? . . . Frank Van Winkle here. Listen, I've got a bit of a story for you; quite a bit, as a matter of fact. It's . . . er . . . a little hard to believe, but I want you to trust me on this one. . . . What? . . . Why should you? Well, you owe me one. I believed your story about the three-foot striped bass that got away from you, didn't I? This is an even better tale than that! Are you ready? . . . O.K. Have you ever heard of Hendrick Hudson and his band of men? (*Curtain*)

* * * * *

SCENE 2

TIME: *One year later.*

SETTING: *Same as Scene 1, without coin collection paraphernalia, pad of paper and pen.*

AT RISE: RIP *sits on sofa, watching baseball game on TV. He is now wearing contemporary clothing—designer jeans, tee-shirt, and running shoes—but he still has his beard. The crack of a bat and crowd cheers can be heard coming from TV. GLO-RIA enters from right, carrying cupcake on a small plate. There is a single lighted candle on the cupcake.*

GLORIA: How's the game?

RIP: Terrible. Our team is losing. (*He rises, goes to TV set, and turns it off.*)

GLORIA: You're looking very chipper today, Grandfather Rip.

RIP: Oh, yes. It's amazing what your twentieth-century health spas can do for a body—even one as old as mine. (*He does a few deep knee bends. Spots cupcake*) What do you have there?

GLORIA: It's a cupcake for you.

RIP: Don't tell me it's my birthday already.

GLORIA: No, today's your anniversary. You woke up from your long sleep exactly one year ago today. (*Holds cupcake out to him*) Make a wish. (RIP *closes his eyes and blows out candle.*)

RIP (*Opening his eyes*): I wished that my book would become a bestseller. I hope it comes true, so I can repay Frank and you for all your kindness. (*Starts to eat cupcake*)

GLORIA: You don't have to do that, Grandfather Rip.

RIP: But I want to. (FRANK *enters suddenly up right. He carries newspaper.*)

FRANK (*Excitedly*): Here it is! (*Points to newspaper*) The reviews on Grandfather Rip's book.

RIP: Are they good?

FRANK: Better than good. Listen: (*Reads from newspaper*) "The long-awaited book by Rip Van Winkle, Jr., the man who created such a commotion in the scientific community last year when he awakened from his two-century-long sleep, has finally been published. *Memories of the Eighteenth Century* is definitely headed for the top of the bestseller list. Leading authorities on life in Colonial America have unanimously praised this book." (FRANK *looks up.*) They have a whole page of comments by various historians. Let me read one to you. (*Reading*) "Before the publication of this book, all we could do was speculate about some of the details of everyday life in

the eighteenth century. Now we have all the facts from someone who was actually there." (*He puts newspaper down.*) It
looks like a winner, Grandfather Rip.

RIP: Excellent!

GLORIA: Frank, Grandfather Rip wants to give some of the
money from his book sales to us.

FRANK: I won't hear of it!

RIP (*Chuckling*): Then don't listen, but you're going to get it
anyway.

FRANK: Well, I guess that's up to you, Grandfather Rip. . . . By
the way, I've invited a friend of mine who's a lawyer to come
over today. He can advise you about any legal matters con-
cerning your book. (*Doorbell rings.*) He may be here now.
(GLORIA *goes to door and opens it.* MR. MILTON *is standing
in doorway, carrying a small attaché case.*)

GLORIA: Yes?

MR. MILTON: Good evening, ma'am. My name is Marvin Milton. I'm from the Internal Revenue Service. Is Mr. Rip Van
Winkle, Jr., available?

GLORIA: Yes, he is. Come in. (MR. MILTON *enters.*)

RIP (*To* FRANK): Internal Revenue Service? What's that?

FRANK: He's a tax collector.

RIP (*Frowning*): Uh-oh.

MR. MILTON (*Crossing to* RIP): Mr. Rip Van Winkle, Jr.?

RIP: Yes.

MR. MILTON (*Sitting in armchair, opening case*): There seems
to be a problem with your income tax, Mr. Van Winkle. (*Takes
notebook from case*)

FRANK: That's ridiculous. He's never even filed an income
tax return.

MR. MILTON: That's the problem. (*To* RIP) It seems that you
haven't paid your taxes since . . . (*He flips through some pages
in notebook.*) 1913. Your taxes are seriously overdue, Mr.
Van Winkle.

FRANK: But he doesn't owe any taxes. He hasn't earned money
or held property in over 200 years.

MR. MILTON: Come now, sir. Be realistic.

RIP: But I was asleep for all those years!

MR. MILTON: That's your story. Do you have any witnesses?

RIP: Well . . . (*Thinking*) No, actually. Unless you can count Hendrick Hudson and his men.

MR. MILTON: Hudson? (*Takes ledger book from his case and thumbs through it*) Hudson, Hudson . . . I have a Harry Hudson, a Hubert Hudson, a Harvey Hudson. (*He looks up.*) No, I'm afraid I don't have a Hendrick Hudson on my tax roles.

RIP: I'm not surprised. He died in 1611. (MR. MILTON *stares at* RIP *in disbelief.*)

MR. MILTON: I see. Well, without any witnesses—any *living witnesses,* that is—you'll just have to pay up, I'm afraid.

RIP: How much do I owe?

MR. MILTON (*Checking notebook again*): With compound interest on the unpaid principal, late charges, and various other penalties . . that comes to $1,528,630.53.

RIP (*Jumping up*): What!

FRANK: Calm down, Grandfather Rip. We'll work this out. (RIP *sits.*)

GLORIA: Certainly. Your book will earn more money than that. And then there are paperback and movie rights. You'll have plenty of money left over. (*Doorbell rings.*)

FRANK: Excuse me. (*Moves to door, opens it.* JOHN DIEDRICH, *carrying briefcase, is standing in doorway.*)

JOHN: Rip Van Winkle, Jr.?

FRANK: No, he's over there. (*Points to* RIP)

JOHN (*Entering and moving to* RIP): Mr. Van Winkle, I'm John Diedrich.

RIP (*Startled, rising*): John Diedrich! The banker?

JOHN: Yes, but the John Diedrich you remember was my great, great, great . . .

RIP (*Interrupting him*): Yes, yes. What do you want?

JOHN: There's this matter of an overdue loan, Mr. Van Winkle.

RIP (*Shocked*): What? I never borrowed money from John! (*Recalling*) Wait a minute—you're not referring to that dime he lent me to pay for a cup of tea and biscuits at the inn, are you?

JOHN: I'm afraid I am, sir. (*Takes small notebook from an inside jacket pocket and flips open to a page*) On June 27, 1786. We have your signed I.O.U.

RIP (*Taking a dime from his pocket and handing it to* JOHN): Here's your dime; now we're even.

JOHN: Not exactly. You see, with the interest compounded over the centuries, overdue charges, service fees, etc., you owe us $5,433.68.

RIP: On the loan of a dime? That's highway robbery! I won't pay!

JOHN: I'm afraid we'll have to sue, then.

RIP (*Furiously*): Sue! Why, you're just like your ancestor—a low-down, sneaky . . .

FRANK (*Interrupting him*): Now, now, Grandfather Rip. Let's not have him suing you for slander, too. (*Doorbell rings again.*)

RIP (*Furiously*): Who's that—someone else I owe money to? (FRANK *goes to door, opens it.* BILL PARKER, *carrying attaché case, is in doorway.*) Look! Another character with an attaché case! How much money do you want, buddy?

FRANK: Grandfather Rip, this man doesn't want to take your money. In fact, he'll probably save you some. (*To* BILL) Hi, Bill, come on in. Don't mind Rip; he's a little excited right now. (*To* RIP) This is Bill Parker, the lawyer I was telling you about. (*To* BILL) Grandfather Rip is having a bit of a problem with these two gentlemen. (*Indicates* JOHN *and* MR. MILTON)

BILL: Oh? What seems to be the problem?

MR. MILTON (*Rising*): Mr. Van Winkle owes the U.S. Government over 80 years of back taxes. I'm from the I.R.S., and I'm here to collect.

JOHN: And I'm a banker. Mr. Van Winkle is more than 200 years overdue on a loan.

BILL: Very interesting. (*To* RIP) There's nothing for you to worry about, Mr. Van Winkle. You don't owe a cent to either of these men.

RIP: I don't? Whoopee! (*Leaps for joy*)

JOHN (*To* BILL): See here, my good man, what is all this nonsense? I have a signed IOU.

MR. MILTON: And I have official U.S. tax records.

BILL: Has either of you gentlemen heard of the statute of limitations? I'm glad to say Mr. Van Winkle's indebtedness expired long, long ago.

MR. MILTON: But that's not fair!

BILL: It's very fair, sir. In fact, you for one should be very happy that there is such a thing as the statute of limitations. If there weren't, the U.S. Government would owe Mr. Van Winkle an awful lot of Social Security money. He turned 65 a very long time ago.

MR. MILTON: That's true, isn't it? (*To* RIP) Ah, good day, Mr. Van Winkle. I don't believe we have any further business to conduct.

JOHN: I guess I have no further business with you, either, Mr. Van Winkle. Goodbye. (JOHN *and* MR. MILTON *exit.*)

RIP (*To* BILL): I'm mighty glad you showed up when you did, Mr. Parker. I thought I was going to end up a pauper before I had a chance to be rich.

BILL (*Laughing*): Glad to be of service, Mr. Van Winkle.

RIP: Call me Rip. Say, I feel like celebrating. Let's all go out somewhere—my treat. We can start with a nice dinner at a fancy restaurant, and then maybe catch a good movie afterwards.

GLORIA: Or go bowling, perhaps.

RIP: Bowling? Are you kidding? The last time I went bowling I woke up two centuries later! (*Softening*) And I wouldn't want that to happen. I kind of like this century, and the people in it. (*He puts one arm around* GLORIA, *the other around* FRANK.)

FRANK: I don't think you'll have any problem at this bowling alley, Grandfather. They don't serve any brew stronger than gingerale.

RIP: Well, O.K. (*They all start for the door, but* RIP *stops.*) But this time, all of you will have to spot me twenty pins! (*Curtain*)

THE END

Production Notes

THE RETURN OF RIP VAN WINKLE, JR.

Characters: 5 male, 1 female.

Playing Time: 20 minutes.

Costumes: Mr. Milton, Bill Parker, and John Diedrich, business suits. Frank and Gloria, contemporary clothing. Rip wears threadbare eighteenth-century clothing—dull-colored pullover shirt, pants belted with old-fashioned belt buckle, and boots, the tops of which are rolled down. He wears a long white beard and cloth cap. There are a few coins in his pocket. In Scene 2 he wears designer jeans, tee-shirt, and running shoes.

Properties: Coins and coin folders; book; magnifying glass; pad of paper; pen; cupcake with candle; small plate; newspaper; 3 attaché cases; 2 notebooks; ledger; dime.

Setting: The Van Winkle living room. There are sofa and armchair left of center, TV down right, telephone on small stand next to TV, and small desk down left. Front door is along upstage wall, right of center. Open doorway is along right hand wall.

Sound: Knocking at door; sound of crowd at baseball game; doorbell.

Arise, Sparta!

by E.M. Nightingale

Helen meets her match. . . .

Characters

MENELAUS, *King of Sparta*
HELEN, *his wife*
THREE HANDMAIDENS
HERALD
PARIS, *Prince of Troy*
CYRUS, *Minister of Trade*
SERVANT

SETTING: *Courtyard of Menelaus' palace in Sparta, 1200 B.C. A table, bench, and stool are down right.*

AT RISE: MENELAUS *sits on stool, his elbows resting on table, as he reads from parchment scroll. He wears a toga and a crown.*

MENELAUS (*Reading*): "Fourteen arrests for assault and battery last night. Council of Elders disrupted by ruffians." (*Shaking his head*) Terrible! The people are getting restless again. We'll need to make another expedition to satisfy their love of adventure. (HELEN *enters left, followed by* THREE HANDMAIDENS, *each carrying a pot of flowers.* HELEN, *young and beautiful, wears a flowing white Greek-style gown and a jeweled tiara.*)

HELEN (*To* HANDMAIDENS): Put one pot there (*Points right*), one there (*Points center*), and one there. (*Points left.* HANDMAIDENS *obey, then exit.* HELEN *nods approvingly.*) That should make the courtyard look prettier.

MENELAUS (*Glancing around*): What's all this about?

HELEN (*Walking toward him*): We're having a garden party tonight.

MENELAUS: It's the first I've heard of it.

HELEN: I was keeping it as a surprise.

MENELAUS: Parties, parties, parties! Why, you've had four in the last five days!

HELEN: Yes, but this is to raise funds for charity. After all, members of the royal house must show a proper concern for the welfare of the people. Spartans lead such dull lives! I have to compensate somehow for being the victim of a political marriage.

MENELAUS (*Aside, bitterly*): And I'd like to lay my hands on those politicians. (HERALD *enters left.*)

HERALD (*Stopping, announcing*): His Highness, Prince Paris of Troy. (PARIS *enters left, moves center, as* MENELAUS *rises to greet him.* PARIS, *young and handsome, carries helmet on his right arm.* HERALD *exits left.*)

PARIS (*Bowing to* MENELAUS): Greetings, O noble King!

MENELAUS: A pleasure, a pleasure! It's not often we have guests from so far away as Troy. What brings you to Sparta? (*Stops, suddenly, as* HELEN *approaches*) Oh—this is my wife, Queen Helen. (*Points to* PARIS) Helen, this is Paris, Prince of Troy.

PARIS (*Looking her over*): Delighted. (*Bows low*)

HELEN (*Smiling*): Charmed. (*Flirtatiously*) We've heard that the men of Troy are so handsome and so . . . (MENELAUS *clears his throat, and she stops.*)

MENELAUS: As I was saying, what brings you to Sparta? Surely, this isn't just a social call.

PARIS (*Looking at* HELEN, *who smiles*): But I wish it were. My father, King Priam, has sent me to try to renegotiate the trade treaty between our two nations. A gross imbalance of payments has developed. We're now importing far more than you're buying from us, and we desire a more equitable agreement.

MENELAUS: Well, you've come to the wrong department. I'm the King. I'm not supposed to know anything about business. You'll have to see Cyrus, my Minister of Trade.

PARIS: Where do I find him?

MENELAUS: You don't. Rest a while. (*They cross and sit on bench.*) He's out hunting with the Benevolent and Paternal Order of Swineherds. About the only time I see him is when he wants his salary.

PARIS: I gather, then, that my stay here may be a long one. (*Smiles at* HELEN) How pleasant! There are so many—ah— lovely sights here.

HELEN (*With a curtsy*): Tell us what's happening in Troy.

PARIS: Oh, the usual scandals in government. The high priest of Athena was caught red-handed selling articles out of the temple treasury to a gang of Scythian smugglers. Our Minister of Finance is being tried for misappropriation of funds.

MENELAUS (*Wryly*): Sounds just like home. (*Claps hands, then looks at* HELEN) I wish I could find an excuse to escape this madhouse for a while and visit Troy. (SERVANT *enters.*) Bring us refreshment. (SERVANT *bows and exits.*)

PARIS (*Sighing*): There's a movement afoot in the palace to have my father, King Priam, removed from the throne and secluded in some comfortable cave.

HELEN (*Sitting on stool*): What on earth for? I've never met him, of course, but I'm sure he's a terribly nice old man.

PARIS: He's accused of disturbing the peace. He keeps everybody awake with his nightmares, in which he says he sees Troy burning. (SERVANT *reenters right, carrying carafe and three filled goblets on tray. He sets tray on table, passes out goblets and exits.*)

MENELAUS: Ridiculous! Who'd want to burn a garden spot like Troy? Has he consulted a physician?

PARIS: Yes, and he was advised to follow a diet of gruel and take a hot bath every night. Of course, he has done neither. A diet of gruel is beneath a king's dignity, and he has never taken a bath in his life. He says it dehydrates the skin. (CYRUS *enters, and goes to table.*)

CYRUS (*Bowing*): Your Majesty, I have returned.

MENELAUS (*Aside*): My day is ruined. (*To* CYRUS) Did you have any luck, Cyrus?

CYRUS: Oh, yes, a beautiful three-point buck.

MENELAUS (*Brightly*): Fine, we'll have steaks tonight.

CYRUS: Oh, no, Your Majesty, I sold the buck at the market.

MENELAUS (*Sighing*): Everybody eats well but the King. Oh, by the way, Cyrus, (*Gestures*) this is Paris, Prince of Troy. He wants to have some words with you. (CYRUS *and* PARIS *nod to each other.*)

CYRUS: I'm flattered. Very few people do.

MENELAUS: Now, tell me, Cyrus, what news do you bring?

CYRUS: A delegation from the Corinthian Boosters Club has just arrived. After their long walk, they were in too great a state of disarray to be admitted through the main gate. Consequently, I let them in through the back door. They're presently having lunch in the kitchen.

MENELAUS: And what did they want besides a handout?

CYRUS: They have a wonderful idea for a barter deal involving Athenian olive oil, their copper pots, and our barley.

MENELAUS: That sounds good. Get on with it.

CYRUS: Excuse me, Your Majesty, but I believe you should attend the meeting that is to begin almost at once in the Blue Room.

MENELAUS: But I don't know anything about foreign trade.

CYRUS: Quite true, but the mere presence of your royal personage would enhance our cause when the bargaining begins.

MENELAUS (*Resigned*): Oh, as you wish. (*To* PARIS) Excuse me. (*Rises and goes right*) I don't know why I ever allowed myself to become a king. (*To* HELEN) See if you can keep our guest amused while I'm gone, Helen.

HELEN (*Looking at* PARIS): You have nothing to worry about. (MENELAUS *and* CYRUS *exit.* HELEN *rises and walks toward* PARIS; *coyly*) Now, how shall I entertain you, noble prince? (PARIS *puts his helmet and goblet on table, rises and moves over to her.*)

PARIS (*Gazing into her eyes*): It would be sufficient if I could stand here and look at you.

HELEN: My husband said something like that to me once . . . but he had a fever at the time. Tell me, do you like parties?

PARIS: Very much.

HELEN: Menelaus doesn't. All he likes to do is sleep and pick apples.

PARIS: Why apples?

HELEN: Our chef told him they were good for digestion. What sort of parties do you have in Troy?

PARIS: All sorts: wild ones, mild ones, and those in between.

HELEN: It sounds fascinating.

PARIS: We also have marvelous festivals, horse races, foot races, and wrestling matches. And our gourmet repasts are prepared by masters of the culinary arts.

HELEN: Here, everything is dietetic. (*Musing*) Yes, I'm sure I'd love Troy.

PARIS (*Putting his arm around her*): There's only one way to be certain . . . go there.

HELEN (*Slyly*): But I couldn't do that without a companion to protect me on the journey.

PARIS: You're looking at him. You and I could make beautiful music together, Helen.

HELEN: Yes, I feel that we were made for each other, but (*Stops and looks away with a sly expression*)—but, no, Menelaus would never give his consent.

PARIS (*Scornfully*): We needn't wait for that.

HELEN (*Pretending surprise*): You mean we should run away?

PARIS: Of course. Listen, I know of a ship that's sailing for Troy tomorrow morning. If we leave right now, we can catch it, but we must get started right away, before the King returns. What do you say? (*Pauses*)

HELEN (*Coyly*): It's against all my principles, but I say, "Yes."

PARIS (*Embracing her*): Darling! (*They kiss. He crosses to table, picks up helmet, then goes back and takes her hand.*) Come, there's no time to lose. (*They hurry out left, as* MENELAUS *and* CYRUS *enter right and move center.*)

MENELAUS (*Angrily*): . . . and as a ruling monarch, I've a certain dignity to maintain. I will not bargain with a pack of unwashed Corinthians! Tell them to go bathe in the river. I'll talk with them tomorrow.

CYRUS: Yes, Your Majesty. (*Turns to leave, then stops, as* THREE HANDMAIDENS *enter right.* 1ST HANDMAIDEN *carries small table,* 2ND HANDMAIDEN, *a wooden box, and* 3RD HANDMAIDEN, *a ceramic pot.* 1ST HANDMAIDEN *stops center and sets table down. The other two place box and pot on it, and all three stand aside in line.)*

MENELAUS (*Moving center*): By the Delphic Oracle, what *is* this?

1ST HANDMAIDEN: Her Majesty is having a lottery tonight.

2ND HANDMAIDEN: To raise additional funds.

3RD HANDMAIDEN: For charity.

MENELAUS (*Annoyed*): Yes, the Queen has told me. What will the prize be?

1ST HANDMAIDEN: Your gold-studded chariot harness, sire. (HANDMAIDENS *exit.*)

MENELAUS: Next time, I suppose the prize will be the Royal Palace. I'd abdicate tomorow, if I could find some fool to take my place. While Helen is at it, I wish she'd raise some funds for me. (HERALD *enters excitedly, goes center.*)

HERALD (*Excitedly*): Your Majesty, Your Majesty! Something terrible has happened.

MENELAUS (*Indicating table*): I already know about it.

HERALD: Oh, no, you couldn't. You see, I was resting under a tree—

MENELAUS (*Interrupting*): As usual.

HERALD: When Her Majesty and Prince Paris trotted past. She was riding your prize gray gelding. They were very excited and didn't see me. From what I could hear, I gather she's running away to Troy with him.

MENELAUS (*Almost speechless*): Are you positive? (HERALD *nods.*) Do you mean to tell me that the Prince, a guest in my house, had the bad manners to abduct my wife?

HERALD: I wouldn't exactly call it an abduction. She looked very happy.

MENELAUS (*Angrily*): Ungrateful hussy! (*Paces back and forth*)

CYRUS: I'll set the Royal Guard on their trail.

MENELAUS (*Thoughtfully, with a slow grin*): No, don't do that.

CYRUS (*Horrified*): You mean you're going to let them get away?

MENELAUS: I most certainly am.

CYRUS (*Protesting*): But you'll lose the respect of your people.

MENELAUS (*Wryly*): Since when have I had that, anyway?

CYRUS: It will be a blot on your escutcheon.

HERALD: Even if you don't care about the Queen, Your Majesty, you still must consider the horse's feelings.

MENELAUS: Good riddance, I say. That creature eats too much. (*Thoughtfully*) It's too bad, though. I was becoming quite fond of the young fellow Paris—I would have liked to retain his friendship. Thirty days with her, and he'll hate me for not trying to get her back. (*Rubbing his hands together*) Oh, jolly, jolly, now I can pick apples all day and sleep ten hours a night.

CYRUS (*Thoughtfully*): You know, Your Majesty, Sparta's financial position is quite unsound, and its coffers are sadly depleted.

MENELAUS (*Sighing*): Ah, well . . .

CYRUS: Also, our counter intelligence agency states that Troy's temples are stacked to the ceiling with gold and silver.

MENELAUS: Gold and silver, eh? (*Thinks*) Interesting, that. (*Begins to pace slowly back and forth*) H-m-m, gold and silver! In other words, if we had such a treasure, it would be enough to reestablish our credit.

CYRUS (*Eagerly*): Oh, yes, Your Majesty, more than enough.

MENELAUS: Very interesting.

CYRUS: And everyone knows that King Priam has chests full of precious stones.

MENELAUS: He *does?* How fascinating!

CYRUS: And the Trojan women are reputed to be extremely beautiful.

MENELAUS: You can forget about them. (*Pacing again*) Well, well, silver and gold, and precious stones. (*Stops pacing*) I've reconsidered. (*Majestically*) There's no doubt about it. It's a matter of honor. With the abduction of Helen, Greece has been shamed, my name has been blackened. There is but one recourse. Revenge! (*Draws his sword. Others do likewise.*) Our duty is clear. (*They wave their swords.*)

MENELAUS, CYRUS, and HERALD (*Together*): Spartans, arise! On to Troy! (*They march off, as curtain falls.*)

THE END

Production Notes

ARISE, SPARTA!

Characters: 5 male; 4 female.

Playing Time: 15 minutes.

Costumes: All men wear sandals, short skirts, tunics, and short swords on studded leather belts, except for Servant, who wears shorts and a short cloak. Menelaus also has a purple toga and crown. Paris and Herald wear helmets with decorated combs. A bright gown with jeweled belt, jewelry, and tiara for Helen. Handmaidens are barefoot, wear togas, and identical flowers in their hair.

Properties: Table, wooden casket, ceramic pots, metal carafe with three goblets, tray, and scroll.

Setting: The courtyard of Menelaus' palace in Sparta. A bench and table with stool left of it are down right. Exits center, right, and left.

Lighting and Sound: No special effects.

Graduation Address

by *Robert Fontaine*

Brian gets more help with his speech than he bargained for. . . .

Characters

BRIAN, *valedictorian*
ROSIE ⎫
TOM ⎪
DARA ⎬ *his friends*
PETE ⎭

AT RISE: BRIAN *is reading paper; he also holds pencil.* ROSIE, TOM, DARA, *and* PETE *stand around him.*

BRIAN: "I stand here proudly to address you. We, the graduating class of old Chutney, are going forth, bearing the torch of learning onward and upward, ever and ever forward!" (*Looks up; pleased*) Not bad, huh?

ROSIE: Wow, Brian, it's pretty dramatic. (*Hesitates*) There is one little thing, though. I have a problem with the part where you say, "I stand here proudly to address you." It's pretty obvious you're standing there, isn't it?

TOM: Rosie's right. And another thing—naturally you're proud. I mean, if you *say* you're proud, some people might think that maybe the rest of us aren't proud.

PETE: Good point, Tom. And while you're making changes, Brian, you might want to cut out the part about how you're there to address people. They'll know you're not there to do card tricks, or try to sell them something.

BRIAN (*Musing*): I see what you mean.

ROSIE: One other thing. Everyone knows we're the graduating class of old Chutney.

51

TOM: Right. And how often do you see someone bearing a torch, except in the Olympics? Besides, what is a torch of learning, anyway?

DARA (*Nodding*): It's obscure.

PETE: Now, what about "onward and upward, ever and ever forward"? Isn't that self-evident? No one expects us to go backward and downward, ever and ever retreating. (*Pauses*) Of course, if I don't decide what I want to do with my life pretty soon, that may be just where I'm headed!

BRIAN: O.K. You've all made your points, and I agree. I'll cut some of these things out. (*Crosses out lines on paper*) Maybe you'll like the next section better. (*Reads*) "We are the coming generation, and before us lies the future."

DARA (*Interrupting*): Hold it! You have to take that out.

BRIAN: Why? I think it's powerful.

DARA: The future can't lie behind you, and of course, we're the coming generation.

BRIAN (*Annoyed; crossing out more lines*): I'm beginning to wonder why I asked you all to listen to this speech. I'm going to have to write the whole thing over.

ROSIE: But think of the great speech you'll have when we're through!

BRIAN: I hope so! Let me see, where was I? Oh, yes. (*Reads*) "On us weighs the burden of shaping the world closer to the heart's desire. We, and we alone, must do the task of putting our shoulders to the wheel and rowing bravely upstream until the glorious mountain peak of happiness and security is reached . . . "

TOM: Whoa! "On us weighs the burden"? (*Touches shoulder*) I don't feel anything.

ROSIE: It means we have a job to do.

TOM: O.K. But how about "shaping the world closer to the heart's desire"? What does that mean? That we should make the world square?

PETE (*Laughing*): Maybe we could squeeze it into a football.

DARA: Or a soccer ball. (*All except BRIAN laugh.*) Brian, Tom's right. "Shaping the world" has to go.

BRIAN (*Miffed*): I was just trying to be poetic. (*Crosses out*)

ROSIE: Now, what about "putting our shoulders to the wheel and rowing bravely upstream"?

PETE: Why can't we row downstream?

DARA: You can't put your shoulder to the wheel and row at the same time. Not unless you have three arms.

ROSIE: It's also a mixed metaphor.

TOM: And people don't put their *shoulders* to the wheel anyway.

PETE: That phrase about reaching happiness on a glorious mountain peak bothers me. Why does happiness have to be on top of a mountain?

BRIAN (*Angrily*): All right! I'll cut it out. (*Crosses out more lines*)

DARA: Listen, Brian, why not just say something like, "We have a job to do, and we'll do it"? That's nice and vague.

TOM: *Too* vague. How about: "We, the cavalry of tomorrow, shall charge across the corpses of poverty, ignorance, and prejudice."

BRIAN (*Shaking head*): And you think what I wrote is too dramatic!

DARA: Tom, that's horrible.

PETE: Hey, how about "the submarines of tomorrow shall speed under the shoals of injustice"?

ROSIE: Give me a break!

BRIAN (*Running hand through hair*): I don't believe this.

TOM: What do you have left, Brian?

BRIAN (*Bitterly*): Not much. (*Reads*) "Dr. Clune, distinguished guests, teachers, and students . . . *I thank you*"!

OTHERS (*Ad lib*): I love it! It's terrific! Short and to the point! Read it again! (*Etc.*)

BRIAN (*Reading*): "Dr. Clune, distinguished guests, teachers, and students . . . I thank you." (*All cheer and clap* BRIAN *on back as curtain closes.*)

THE END

Deputy Toby

by *Theodore G. Kottke*

Clever pranks outwit
corrupt mayor. . . .

Characters

TOBY, *young man about town*
SHERIFF JOHN THOMPSON
ALICE THOMPSON, *his wife*
MAYOR ALVIN JONES
LUCILLE JONES, *his wife*

SCENE 1

TIME: *The present.*
SETTING: *Living room of the Thompsons' home. There are several packing boxes, furniture covered with sheets, table. Door is situated so audience can see people approach it from outside.*
AT RISE: TOBY *enters, crosses downstage and addresses audience.*
TOBY: Hi. I'm Toby. (*Emphatically*) Toe-Bee, the most fun-loving, red-headed, freckle-faced fella you'll ever meet. Yep, as the letter said to the stamp, you stick with me and we'll go places! (*Noises are heard offstage.*) Here come the Thompsons. John Thompson is the new Sheriff of Mt. Pleasant County. He and his wife just moved in. Let's see what they have to say. (*TOBY stays downstage. SHERIFF and ALICE THOMPSON enter. He is carrying a large cardboard box.*)
ALICE: It's so exciting, moving to a new city. (*Proudly*) I'm so proud of you, John! Just think—two years ago you were a deputy, and now all your hard work has been rewarded. (*He puts box down and she hugs him.*) Come on, Sheriff, let's get

54

these things unpacked so we'll be ready for our company. (*They start unpacking. After a moment*) John?

SHERIFF: Yes, Alice?

ALICE: When the mayor and his wife visit, could you talk to him about the salary you'll be getting? It seems so small, considering you're the sheriff of such a large county.

SHERIFF (*Sighing*): It's too late for that, Alice. I've already signed a contract. I think we'll have to wait.

ALICE: I suppose so, but it's still unfair. (*They continue to unpack.*)

TOBY (*To audience*): Sheriff John Thompson is the calmest and most mild-mannered man I've ever eavesdropped on! He's so gentle, I'll bet he wouldn't take honey from a beehive. He wouldn't want to bother the bees. Ha-ha. Well, folks, it's time for this Toe-*Bee* to put some vinegar into this new sheriff. Toe-*Bee* will pierce, pinch, nettle, sting, and yes, even nip his good-natured hide. (*He runs to door, knocks.*) Just watch me—I'll get him going.

ALICE: Oh, that must be the mayor and his wife. I'll run upstairs and get ready. (*She exits.*)

SHERIFF (*Crossing to door, opening it*): Why, hello. Can I help you?

TOBY: Toby is my name and unpacking is my game. Hire me and I'll help you move in.

SHERIFF (*Amused*): Are you willing to work hard?

TOBY: Well, Sheriff, the world is full of willing people, some willing to work hard and others willing to let them.

SHERIFF: That's certainly true enough, but which are you?

TOBY: The willing one!

SHERIFF: Are you a speedy worker?

TOBY: I guarantee fast service, no matter how long it takes me.

SHERIFF: Before I hire you, Toby, I must tell you that this job requires someone who is responsible.

TOBY: You've got the right man, Sheriff. Everywhere I've worked, when something went wrong, I was responsible.

SHERIFF: I hope you're not lazy.

TOBY: Nope, but I'm very wise.

SHERIFF (*Laughing*): O.K., I'll give you a try. If we hurry we can get the house in order before the mayor arrives.

TOBY: I'm only too happy to oblige. (*He starts unpacking hurriedly, and drops a dish.*) Whoops!

SHERIFF: Careful there, Toby. Slow down. (TOBY *starts to work very slowly.* MAYOR *and* LUCILLE *enter, cross to door, knock.*) Toby, I think our visitors are here. Would you answer the door? I'll get my wife. (SHERIFF *exits.* TOBY *wildly dusts room. Knock is heard again.* TOBY *stops dusting, opens door.*)

TOBY: Good day, Mr. and Mrs. Mayor. Come in. (MAYOR *and* LUCILLE JONES *enter.* MAYOR *is pompous,* LUCILLE *a snob.* TOBY *shakes hands with* MAYOR, *lets out a loud sneeze.*)

LUCILLE (*Horrified*): You shouldn't sneeze before the mayor!

TOBY: Sorry, sir. I didn't know it was your turn. (*Shakes hands with* LUCILLE)

LUCILLE: How do you do?

TOBY: How do I do what?

LUCILLE (*In condescending tone*): How do you find yourself?

TOBY: Do I look lost?

MAYOR: You don't understand. How do you feel?

TOBY: With my fingers, of course. Why do you keep asking me all these silly questions?

MAYOR (*Angrily*): Toby, what are you doing here?

TOBY: The new sheriff hired me to help them move in. When I show him how well I work, he just might hire me as his deputy.

LUCILLE: Very unlikely. You have to know something about the law.

TOBY: I know Cole's Law.

MAYOR: What's that?

TOBY: Always mix chopped cabbage with mayonnaise.

LUCILLE (*Haughtily*): Young man, apologize to the mayor for your impertinence.

TOBY: O.K., I apologize. Here's a present for you. (*He hands beans and glass of water to* MAYOR.) Swallow these—they're smart pills.

MAYOR: These aren't smart pills. They're lima beans!

TOBY: See? You're getting smarter already.

LUCILLE: How dare you!

TOBY (*To* LUCILLE): Now, let's see how smart you are. What is H, I, J, K, L, M, N, O?

LUCILLE: Oh, for heaven's sake! This is ridiculous! How should I know?

TOBY: The chemical formula for water, H to O. (TOBY *takes glass of water from* MAYOR *and drinks it.*) I can spell "mousetrap" with only three letters: C, A, T!

MAYOR (*Upset*): Toby, stop it! Come, Lucille, we're leaving. (*They turn to exit just as* SHERIFF *and* ALICE *enter.*)

SHERIFF: Toby, please wait outside. (TOBY *crosses downstage, addresses audience.*)

TOBY: I don't know about that mayor. This brain (*Points to his head*) tells me to be very suspicious! Maybe we'd better keep our eyes on him. (TOBY *watches during following.*)

MAYOR (*Clearing throat; pompously*): Sheriff Thompson, on this auspicious occasion, I would like to welcome you to Mt. Pleasant County. May your time spent enforcing the laws of our fair state, county, and city be carried out in a manner showing no prejudice to . . .

LUCILLE (*Impatiently*): Yes, yes, Alvin, very nice. Why don't you have your talk with Sheriff Thompson now and save your speech for the Fourth of July?

MAYOR: Oh, yes. A nice chat with our new sheriff seems to be in order at this time.

ALICE: John, I'll take Mrs. Jones on a tour of the house while you talk to the mayor about law, order, and (*With meaning*) *financial* matters. (ALICE *and* LUCILLE *exit.*)

MAYOR: I'm always ready to talk law and finances.

SHERIFF: Mayor Jones, I'm looking forward to a friendly, productive partnership here in the Mt. Pleasant area. My wife and I are . . .

MAYOR (*Interrupting*): Before you get too excited, let's set the ground rules.

SHERIFF: Ground rules? What do you mean?

MAYOR: Do you have any idea how expensive it is to live today and to finance municipal government?

SHERIFF: Of course, I'm well aware of costs. . . .

MAYOR (*Imperiously*): Stop interrupting me! Your job here will last a lot longer if you learn to keep quiet and pay attention. Now, any real money around here comes from one place—kickbacks! For every traffic ticket you write, all the supplies you order and every insurance policy negotiated, we will skim a little off the top. Just enough to line our pockets with a little extra green.

SHERIFF (*In disbelief*): I don't believe I'm hearing this.

MAYOR: Quiet! I've been doing this for years. No one can prove anything. My creative bookkeeping is foolproof. And with the extra money, I can buy the votes to keep me in this very safe and profitable office. If you go along with this we can make a lot more money. Well, are you with me? (ALICE *and* LUCILLE *are heard talking offstage.*) Wait! They're coming back. I'll give you until tomorrow morning to think this over.

SHERIFF: I think you'd better go. (ALICE *and* LUCILLE *enter.*)

ALICE: Oh, John, Lucille has been telling me about their beautiful estate and their extensive travel. In fact, she invited us to go with them to the Caribbean this winter.

LUCILLE (*In patronizing tone*): Yes, our yearly trip to the islands is so invigorating.

SHERIFF (*Sternly*): Our guests are leaving now, Alice.

MAYOR (*Unctuously*): We don't want to bother you two on your first full day in Mt. Pleasant. I hope we can see a lot of each other in the very profitable years ahead. Come, Lucille. (MAYOR *and* LUCILLE *exit.*)

ALICE: John, you were so rude to them!

SHERIFF: Start packing, Alice. We're leaving. The sooner we're out of here the better.

ALICE: Why? What happened?

SHERIFF: Bribes! Kickbacks! Payoffs! And the mayor informs me that I'll have to participate in his illegal schemes. I'll have to break the same laws I've sworn to uphold if I want to remain sheriff of Mt. Pleasant County.

ALICE: Oh, John, how awful. You're right, we can't stay here. We'll find an honest place and start fresh. (*They start packing.*)

TOBY (*Addressing audience*): Well, it looks pretty gloomy to me. The mayor is bad and the good sheriff is sad. (*Pacing*) What to do, what to do. Hey, I've got it! If we can get the sheriff really angry, get his dander up, maybe he'll want to stay and do something to change things around here. I think I'll iron a four-leaf clover and press my luck. While I help the Thompsons pack, I'll set up a trick or two in their house. Mr. and Mrs. Sheriff only *think* they are leaving. (*Curtain*)

* * * * *

SCENE 2

TIME: *The next morning.*

SETTING: *The same, except that pair of shoes—one nailed to the floor—is on stage.*

AT RISE: SHERIFF *enters, wearing undershirt, slacks, and slippers, and carrying shirt.*

SHERIFF (*Yawning; to himself*): What a terrible night's sleep I've had. Guess I have a lot on my mind. (*He starts to put on shirt, but left cuff is sewn together.*) What's wrong with this shirt? (*He takes off shirt, pulls cuff open, puts it back on, then finds that the right cuff is also sewn together.*) Oh, for heaven's sake! (*He gets a little more upset. He takes off shirt, pulls the other cuff open and puts shirt back on. When he tries to button the shirt he finds that the button holes are also sewn together.*) That's it! I give up! (*He rips it off, throws it aside. He sits, takes off his slippers and puts on his shoes.*) Well, that's better. (*He gets up to walk, when he discovers shoe nailed to floor. He lets out a loud yell as he falls. ALICE enters, watches in amusement. SHERIFF sits again, takes his foot out of the nailed-down shoe and puts his slipper back on.*)

ALICE (*Solicitously*): Poor John! Having trouble waking up this morning? Let me pour you some coffee. (*Disgruntled, JOHN sits at table. ALICE pours him a cup of coffee. He puts spoon of sugar in it, drinks it and lets out a horrible yowl.*)

SHERIFF: Ugh! Who changed the sugar to salt? Oh, that tastes awful. Who is doing these things to me? (*Yelling*) When I find out I'll put 'em in jail and throw the key away!

ALICE: How can you? If we leave Mt. Pleasant, you won't be the sheriff and you won't have a jail to use.

SHERIFF (*Still outraged*): I don't care. I'll get whoever did this and teach him a lesson. (*Loud knock on door.* MAYOR *bursts in.* SHERIFF, *still upset, confronts* MAYOR.) What do you think you're doing here? You'll wait outside until I invite you in and not one second sooner!

MAYOR (*Arrogantly*): Hold on, there! I'm your boss, and I'll do what I want.

SHERIFF (*Angrily*): No, you won't! When I got up this morning I was going to leave this town, but now, I'm going to stay and do it right by putting people like you behind bars. So, listen to me—*I'm* the one who's staying, and *you're* the one who's leaving. (SHERIFF *grabs* MAYOR *by the back of his shirt and pants and throws him out the door, making a kicking motion.*) I'll give *you* kickbacks!

ALICE (*Proudly*): Wow, that's quite a change from yesterday! (TOBY *appears at door.*)

TOBY (*Entering*): When I was coming up the street just now, I passed the mayor. He was yowling, howling, hollering, clamoring, and yammering like a stuck pig!

SHERIFF: Good! I'm planning to arrest him and have him behind bars in short order.

ALICE: Hurrah for Sheriff Thompson! (*She hugs him.*)

TOBY (*Slyly*): So, Sheriff, how was your coffee this morning?

SHERIFF (*Puzzled*): My coffee? Well, it—(*Suddenly*) So it was you! You booby-trapped me. I should have known! (*He shakes* TOBY'*s hand.*) You know, Toby, that was good work. I'll be needing a deputy to help me out now that I'm staying on in Mt. Pleasant County. Would you like the job?

TOBY (*Delighted*): I'll be happy to oblige, Sheriff! You know I'm very wise. . . .

SHERIFF: O.K., let's see how wise you are. What would you do with a prisoner who doesn't behave?

TOBY: No problem, Sheriff. If a prisoner doesn't behave, I'll kick him out! (*All laugh as curtain closes.*)

THE END

Production Notes

DEPUTY TOBY

Characters: 3 male; 2 female.

Playing Time: 15 minutes.

Costumes: Toby wears country-style clothes—overalls or jeans, flannel shirt and straw hat. He also has red hair and freckles. Sheriff wears uniform in Scene 1; shirt, pants, slippers in Scene 2. Others wear modern dress.

Properties: Packing boxes holding books, china, other household items; beans; glass of water; coffee pot, cups, bowl of sugar; pair of shoes, one nailed to a piece of plywood; shirt with cuffs and buttonholes sewn together.

Setting: Thompsons' living room. There are packing boxes all around, a couple of pieces of furniture covered with plastic or sheets, and a table. Working door situated so that audience can see people approaching door from outside.

Lighting and Sound: No special effects.

Your Money Cheerfully Refunded

by Albert K. Schaaf

Return of the rebellious robot . . .

Characters

CUSTOMER
CLERK

SETTING: *Refund desk in a department store. There is a counter or a desk center, with a telephone on it and a chair behind it.*

AT RISE: CLERK *sits behind desk, as* CUSTOMER, *carrying a large package, approaches.*

CLERK (*Pleasantly*): Good morning. May I help you?

CUSTOMER: Yes, I'd like to return my robot . . . well, actually, it's my son's robot. He's eight years old.

CLERK: Well, we can't take anything back after eight years!

CUSTOMER: No, no. My son is eight years old. I bought the robot last week.

CLERK: I see. Is that Richard Roberts, the Robust Robot?

CUSTOMER: What?

CLERK: The name of the toy. Is it Richard Roberts, the Robust Robot?

CUSTOMER: I guess so. I didn't ask him his name.

CLERK: I beg your pardon?

CUSTOMER: Oh, I know that sounds silly, but that's why I want to return this thing. It's almost human. In fact it's superhuman.

CLERK: Really? We haven't had any other complaints about Richard Roberts.

CUSTOMER: Well, this one's defective.

CLERK: In what way?

CUSTOMER: Well, it's supposed to shoot a fake laser beam from a laser gun in its hand.

CLERK: Of course. Doesn't it do that?

CUSTOMER: Yes, but every time it shoots the laser beam, the garage door opens.

CLERK: Hm-m-m. That's odd.

CUSTOMER: I'll say. Last night it kept changing the channels on the TV. . . . Oh, and another thing—it doesn't go "clang, clang."

CLERK: "Clang, clang"?

CUSTOMER: On the television commercials, it walks slowly across the floor going "clang, clang, clang, clang." This one doesn't make any noise at all. It just sneaks around.

CLERK: That might be a relief.

CUSTOMER: I would have thought so, too, but yesterday it sneaked into the baby's room and carried her into the back yard.

CLERK (*Surprised*): That's amazing!

CUSTOMER: And do you know this thing takes thirteen batteries?

CLERK: Really?

CUSTOMER: Size "D." It cost me $25 just to get him started.

CLERK: But you could have taken the batteries out and stopped the robot from doing anything.

CUSTOMER: That's what I thought. Then the latch to the battery box jammed and the on-off switch broke off the first time my son turned it on. That thing's been sneaking around my house for four days like something from another world.

CLERK: It's a good thing it hasn't been going "clang, clang" all that time, isn't it?

CUSTOMER (*Wearily*): Please, can I just return Roger What's-his-name?

CLERK (*Pointing*): Roger is that rabbit doll over there. This is Richard Roberts.

CUSTOMER: Whatever.

CLERK: I'll call my manager and make sure it's all right to refund your money.

CUSTOMER: Thank you. (CLERK *picks up phone.*)

CLERK (*Into phone*): Mr. Prentice? I have a man here with a robot that opens garage doors and doesn't go "clang, clang". . . . No, sir, the man doesn't want to go "clang, clang"; he wants the robot to . . . well, no, he doesn't want the robot to either. The toy seems to be defective. . . . The laser gun doesn't work right, and the on-off switch broke. . . . (*Addressing* CUSTOMER) Was there anything else wrong with it?

CUSTOMER: Only one eye lights up.

CLERK (*Into phone*): Mr. Prentice, I think we should give a full refund. The toy seems completely defective. . . . All right. I'll check it. (*Hangs up phone*) I think we can refund your full purchase price.

CUSTOMER: I should hope so.

CLERK: But I have to be sure about the defects. May I have the box? (*Reaching for box*)

CUSTOMER: Careful. Don't tilt it like that, it will . . .

CLERK (*Holding hands out, palms upward*): I feel water falling on me.

CUSTOMER: I'm afraid Richard Roberts turned on your sprinkler system.

CLERK: I'm getting soaked! (*Looks off*) And look! It stopped the escalator! (*Starts to run off*)

CUSTOMER (*Following*): Wait! You owe me $129.95!

CLERK (*Stopping for a moment*): Let Richard Roberts open the cash register and take it yourself! (*Exits, as curtain falls*)

THE END

The Three Little Pigs and Friends

by Val R. Cheatham

A hilarious spoof of a
favorite story . . .

Characters

DIRECTOR
ANNOUNCER
HOGNEY DANGERFIELD
SHAKESPIG
ALBERT SWEINSTEIN
BIG BAD WOLF
MAKE-UP
AGENT
WRITER

SETTING: *Countryside set in TV studio. Brick house is up center; audience must be able to see inside house, where there are chairs and table. See Production Notes. Podium is outside the house. Stool is at far left, near exit.*

AT RISE: ANNOUNCER *stands by podium.* DIRECTOR *enters, carrying clipboard. He wears one-ear headset and simulated neck mike, crosses to center, and surveys stage.*

DIRECTOR: All right, let's get started. (*Talks into mike*) Ready, control? Three Pigs set, take one. 5 . . . 4 . . . 3 . . . 2 . . . 1. (*Points to* ANNOUNCER; *moves to side of stage*)

ANNOUNCER: Here it is: Live, on tape, from the Pigstylish Pen in New Pork City! Yes, ladies and gentlemen, Ham Box Office presents "The Three Little Pigs." You remember them. The first little pig, Hogney Dangerfield, (HOGNEY DAN-

GERFIELD *enters and crosses to brick house)* built his house of straw. *(Snidely)* That alone should tell you how smart he is. *(Taps forehead, looks knowingly at audience)*

HOGNEY: I saw that! No respect! I get no respect from anybody! *(Enters house)*

ANNOUNCER: The second little pig, Shakespig, is a little smarter. He made his house of sticks. His problem is his ego. He thinks "all the world's a stage." (SHAKESPIG *enters.)*

SHAKESPIG *(Speaking with exaggerated motions and inflection)*: Hark! 'Tis true! All the world's a stage and the players merely have second billing to me, the star. *(Enters house and poses by table)*

ANNOUNCER: And of course, as you all know, the third snout-hearted little fellow . . . *(Chuckles)*

DIRECTOR *(Crossing to center)*: Cut! Cut! That's enough. Let's stop the pig puns and get on with it.

ANNOUNCER: Sorry, I just wanted to "ham" it up a bit. *(Chuckles)*

DIRECTOR *(Into mike)*: Ready . . . take two! *(Points; moves to side as before)*

ANNOUNCER: The third little pig made his house of bricks. (ALBERT SWEINSTEIN *enters.)* His name is Albert Sweinstein. Everyone calls him a genius, because of this theory he developed: The harder the wolf blows, the sooner a poorly built house will fall down.

ALBERT: I call that my "theory of relatives," because that's what it gets me—relatives—a whole house full. Serves me right for building a nice, strong brick house. *(Shrugs shoulders and enters house)*

ANNOUNCER: Now, before you all go hog wild with "hamticipation," let our show begin! *(Sits on stool)*

ALBERT: Good morning, my two brothers.

HOGNEY: Good morning? For it to be a good morning, I would have to get some respect. But, do I get respect? Never! In fact, just this morning I stepped out to get the paper and was run over by the Welcome Wagon.

SHAKESPIG *(Dramatically)*: Alas and alack.

ALBERT (*Glaring at* HOGNEY): I have a theory that unless one works his legs as much as his mouth, chores never get finished. Tell me, Hogney, have you gathered the eggs, milked the cows, made the beds, or started breakfast?

HOGNEY: How can I? I never get any respect. The mailman doesn't even ring my bell.

SHAKESPIG: A bell by any other name would chime as sweet. A bell, a bell, my pigdom for a bell.

WOLF (*Entering*): Hey, in there—(*Swaggers over to house*) It's the Big Bad Wolf. Get up off those curly tails, pack your suitcases, and get ready to move out, 'cause I'm gonna huff, and puff, and bl-lo-o-w-w your house down!

DIRECTOR: Hold it, Wolf. (*Walks over to* WOLF)

WOLF: What do you mean?

DIRECTOR (*Grimacing*): Your make-up is terrible! It's not right under these lights.

WOLF: It isn't?

DIRECTOR: No! The shadows are all wrong. You look much too happy.

WOLF: Happy? But I don't feel happy.

DIRECTOR (*Ignoring him*): I think we can fix it. (*Calls off*) Make-up!

MAKE-UP (*From offstage*): Make-up coming! (*Runs in, holding oversize powder puff, flaps it twice across* WOLF's *face, then runs out.* WOLF *coughs and fans air.*)

DIRECTOR: That's better. Now, before we continue, tell me— do we have your agent's name and phone number on file?

WOLF: My agent? What do you mean?

DIRECTOR: You know . . . the one who negotiates your salary, house, and vacations—all the fringe benefits.

WOLF: I don't have an agent. I've never had an agent.

DIRECTOR: Oh? And just what is your pay? How long is your vacation?

WOLF: Pay? Well, actually, I've never been paid. And I haven't had a vacation in years.

AGENT (*Entering*): No pay? No vacation? No fringe benefits? Well, kid, what you need is an agent—me! Stand up straight (*Straightens* WOLF's *posture*) when I talk to you. I'll handle you for 40% of the gross, plus expenses. We'll start by demanding one thousand per show. Then we'll do commercials—let me see your teeth. (*Looks into* WOLF's *mouth*) We'll cut a hit record . . . which do you prefer, country or rock? Why, in no time at all, I'll have you right where you belong—Hollywood!

WOLF (*Excitedly*): Do you mean it?

AGENT: Of course, Wolfie, I'll make you a star!

DIRECTOR: Hold it! What about the director's cut?

AGENT: Don't worry, everyone will get his piece of the pie—or slice of bacon, in this case.

ALBERT (*To pigs*): I don't like the sound of that.

WOLF (*Dreamily*): Wow! Me, a star!

AGENT: Let me see your profile. (*Studies*) Hmm-m-m-m . . . A little make-up would help. (*Calls off*) Make-up!

MAKE-UP (*Off*): Make-up coming! (*Enters, slaps* WOLF *with an oversize puff, as before.* WOLF *coughs and fans away excess.* MAKE-UP *exits.*)

AGENT: Good! Now remember, Wolf, stay away from girls in red riding hoods, and don't call me, I'll call you. (*Exits*)

WOLF (*Smugly*): How about that, Pigs? Soon you won't have the Big Bad Wolf to kick around anymore.

HOGNEY: No respect! I get no respect! First somebody stole my car, then they came to my house and stole my watchdog.

SHAKESPIG: Alas, poor mongrel, I knew him well.

WOLF (*Happily*): I won't have to huff and puff or listen to the addled theories of that boring boar.

ALBERT: I also have a theory that the more energy one uses to operate the mouth, the more it reduces the relative amount left to operate the mind.

WOLF (*Angrily*): Oh, yeah? Well, let me tell you—

DIRECTOR: O.K. , enough, enough. We don't have all day. Come on, Wolf, you aren't a star yet. Let's get on with this.

WOLF: Get on with what?

DIRECTOR: You know what: The scene—The Three Little Pigs! Now, hurry up.

WOLF: All right, all right. Ah, where were we?

DIRECTOR: You were about to "huff and puff and blow the house down." Take 3, ready. (*Points, returns to side of stage*)

WOLF: O.K., I remember. (*Quickly and with very little expression*) I'm gonna huff and puff and blow your house down.

ALBERT: Hm-m-m ... It is my theory that the Wolf's problem is believability. He must make the audience truly believe he is going to blow our house down, even though it is brick, and he, in fact, cannot.

WOLF: You think you're so smart! Well, my fine little sausages, I'm going to have myself a "ham-let" sandwich! (*Overacting*) Are you ready? One ... (*Takes deep breath*) two ... (*Takes another deep breath*) three—(WRITER *enters.*)

WRITER: Hold it! Ho-o-o-o-ld it! That's not in the script, and you know it.

WOLF: Huh? Who are you?

WRITER: The script writer, that's who, and that's not in the script! You should know the lines. You've been over them a thousand times.

WOLF: Well, of course I know the lines. They're as clear as the hair on my chinny chin chin.

WRITER: Then you should know it's not "ham-let sandwich"; it's "I'm going to huff, and puff, and blo-o-o-w your house down!"

WOLF: I know that, I just thought—

WRITER (*Angrily*): You "just thought"? No, all script changes must have the writer's approval.

WOLF: But I just switched a few words! It's nothing, really.

WRITER: Nothing? You say a script change is nothing? I have a Pulitzer Prize, two Oscars, and an Emmy for script writing and you want to change my words? It's writers like me who have come up with the immortal "ring around the collar" and "plop, plop, fizz, fizz." No! There will be no changes whatsoever. And another thing, your make-up is all wrong. (*Calls off*) Make-up! (*Exits*)

MAKE-UP (*Off*): Make-up coming! (*Enters, slaps* WOLF *with puff, exits*)

WOLF (*Coughing and gasping for breath as he fans away powder*): I'm going to huff (*Coughs*) and puff (*More coughs*), and blo-o-o-w-w your house (*Coughs*) down. (*Drops to knees*)

DIRECTOR: Hold it. (*Walks to center, and simulates listening to message in headset*) O.K., people, cut! Strike the production! It's all over.

WOLF (*Still on floor*): What . . . are you . . . talking about?

PIGS and ANNOUNCER (*Ad lib; confused*): What's wrong? What's going on? No respect! (*Etc. All gather at center.*)

DIRECTOR: The word just came from the producer. The sponsor, Good Ole Boys Sausage, Bacon, and Pickled Pigs Feet, says the show is bad for their image. The program has been cancelled.

HOGNEY: Cancelled! What have I been saying all along? No respect! (*Exits*)

SHAKESPIG: All's not well that ends. (*Exits*)

ALBERT: Say, that could be a new theory: Cancellations are due to relative lack of sponsors. (*Exits*)

ANNOUNCER: I know what the problem was. We should have had more class, more sophistication. We should have exchanged dialogue in Latin (*Chuckles*)—Pig Latin. (*Exits, laughing*)

WOLF (*Coughing*): Pig Latin? Pig Latin! What a terrible joke to make up!

MAKE-UP (*Off*): Make-up coming!

THE END

Production Notes

THE THREE LITTLE PIGS AND FRIENDS

Characters: 9 male or female.

Playing Time: 10 minutes.

Costumes: Appropriate animal costumes for Pigs and Wolf, with false ears, tails, etc., or actors may wear everyday clothes and hold signs indicating WOLF, SHAKESPIG, etc.

Properties: Clipboard, headset, simulated neck mike, oversize powder puff with small amount of powder on it.

Setting: Countryside set in TV studio, with brick house up center. House may be cardboard folded at 90 degrees (to show two sides) with large cutout window and door. Audience must be able to see inside house, where there are chairs and table. Stool at far left, near exit.

Lighting and Sound: No special effects.

That Figures!

by Helen Louise Miller

Math: Anyone can do it . . .

Characters

MR. TOM FINCH
MRS. MONA FINCH
CHARLIE FINCH ⎤ *their children*
LIBBY FINCH ⎦
KAREN, *babysitter*
MR. WIZARD
JANE ⎤ *Libby's friends*
MARCIE ⎦
RADIO ANNOUNCER, *offstage voice*

TIME: *Present; just after breakfast.*
SETTING: *The Finch dining room. At center is table set for breakfast, and four chairs. Door left leads to front hall; door right leads to kitchen. There are several windows up center with a low bookcase under them. Radio is in bookcase. Telephone is on small table near door left. Other chairs, buffet, or china cabinet complete furnishings.*
AT RISE: *MR. FINCH and LIBBY FINCH are at table. MR. FINCH is finishing breakfast. LIBBY is pretending to be absorbed in reading paper. MRS. FINCH is straightening CHARLIE's tie.*

CHARLIE: Ow! Not so tight, Mom. Do you want to strangle me?
MRS. FINCH: Of course not. What I want you to do is speak up loud and clear. No mumbling. I want to hear everything you and Dad say on TV.
MR. FINCH (*Nervously*): I'll probably open my mouth, and nothing will come out.

71

MRS. FINCH: Tom, you can't be nervous. You've been on TV before.

MR. FINCH: But this is live. The other shows have all been taped.

MRS. FINCH: Well, then, just pretend it's being taped. Anyway, you have no reason to be nervous. You two are the best team in the area. I know you'll give the other contestants a run for their money.

CHARLIE: Don't be so sure. The competition this time is tough.

MRS. FINCH: Well, just remember—win or lose, Libby and I will be proud of you. (*Turns to* LIBBY) Won't we, Libby?

LIBBY (*Pretending not to hear*): What did you say?

MRS. FINCH: I just said we'll be proud of Dad and Charlie when we see them on *Mad About Math*.

LIBBY (*Still reading paper*): I don't see what's so wonderful about a dumb old math show.

MRS. FINCH: Libby! What a rude thing to say!

CHARLIE: She's just mad because she's so bad in math.

LIBBY (*Heatedly*): I'm not mad. I'm just not interested. I'm going to be a writer when I grow up, so I won't need math. (*Defensively*) Anyway, one wonk in the family is enough.

MRS. FINCH: Libby, you're being really mean. Apologize to your brother this instant! (LIBBY *sulks*.)

CHARLIE: That's O.K., Mom. I don't need an apology. (*To* LIBBY) But you know, you're wrong about not needing to know math. You'll have to learn how to add so you can count up all the rejection slips you get when you're a writer.

MR. FINCH (*Sternly*): Charlie!

LIBBY (*Enraged; throwing paper at* CHARLIE): You brat!

MRS. FINCH: Children! Enough!

MR. FINCH (*Looking at watch*): Listen, we have to go. Libby and Charlie, we're going to have a little chat this afternoon about all of this. (*To* MRS. FINCH) Wish us luck.

MRS. FINCH (*As* MR. FINCH *and* CHARLIE *exit*): Good luck! We'll be watching you! (*Turns to* LIBBY) Libby, what's gotten into you?

LIBBY (*Apologetically*): I'm sorry I picked on Charlie, Mom—I really am. It's just that he thinks he's so smart because he can do all kinds of problems in his head, and he always gets the right answers.

MRS. FINCH: But don't you think that's quite an accomplishment?

LIBBY: Well, sure, but it always makes me feel so stupid.

MRS. FINCH: Look how easily you write poems and stories. Just as Charlie's clever with numbers, you're clever with words.

LIBBY (*Halfheartedly*): I guess.

MRS. FINCH: It's true. And I'll bet you could be good in math, too, if you made up your mind to work harder at it.

LIBBY: But I don't enjoy it.

MRS. FINCH: We'll talk more about this later. I told Mrs. Garner we'd be over soon to watch the show. It certainly is a nuisance that our TV is broken now, of all times.

LIBBY: Mom, would you mind if I stayed home? Listening to all those problems makes my head ache.

MRS. FINCH (*Disappointed*): Well, I certainly don't intend to force you to go. You can stay home if you like. But don't be a bother to Karen.

LIBBY: I won't, Mom.

MRS. FINCH: I told her she could bake some cookies for a school party while the baby is asleep, so maybe you could give her a hand with that.

LIBBY: Sure.

MRS. FINCH: If you need me for anything, you know Mrs. Garner's number.

LIBBY: O.K. I'll be fine. (MRS. FINCH *turns to exit.*) Mom?

MRS. FINCH (*Turning*): Yes, Libby?

MRS. LIBBY: Even though I'm not watching Dad and Charlie on TV, I'll be rooting for them. (MRS. FINCH *nods, smiles, exits. After a pause,* LIBBY *buries her head in her arms and begins to sob. She raises head and yells.*) Stupid math! I hate it! I hate it! (*Buries head again.* MR. WIZARD *enters, watches* LIBBY *for a while, then clears throat softly.*)

MR. WIZARD: Excuse me. Are you Libby Finch?

LIBBY (*Startled; sitting up*): Who are you? How did you get in here? (*Shakes head*) I must be dreaming.

MR. WIZARD: I'm Mr. Wizard, and I was instructed to pay a call on (*Consulting card*) Libby Finch.

LIBBY: Mr. Wizard? I really am dreaming. (*Puts head down again*)

MR. WIZARD: But you are Libby Finch.

LIBBY: Yes, but I can't talk to you now. I can't talk to anyone now.

MR. WIZARD: Why not?

LIBBY: Can't you see I'm busy? I'm busy crying. I'm very upset.

MR. WIZARD: Yes, I know. You're upset about math, aren't you?

LIBBY (*Looking up*): How did you know?

MR. WIZARD: I told you my name is Mr. Wizard, and we wizards know a lot. For example, I'll bet I can tell you *why* you're upset about math.

LIBBY (*Miserably*): Don't bother. I know that without being told.

MR. WIZARD: But I'm going to tell you anyhow. You see, I love to talk—especially when it's about math.

LIBBY: Well, I don't. I hate math and everything about it.

MR. WIZARD: That's just your trouble. You're miserable about math because you hate it, and you hate it because you think you can't do it.

LIBBY: I *know* I can't do it, and if you don't believe me, just look at my report card. (*Pulls it out from book in bookshelf behind her*)

MR. WIZARD: So *that's* where you've been hiding it.

LIBBY (*Wryly*): You knew that, too.

MR. WIZARD: Of course. I'll bet I can even tell you what you're going to say next.

LIBBY: Give it a try. (*Tosses report card on table, but misses; it drops to floor unnoticed*)

MR. WIZARD: You're going to say that you can't be bothered with math because you'll never need it.

LIBBY (*Astonished*): That's right. If I really thought I'd have any use for it, I'd do some of these wretched old math problems. But as it is, it's just a waste of time.

MR. WIZARD: Suppose I could show you that you probably use math about twenty times a day?

LIBBY (*Laughing*): Twenty times a day! That's ridiculous!

MR. WIZARD: Well, maybe not twenty, but at least . . . seven. Seven is a lucky number!

LIBBY (*Skeptically*): I'd still say it was pretty unlikely.

MR. WIZARD: I'll tell you what. I'll make a bargain with you. If I can show you that problems dealing with numbers keep popping into your everyday life at the rate of seven a day, will you promise to get down to business and work hard on your math problems?

LIBBY: Well, O.K. But I'm afraid you'll get the bad end of the bargain.

MR. WIZARD: Let me worry about that. Now, here's the plan. First of all, we have to keep score. (*Hands score card to* LIBBY) Every time a situation arises in which you have to do any sort of counting or figuring, a bell will ring. That will be the signal that I've scored another point, and you have to stop whatever you're doing and mark the score card. Will you do that?

LIBBY: Why not? It sounds like fun.

MR. WIZARD (*Reassuringly*): Numbers really *are* fun, if you just learn to appreciate them.

LIBBY: Now you sound just like my Dad.

MR. WIZARD: Is it a bargain?

LIBBY: It's a bargain. (*They shake hands.*)

MR. WIZARD: By the way, you dropped your report card on the floor. (*As* LIBBY *stoops over to pick it up,* MR. WIZARD *quickly exits.*)

LIBBY: Here it is, Mr. Wizard. (*Noticing that* MR. WIZARD *is gone*) Where did you go? (KAREN *enters, carrying cookbook.*)

KAREN: Libby, did your mother leave yet?

LIBBY: Yes. A little while ago.

KAREN: Oh, dear. I have a question about this recipe.

LIBBY: Can I help you?

KAREN: Well, this recipe for oatmeal cookies makes four dozen, but I want to make six dozen, and I don't know if I have enough oatmeal.

LIBBY: How many cups does it call for?

KAREN: Three.

LIBBY: O.K. (*Thinking*) So you want to make one and a half times the recipe. Half of three is one and a half—so if you add three plus one and a half, that's four and a half cups of oatmeal.

KAREN (*Impressed*): Wow! That was quick. And I always thought you had trouble with arithmetic. Thanks! (*Exits*)

LIBBY (*Suddenly*): I used math! (*Doorbell is heard.*) Where's that score card? (*Grabs score card and writes on it hastily, then, as she exits*) That's one point for Mr. Wizard. (*Offstage*) Oh, hi, Jane. Come on in. (*She reenters, followed by JANE, who carries colored paper.*)

JANE: What are you doing?

LIBBY: I'm helping Karen bake oatmeal cookies and babysit.

JANE: Yum, oatmeal cookies! (*Excitedly*) Guess what? My parents said I can have a party for my birthday.

LIBBY: Great! That'll be fun.

JANE: Remember those place cards you had for your party last year?

LIBBY: Sure.

JANE: Well, I brought this paper over and thought maybe you'd show me how to make them.

LIBBY: It's easy. (*Takes paper from JANE*) How many do you need?

JANE: Twelve.

LIBBY: O.K. This paper is just the right size. (*Demonstrating*) Now, you fold the sheet in half, like this. Then fold it again, and then again. That gives you eight place cards out of that sheet. So we'll just need half a sheet for the other four. That will make twelve place cards.

JANE: Gosh! Charlie should hear you now. He doesn't think you can do fractions.

LIBBY: Fractions? Who said anything about fractions?

JANE: *You* did! You just divided a paper into halves, then into fourths, then into eighths!

LIBBY: Oh, no!

JANE: What's the matter? (*Doorbell is heard.*)

LIBBY: Oh, nothing. Nothing at all! Excuse me while I fill out this little card. (*Writes on score card*)

JANE: Do you want me to see who's at the door?

LIBBY: Oh, would you, Jane? Thanks. (JANE *exits*.) Oh, dear, that's two points for Mr. Wizard.

JANE (*Reentering*): It's the paper girl. She says you owe her for three weeks, but last time your mother paid her a week in advance, so she thinks it's only two weeks. She says she's short on change, so she hopes you have the exact amount.

LIBBY: Good grief! That's complicated. (*Phone rings*.) Would you tell her I don't have enough to pay her, and ask her to come back in a couple of hours, when my mother will be home?

JANE: Sure. (*Exits*)

LIBBY: Another point for Mr. Wizard! (*She answers phone, cradles it on her shoulder while she marks score card again*.) Hello. . . . No, I'm sorry, you have the wrong number. (*Hangs up. JANE reenters*.)

JANE: Everything's all set with the paper girl.

LIBBY: Thanks, Jane.

JANE: Now, back to the place cards.

LIBBY: You know, so much is happening around here, I'd rather help you another time. Why don't you drop by tomorrow morning? Things will be calmer then, I'm sure.

JANE: O.K. But just one more quick question. How much ice cream do you think I should buy for twelve?

LIBBY (*Musing*): I'd say two quarts would be plenty. (*Timer goes off*.)

JANE (*Puzzled*): There sure are a lot of bells in this house.

LIBBY: Must be the timer for Karen's cookies. Oh, dear! Where's that score card? I seem to be running into figures everywhere! (*Marks score card*)

JANE: You're awfully mysterious about that card. What is it, anyway?

LIBBY: Well, it's sort of a secret for now, Jane. I'll tell you about it some day.

JANE: O.K. Listen, I think I'd better go. You seem to have a lot on your mind. I'll see you tomorrow.

LIBBY: O.K. Bye, Jane. (JANE *exits*. LIBBY *sighs heavily, sinks into sofa*.) What a morning! I need a break. At least the radio won't be firing math problems at me. (*Turns on radio. Closing strain of music is heard, then* ANNOUNCER's *voice.*)

ANNOUNCER: Don't miss the sensational values at Roger's Shoe Barn, now in progress. Shoes with a red sticker, fifteen percent off. Shoes with a yellow sticker, twenty-five percent off. And shoes with a blue sticker, forty percent off! Think what you'll save on shoes for the whole family when you come to Roger's! (LIBBY *shuts off radio in disgust, then looks up at ceiling in anticipation.*) O.K., little bell, where are you? (*Doorbell rings.*) Ah, right on schedule. (*Fills in score card*) Mr. Wizard isn't giving me a minute's peace! (*Bell rings again.* LIBBY *yells off.*) Coming! (MARCIE *enters, carrying book.*)

MARCIE: Hi! Anybody home?

LIBBY: Oh, hi, Marcie.

MARCIE: I don't mean to barge in like this, but I thought the doorbell might be broken.

LIBBY (*Wryly*): I wish. . . . So—what's up?

MARCIE: I came to see if you want to come downtown with me.

LIBBY: Where are you going?

MARCIE: Well, first I have to stop at the library to return this overdue book for my mother. She must owe a fortune on it. It was 5¢ a day, plus an extra fee of 2¢ a day after the first two weeks, and she's had it over a month. At this rate, she'll owe enough to buy the book. I can't even figure it out. (*Phone rings.*)

LIBBY: *Figure!* (*Answers phone*) Hello. . . . (*Annoyed*) No, this is the same number you called a while ago. (*Hangs up, marks score card*)

MARCIE: I read the book, too, while my mother had it. It's all about a murder in a town that was on the border between the Eastern Standard and Central Time zones. The murderer was tripped up on his alibi because of the difference in time between the two zones.

LIBBY (*Holding hand to head*): Marcie, please—let's not talk about numbers, O.K.?

MARCIE (*Enthusiastically*): But, listen! All those time zones never meant anything to me when we studied about them in school, but in this story it was a matter of life and death. (*All sorts of bells begin to ring at once—doorbell, telephone, timer, alarm clocks, striking clocks, etc.)* Libby! What's going on?

KAREN (*Running in*): Libby, there must be something wrong with the electrical system! Maybe we should leave the house!

LIBBY: Karen, trust me—everything's fine. (*Bells stop ringing.*) I—ah—got bored and I set lots of things to go off at the same time. It was dumb, I know, but—(*Sheepishly*) I'm sorry.

KAREN (*Looking at her strangely*): All right. I just hope the baby doesn't wake up before I finish these cookies! (*Exits*)

MARCIE: I guess there's never a dull moment in this house! So—do you want to come downtown with me?

LIBBY: Not this time, Marcie. I . . . I have some things to do. But thanks for asking.

MARCIE (*As she exits*): O.K. I'll talk to you tomorrow. Bye! (*Exits*)

LIBBY (*To herself*): What a day! (MR. WIZARD *enters right.*)

MR. WIZARD: Well, things got pretty hot for you there for a while. Do you have your score card ready?

LIBBY: I do. (*Hands card to him*) You win. I guess you must have been right all the time.

MR. WIZARD: It's nice of you to admit it.

LIBBY: Now that you've won, what do you want me to do?

MR. WIZARD: I want you to take another look at that report card you were trying to hide when I came in.

LIBBY (*Getting it from table*): Well, it still has a terrible grade in math.

MR. WIZARD: Take a look at what it says on the back.

LIBBY (*Reading*): "With a little effort and serious application Libby could make real progress in this subject, but she doesn't seem to take any interest in it."

MR. WIZARD: Now that you've seen what a big part math plays in your everyday life, how about that *effort* and *application*, Libby?

LIBBY: I'll make another bargain with you, Mr. Wizard. Stop by in a couple of months, and I'll show you a report card that'll really dazzle you.

MR. WIZARD: It's a deal. In the meantime, I think your whole family would be happy if you looked in on the second half of that TV program. You *do* want your father and brother to win, don't you?

LIBBY: Of course I do! And who knows? Maybe someday I'll be the one on *Mad About Math. (All sorts of bells go off again.)*

MR. WIZARD: See? You just can't get away from math, Libby.

LIBBY *(Giggling):* That figures! *(Quick curtain)*

THE END

Production Notes

THAT FIGURES!

Characters: 3 male; 5 female; male or female for Radio Announcer.

Playing Time: 20 minutes.

Costumes: Modern, everyday dress. Charlie and Mr. Finch wear jackets, ties. Mr. Wizard, black robe and tall, peaked hat, both of which are decorated with white plus, minus, multiplication, and equal signs.

Properties: Newspaper; book; report card; score card; pencil; cookbook; colored paper.

Setting: The Finch dining room. Table center is set for breakfast. Door left leads to front hall; door right leads to kitchen. There are several windows up center and low bookcase under them. Radio is in bookcase. Telephone is on small table near door left. Chairs, buffet, or china cabinet complete furnishings.

Lighting: No special effects.

Sound: Doorbell; oven timer; telephone; alarm clock; striking clock.

The Last Time I Saw Paris

by Lewy Olfson

Beauty contest on Mount Olympus . . .

Characters

ATHENE
HERA
APHRODITE
PARIS

SETTING: *Mount Olympus. Stone benches stand left and right.*
AT RISE: HERA *is seated on one bench, polishing a thunderbolt, of which there is a pile on the floor beside her.* ATHENE, *seated on other bench, pushes her helmet back, then stretches and yawns.*
ATHENE (*Impatiently*): Another boring day on Mount Olympus.
HERA: Now, now, Athene. Why don't you take up some hobby? You're so good at arts and crafts I don't see why you can't keep busy. (*She blows on thunderbolt, then rubs it hard with cloth, and holds it at a distance to inspect it.*)
ATHENE (*Shaking her head*): Do you call polishing thunderbolts keeping busy? Pretty dull, if you ask me.
HERA: Well, why don't you go inspect your olive grove?
ATHENE (*Bored*): If you've seen one olive tree, you've seen them all.
HERA: Then how about reading a good book? After all, you *are* the goddess of wisdom.

81

ATHENE: Books bore me. (*Rises and begins to pace back and forth restlessly*) I want something new to happen—something exciting!

HERA: You could always see how your friend Jason is getting along with the *Argo*.

ATHENE: He's away on a shakedown cruise before sailing off after the Golden Fleece, and you know I always get seasick. Oh, there's simply nothing to do.

HERA (*Sarcastically*): I feel sorry for you. I never have trouble keeping busy—Only the other day when I went down to Earth I got involved in an interesting case.

ATHENE (*Bored*): I can just imagine!

HERA: No, really. It was a sad case, rather touching, in fact. There was this young musician, Orpheus, who had lost his wife, Eurydice. She was killed and ended up in Hades.

ATHENE: Oh, that's too bad.

HERA: His pleas really got to me, so I arranged for him to go down to Hades to try to get his wife back.

ATHENE: How did he make out?

HERA: Last I knew, he was down there playing his lyre, and it looked as if he would charm them all and get her back.

ATHENE: Well, Hera, that may be great for you, but that's not what I call exciting. I'd like some real adventure.

HERA (*Looking offstage*): Maybe it's on its way. Here comes Aphrodite with the mail. Perhaps there's a letter for you from Odysseus.

ATHENE: I think he has his hands full with Penelope. (*Sighing*) I'm sure Aphrodite gets plenty of mail. After all, she's goddess of love. Everyone writes to her with problems. She ought to set up a marriage counseling service to answer all those "Dear Aphie" letters. (*Sighs*) But me—all I ever get is catalogues from mail-order houses selling do-it-yourself kits. (APHRODITE *enters, a bag over her shoulder, holding some letters.*)

APHRODITE (*Waving letters as she approaches* HERA *and* ATHENE): Ladies, the afternoon mail is here.

ATHENE: Anything for me?

APHRODITE: Just a bill from your helmet polisher. (*Hands her envelope, then turns to* HERA) And there's a bill for you from your sandal shop. Those gold sandals certainly must set you back a lot. (*Reaches into bag for letters and hands* HERA *envelope, then looks at postcard in her hand*) And there's a postcard.

HERA: For me? I wonder who—

APHRODITE: It's one of those garish, touristy things. (*Reading*) "Greetings from the Underworld. Having a wonderful time, wish you were here. Signed, Orpheus."

HERA (*Reading it*): Isn't this nice.

ATHENE: Well, so much for the mail as a possible source of amusement for me!

APHRODITE (*Reaching into bag again and pulling out golden apple*): Wait! There was something else. Look! (*She holds up golden apple.*)

HERA: What is it?

APHRODITE: It's a golden apple.

ATHENE: Well, whom is it for?

APHRODITE (*Examining apple closely*): I'm not sure. The label just says, "For the fairest of the fair."

ATHENE (*Suddenly sitting up straight*): The fairest of the fair?

APHRODITE: That's what the label says.

HERA (*Innocently*): Well, Aphrodite, I think it *must* be meant for you. Don't you agree, Athene?

ATHENE (*Shrugging; overly casual*): Probably.

APHRODITE (*With exaggerated modesty*): Why, you must be joking! Surely you don't mean to suggest that I—why, it's too silly for words. I thought surely it must belong to one of *you* two.

HERA (*In mock amusement*): To me? Now, really, Aphrodite, how could anyone possibly think that I could be the fairest of the fair? I mean . . . I'm older than you.

APHRODITE (*Deprecatingly*): Just because you're years older—

HERA (*Overly sweet*): Let's not get carried away. I said I was older, but I didn't say I was *years* older.

APHRODITE: Hera, you know what the Delphic Oracle says: "Age lies not heavily on those who lie lightly."

HERA (*Shaking her head, perplexed*): One of these days we must get a translator for the Delphic Oracle.

ATHENE: But Hera, if *you* refuse the apple, surely you don't think *I* . . . ?

APHRODITE (*Quickly*): But of course, Athene, darling, the apple is yours. Who else on Olympus has a figure like yours?

ATHENE: Well, but what about Hera's velvety skin?

HERA: And what about Aphrodite's hair?

APHRODITE: But really, Hera, when you consider Athene's lovely eyes—

ATHENE: And your perfect nose, Aphrodite! And Hera's mouth. It is just perfection!

HERA: My mouth? But, Athene, your ear lobes—

APHRODITE (*Interrupting*): Athena is right about your mouth, Hera—

ATHENE (*Interrupting*): And there's Aphrodite's posture—

HERA (*Interrupting*): Not to mention your graceful carriage—

APHRODITE (*Raising her hands for silence*): It's obvious none of us can agree as to who really should get the golden apple.

HERA: I suggest you just pitch the silly thing down from the top of Mount Olympus, Aphrodite. Maybe then whoever really *is* the fairest of the fair will find it.

ATHENE: I was going to suggest just returning it to the Post Office marked "Return to Sender, Addressee Unknown."

APHRODITE: You're both right. That's just what I'll do. (*She starts out.*)

HERA (*Jumping up quickly, in alarm*): But—Aphrodite!

APHRODITE (*Stopping, a knowing smile on her face*): Yes?

HERA (*Tactfully*): On second thought . . . not that it really matters, of course, but—well, wouldn't it be rude to just send back the golden apple?

ATHENE: Hera is right, Aphrodite. If someone was good enough to have an apple carved out of solid gold, the least we can do is find someone to accept it.

APHRODITE: I agree. But who?

ATHENE (*Staring off into space*): Well, just to solve the problem . . . as a favor to you . . . I'd be willing to—

HERA: No, Athene, I don't think you should. Since it would be so obvious to everyone that I couldn't *possibly* be the fairest of the fair, *I* should take it. I mean, that would be the right thing to do.

APHRODITE: I simply can't let both of you make such sacrifices. I'm the one who caused the problem by picking the silly thing up in the first place. I should force myself to keep the apple.

ATHENE (*Dryly*): I think we're right back where we started.

APHRODITE: Honestly, how anyone ever expected three women to be able to agree on which one is the most beautiful . . .

HERA: That's it!

ATHENE: That's what?

HERA (*Profoundly*): The one below must go above to find the one in three!

APHRODITE: What?

ATHENE: Don't mind her, she's quoting that Delphic Oracle again.

HERA: What we need is a man—a human being—an earthling.

APHRODITE: That's a marvelous idea, Hera!

HERA (*Closing her eyes, intoning*): Let the first human man to pass beneath this spot be brought before us instantly! I, Hera, command it!

ATHENE (*Jumping up and down*): Oh, this is so exciting! I wonder who it will be?

APHRODITE: I hope he's handsome!

ATHENE: I hope he's intelligent!

HERA (*Dryly*): I hope he appreciates older women. (PARIS *enters. He is a young man, considerably less mature than the goddesses.*)

ATHENE: Behold! He comes!

APHRODITE: Good morrow, stranger!

HERA: Welcome to our dwelling place!

PARIS: Oh, hi, there! Say, do you know what place this is? I think I'm lost.

HERA: What is your name, earth person?

PARIS: My name? I'm Paris, Prince of Troy. Pleased to meet you. I seem to have lost my sense of direction. This isn't one of the suburbs of Troy, is it?

HERA (*Imperiously*): It is for us to question. It is for you to be silent and obey.

PARIS: What? Boy, that's all Greek to me.

HERA: Let your eyes do my bidding, and let your choice be my choice.

PARIS: Say, lady, did anyone ever tell you you sound just like the Delphic Oracle? I'm getting out of here! (*He starts to exit.* APHRODITE, *smiling sweetly, stops him.*)

APHRODITE: Just a moment, kind sir. Please. You will do us a great favor if you stay.

PARIS: Well . . . anything to oblige a pretty woman, I always say.

ATHENE (*Thrusting apple at him*): Do you see this apple?

PARIS (*Taking it happily*): Why, thanks! I haven't had lunch yet, and I love apples!

APHRODITE: No, no. You don't undersand. That's not a real apple. It's solid gold.

PARIS: Solid gold! Wow! I'll bet it must have cost a lot of money—even more than my season ticket to the Olympics.

HERA (*Angrily*): No, no, no! The apple is not for you.

PARIS (*Disappointed*): I was afraid of that.

ATHENE: What we want you to do is give that golden apple to whichever one of us you think is the fairest of the fair.

PARIS: The fairest of the fair? You're all good-looking. I don't see how I could possibly decide which one of you is the prettiest.

HERA (*Patiently*): We understand your problem. All three of us, we admit, are more beautiful than any woman you have ever seen before. But one of us must be just a teeny, tiny bit prettier than the other two. And that's the one you should give the apple to. (PARIS *shakes head, looks confused.*)

APHRODITE: Paris, may I have a private word with you? (*She draws him to one side.*) Obviously, Paris, this whole thing is just sort of a game with us. I mean, none of us really takes it seriously. And since it obviously doesn't make any difference to you which one of us gets the apple, here's what I'll do. If you give me the apple, I'll get you a date with the most beautiful woman in the world: Helen, Queen of Sparta.

PARIS (*Impressed*): Would you really? Do you have her phone number and everything?

APHRODITE: Trust me, Paris. I have connections.

HERA (*Calling*): Paris! Could I have a word with you in private?

PARIS (*Crossing to* HERA): Of course.

HERA (*Soothingly*): Now, Paris, you understand that the choice is to be all your own. But since it's such a problem for you, I'd be glad to help you out. Choose me, Paris, and I'll make you the richest man in the world.

PARIS (*Impressed*): Richer than King Croesus?

ATHENE (*Calling and beckoning with her finger*): Paris . . .

PARIS (*Crossing to* ATHENE): You want to make things easier for me, too, I'll bet.

ATHENE (*In a flirtatious voice*): Give the apple to me, and for the rest of your life you will always be victorious in battle.

PARIS (*Impressed*): Really? Does that mean I could beat up Achilles? He's always showing off his muscles.

ATHENE (*Nodding*): When you get through with him, Achilles will look like a Greek ruin.

APHRODITE (*Calling*): Paris! Are you ready? We're waiting for your decision. (*Goddesses line up, facing him.*)

ATHENE: Paris—remember Athene!

HERA: Paris—remember Hera!

APHRODITE: Paris—remember—Queen Helen of Sparta! Atreus 7–5609!

PARIS (*Tossing apple to* APHRODITE, *who catches it*): Aphrodite, the golden apple is yours!

APHRODITE (*Running off with it, joyfully*): Thanks, Paris! Thanks! (*Exits*)

HERA (*Seething*): Yes, Paris, thanks. Thanks for nothing.

PARIS (*Concerned*): I hope you two aren't upset. I mean, I had to pick one of you—so naturally two had to be left out. But I hope there aren't any hard feelings.

ATHENE (*Overly sweet*): Hard feelings? Why, no. Not at all!

HERA (*With venom*): Why should we care if you picked Aphrodite? Fair is fair.

ATHENE: As a matter of fact, I think we ought to give Paris a present, Hera—something to show him we have no hard feelings.

HERA: Good idea, Athene! Paris, we're going to give *you* a wonderful present, just the way Aphrodite did.

PARIS (*Happily*): You are? What is it going to be?

ATHENE *and* HERA (*Shouting at him in unison*): A Trojan Horse! (*Quick curtain*)

THE END

Production Notes

THE LAST TIME I SAW PARIS

Characters: 1 male; 3 female.

Playing Time: 10 minutes.

Costumes: Ancient Greek robes and sandals for goddesses. Athene wears a helmet. Paris wears a short tunic and sandals laced up to the knee.

Properties: Thunderbolts (cardboard cutouts), letters, postcard, golden apple.

Setting: Mount Olympus. There are stone benches right and left. There is an exit at one side.

Lighting and Sound: No special effects.

Unlucky Cinderella

by Marilee Jackson

If the shoe doesn't fit—improvise!

Characters

CINDERELLA
TWO STEPSISTERS
GERTRUDE, *Cinderella's stepmother*
FATHER
VERY ODDMOTHER
ROYAL SHOE FITTER
ROYAL DRESSMAKER
PRINCE
KING
QUEEN

SCENE 1

TIME: *Once upon a time.*

SETTING: *Cinderella's house, with small table, two chairs, a throw rug, and clothes rack with gown hanging on it. Door up center leads outside. Exits left and right lead to rest of house.*

AT RISE: CINDERELLA *enters, humming as she sweeps.*

CINDERELLA (*To audience*): Oh, hello there. My name is Cinderella. Please excuse my appearance. (*Sighs*) I've been working all day long, same as every day. (*Puts her hand to her ear*) My stepsisters are coming. I had better get busy. (STEPSISTERS *enter left.*)

1ST STEPSISTER (*Looking around*): Cinderella, this place is a mess. Didn't Mother tell you to scrub the floor?

2ND STEPSISTER (*Angrily*): And where is my gown? You were supposed to iron it. You know tonight is the grand ball!

CINDERELLA (*Meekly*): I did scrub the floor.

1ST STEPSISTER (*Getting down on hands and knees*): I can't see my face in it. Scrub it again!

CINDERELLA (*To* 2ND STEPSISTER): And I did iron your gown. (*Fetches it from clothes rack*) Here it is.

2ND STEPSISTER (*Pulling large magnifying glass from her pocket and holding it up to dress*): I see a wrinkle. (*Exasperated*) Can't you do anything right? (STEPSISTERS *exit.* CINDERELLA *bursts into tears.* FATHER *enters from up center.*)

FATHER: Cinderella, why aren't you getting dressed for the ball?

CINDERELLA: Oh, Father. I have too much work and nothing to wear.

FATHER (*Firmly*): We'll see about that. (*Calling*) Gertrude! Come here at once! (GERTRUDE *enters left. She carries scroll and brown paper package.*)

GERTRUDE (*Sweetly*): Yes, my pet?

FATHER: Why must Cinderella work while the other girls do nothing? And why is her closet empty while they have dozens of pretty dresses? (*He folds his arms across his chest and frowns.*) I am waiting for an explanation!

GERTRUDE: Oh, my dear, you have misunderstood! I only asked Cinderella to finish a few chores before the ball. Isn't that fair?

FATHER (*Scratching his head thoughtfully*): A *few* chores would be fair.

GERTRUDE: As for her empty closet, I have thrown away all her old dresses and purchased new ones for her. Wasn't that nice of me?

FATHER (*Giving in*): Very nice of you. Come, Cinderella, dry your eyes and finish your few chores. Then, off to the ball! (*He exits.*)

GERTRUDE (*Handing bundle and scroll to* CINDERELLA): Here is your new dress, and here is your list of chores. You heard what your father said. It is fair for you to finish them before you go to the ball! (*She exits.* CINDERELLA *unrolls scroll, which is long enough to reach floor. Then she unwraps bundle and holds up an ugly dress.* CINDERELLA *bursts into tears.* VERY ODD MOTHER *enters through door.*)

VERY ODDMOTHER: Hello, there, Cinderella!

CINDERELLA (*Tearfully*): Who are you?

ODDMOTHER (*Simply*): Your Very Oddmother, of course. Don't you know how the story goes?

CINDERELLA: Very Oddmother? You must mean, "Fairy God-mother."

ODDMOTHER: Not at all! Fairy Godmothers are so . . . old-fashioned! It is much more pleasant being a Very Oddmother. Now, let me see. I believe this is where you expect me to turn your pumpkin into a coach, mice into footmen, and your plain little shoes into glass slippers. (CINDERELLA *begins to wail loudly.*) I *do* have the right story, don't I? You are Cinderella?

CINDERELLA (*Sniffling*): *Unlucky* Cinderella! (*Cries even louder*)

ODDMOTHER: What's the problem? Don't you want to go to the ball?

CINDERELLA (*Sobbing*): Of course, I do, but I don't have a ball gown.

ODDMOTHER: Then you have no time to waste. First, I will call for my magic dressmaker. (*Waving her wand*) Zip, zip! (ROYAL DRESSMAKER *enters, wearing an apron which holds Velcro-backed lace or ribbon, and Velcro-backed flower appliqués. She wears a tape measure around her neck, and a thimble on her finger.*)

DRESSMAKER: Royal Fashions, at your service. (*Bows*) Hm-m. (*Measuring* CINDERELLA) I think I can handle this. Turn around. (CINDERELLA *obeys.*) And again. (*She turns again.*) Yes, I think you will do quite well.

CINDERELLA (*Miserably*): But I'm trying to tell you—

DRESSMAKER: Stop babbling, girl, and stand still. We have work to do. Now, a bit of ribbon here. (DRESSMAKER *pulls ribbon from apron and attaches it to the skirt of* CINDER-ELLA's *dress and to the cuffs of her sleeves.*) And some pretty flowers there. (*Attaches flower appliqués to* CINDERELLA's *skirt.*) What do you think of that? (*Pulls a mirror out of apron pocket*)

CINDERELLA (*Gazing into mirror*): It's beautiful, but—

DRESSMAKER: But nothing! It is the most beautiful dress I have ever created! Now, walk like this—(*She glides across stage and* CINDERELLA *tries to imitate her.*) No, no. Gracefully, so that your *tiny* feet barely touch the floor.

CINDERELLA (*Protesting*): But that's what I keep trying to tell you. (*Points*) Look at these ugly shoes!

ODDMOTHER: Yes, I see . . . except for those shoes, you look lovely, my dear, lovely! And so, with a wave of my wand—(*Waving wand*) Presto! My Royal Shoe Fitter. (ROYAL SHOE FITTER *enters with a stack of shoe boxes, which have been glued together, off center, to create the illusion of a pile about to topple. Only the top box contains shoes.*) I trust you have brought the most beautiful slippers.

SHOE FITTER: Of course. I have red slippers, blue slippers, gold slippers, silver slippers, every kind of beautiful slipper made!

ODDMOTHER: Well, don't stand there, Cinderella. Try them on. Choose your favorite! (CINDERELLA *begins to cry.*)

SHOE FITTER: What is wrong? Did we forget your favorite color?

CINDERELLA (*Sobbing*): I can't wear any of your pretty little shoes. That's what I've been trying to tell you! (CINDERELLA *lifts up hem of her skirt to reveal oversized feet. Note: She is shoeless, and long cardboard soles have been inserted into the soles of her socks.*) I have big feet!

SHOE FITTER (*Appalled*): She has *huge* feet!

ODDMOTHER: She has *enormous* feet!

SHOE FITTER (*Throwing up his arms*): How did this happen?

DRESSMAKER: Everyone knows that Cinderella has tiny feet.

SHOE FITTER: What will the Prince think when he sees those feet!

CINDERELLA (*Wailing*): Everything is ruined!

ODDMOTHER: Nonsense, my dear. You forget, you have a Very Oddmother. It will just take a little thinking. You can still leave a tiny glass slipper. You will simply have to carry it in your evening bag, and when the clock strikes midnight, you pull it out, drop it, and run home as fast as you can!

SHOE FITTER: But when the Prince goes looking for the owner of the slipper, it will not fit on her foot!

ODDMOTHER: I have plenty of time to deal with that problem. For now, Cinderella, off you go to the ball. (*To* DRESS-MAKER) May we have an evening bag, please? (DRESS-MAKER *produces one.*) The glass slipper? (SHOE FITTER *pulls a shoe from shoebox.* CINDERELLA *places it in her bag.*) Don't forget, when the clock strikes midnight, you must be gone!

DRESSMAKER: Have a good time.

CINDERELLA: Wait! Where is my pumpkin coach? And my little mice footmen and horses?

ODDMOTHER (*In disbelief*): Pumpkins? At this time of year? And if I allowed mice near the palace, all the guests would be terrified.

CINDERELLA: So, how shall I get to the ball?

ODDMOTHER: By magic, of course! Hold on tight! (*Waving wand*) Abracadabra . . . (*Blackout. Curtain*)

* * * * *

SCENE 2

TIME: *A few minutes later.*

SETTING: *Ballroom of the Royal Palace. A candelabra sits on table, which is covered with a rich cloth. The chairs, now covered with fine cloth, stand at center, and are used as thrones for King, Queen, and Prince.*

AT RISE: PRINCE *paces downstage. Every now and then he peers around as if looking for something.* KING *and* QUEEN *are seated on thrones, eating from a box of chocolates.* STEP-SISTERS *are dancing, right, circling one another, bowing, and circling again.*

QUEEN: Why are you so anxious, my son?

PRINCE: I am expecting someone special tonight. It said so in my fortune cookie. (PRINCE *produces a slip of paper from his pocket.*) It says, (*Reading*) "Tonight you will meet the girl of your dreams. You will know her by her long. . . ."

QUEEN (*Expectantly*): Yes?

PRINCE (*Frowning, shaking head*): And then I can't read the rest. I spilled some duck sauce on it. (*Puts fortune back in pocket; with a dismissive wave*) Oh, well, if she's special, I'm sure I will recognize her. (CINDERELLA *enters.* STEP-SISTERS *stop dancing and huddle together, gossiping in low whispers.* PRINCE *sees* CINDERELLA *and gives a start.*) Who is that charming girl? I have never seen her before.

QUEEN: Could she be—?

PRINCE: If only I knew the last word of my fortune!

1ST STEPSISTER (*In stage whisper*): Who is she? She looks a bit like—

2ND STEPSISTER: An awfully lot like—

STEPSISTERS (*Together*): Cinderella!

1ST STEPSISTER: But Cinderella has no beautiful clothes.

2ND STEPSISTER: And Cinderella has no carriage. The palace is a long way from our house.

1ST STEPSISTER: We must be mistaken.

2ND STEPSISTER: It's only our imagination. Cinderella is at home, doing her *few* chores. (STEPSISTERS *giggle at this, then step aside and mime conversation.* PRINCE *leaves throne and approaches* CINDERELLA, *bows to her, and invites her to dance. They dance for a moment, then continue in slight rocking motion, while they speak the following.*)

PRINCE: Where are you from? I have never seen you before.

CINDERELLA: Oh that's because I live a long (*On hearing "long,"* PRINCE *snaps to attention and casts questioning look at audience.*) way from here.

PRINCE (*Intrigued*): And how late will you be staying at the ball?

CINDERELLA: Oh, not very long. (*Again,* PRINCE *reacts to hearing "long."*) I must leave at midnight.

PRINCE (*Excitedly*): Well, since I've been deprived of your charming company all my life, you must save all your dances for me.

CINDERELLA (*Flattered*): Oh, Prince, I could dance with you my whole life long. (*Upon hearing "long" again,* PRINCE *whoops for joy and twirls* CINDERELLA *about gleefully. They continue to dance and mime conversation while swaying.*)

KING (*Pulling watch from his pocket*): It is almost midnight.

QUEEN (*Gesturing to dance floor*): But it has been a wonderful party. Our son seems to be having a marvelous time!

KING: Who is that enchanting girl with him?

QUEEN: I am quite sure I have never seen her before. (*Sound of clock chiming is heard off.* CINDERELLA *gives a start.*)

CINDERELLA (*Woefully*): Oh, I must go! (*Curtsies quickly to* PRINCE) Goodnight, my Prince. (*She runs off.*)

PRINCE (*Calling after her*): Wait! You never told me your name! How will I find you? (*Suddenly a shoe is thrown onto stage from wings.* PRINCE *picks it up with a look of astonishment. Curtain*)

* * * * *

SCENE 3

TIME: *Three days later.*

SETTING: *Cinderella's home. Same as Scene 1.*

AT RISE: CINDERELLA *is sweeping up right corner.* GERTRUDE *and* STEPSISTERS *are gathered together down center.* FATHER *sits at table, reading a book.*

1ST STEPSISTER: Have you heard? The Prince is visiting every house in the village, looking for the owner of a glass slipper he found at the ball.

2ND STEPSISTER: He has proclaimed that whoever owns it will be his bride.

GERTRUDE (*Indignantly*): Hmph! And why shouldn't one of my daughters be his bride? (*To* STEPSISTERS) All you need to do is get your foot into that shoe!

1ST STEPSISTER: I will try, Mother.

2ND STEPSISTER: I will try *harder*, Mother. (*Scowls at her sister*)

CINDERELLA (*To audience*): Oh, woe is me. How will this all end? I am supposed to put on the glass slipper, marry the prince, and live happily ever after. But how can I do it with these feet? (*Lifts up her skirts and looks dolefully at her feet; exits. Knocking on door is heard.*)

GERTRUDE (*Rushing to door and opening it to* PRINCE): Please come in, Your Highness. (*She curtsies to* PRINCE *as he enters. He carries glass slipper.*)

FATHER (*Bowing*): Good Prince! Welcome to our humble home. Please sit down. (*Indicates chair*)

PRINCE (*Sitting*): Thank you. I am so tired. I have been to every house in the village looking for the owner of this slipper. (*Sadly*) If I do not find her here, I am without hope.

GERTRUDE (*Worming her way between* PRINCE *and* FATHER): I should like you to meet our two lovely daughters, Prince.

FATHER: Two? (GERTRUDE *covers his mouth with her hand.*)

1ST STEPSISTER (*Simpering*): How do you do, Your Highness? (*Tries to grab slipper*) Oh, I think the slipper looks just my size.

PRINCE (*Holding slipper just out of her reach; to audience*): I hope not. (*Worriedly*) But, she does have a rather *long* nose. (PRINCE *tries slipper on her foot.* 1ST STEPSISTER *groans, trying to jam her foot into shoe unsuccessfully. Relieved*) I'm afraid you are not the one.

2ND STEPSISTER (*Pushing forward*): Let me try!

PRINCE (*To audience*): I suppose I must. But what if the shoe fits? She does have a rather *long* neck. (*He tries the shoe on* 2ND STEPSISTER's *foot. She tries to push her foot in, but finally gives up.*)

2ND STEPSISTER (*Wailing*): I don't want that smelly old shoe, anyway! (GERTRUDE *consoles her.*)

PRINCE (*In resignation*): Well, that is that. I have failed to find my princess. (VERY ODDMOTHER *peeks in from off right.*)

ODDMOTHER (*Calling off*): Psst! This is where you come in.

CINDERELLA (*Also peeking in from off right*): But the shoe won't fit! I will be a laughingstock!

ODDMOTHER: I have a plan. Go sit by the table, and ask to try on the slipper. (ODDMOTHER *pushes* CINDERELLA *forward to table. Only the audience can see* ODDMOTHER *lift tablecloth and crawl under table.*)

CINDERELLA (*To* PRINCE): I have not had a chance to try the slipper, Your Highness.

PRINCE (*Delighted*): Where did you come from? (*Turning to* GERTRUDE) I thought you said you had only two daughters.

GERTRUDE (*Disdainfully*): Cinderella is my *step*daughter.

PRINCE: Nevertheless, I wish to try it on her. (*To audience*) Despite her ragged clothes, I find her hauntingly familiar. (PRINCE *holds out the slipper.* ODDMOTHER'*s bare foot emerges from beneath tablecloth.* PRINCE *kneels down and places the slipper on the foot.*) It fits!

CINDERELLA (*Astonished*): It does?

FATHER (*Delighted*): Hooray!

PRINCE (*Holding up his hand*): Wait! There is one problem. The slipper fits, but I am also seeking the meaning of my fortune. (*He pulls out slip of paper from pocket.*) It says here that the girl of my dreams will have long . . . (*Pauses*)

FATHER: Long what?

PRINCE (*Frustrated*): That's what I don't know. (*To* CINDERELLA) And unless you have some quality that meets that description, you cannot be the one I am seeking.

CINDERELLA (*Standing; excitedly*): But I do! I do! I have the longest feet you have ever seen! (*She raises her skirts to reveal feet.*)

PRINCE (*Astonished*): My goodness! Your feet *are* long! But the slipper? How did it fit? (CINDERELLA *pulls off the tablecloth and reveals* VERY ODDMOTHER, *still wearing the glass slipper.*)

CINDERELLA: It didn't. My Very Oddmother played a trick on you. We thought you would not want a princess whose feet could not fit into the glass slipper.

PRINCE: Nonsense! That sounds like something that would happen in a fairy tale. (*Proudly*) I am a modern prince. And this is a modern story. (*Kneeling before* CINDERELLA) With your consent, we will be married and live happily ever after!

CINDERELLA (*Winking to audience*): In other words, for a long, long time! (CINDERELLA *and* PRINCE *embrace, striking a pose. Curtain*)

THE END

Production Notes

UNLUCKY CINDERELLA

Characters: 3 male, 6 female, 2 male or female for Shoe Fitter and Dressmaker.

Playing Time: 25 minutes.

Costumes: Long dresses for women. Men wear vests, pants, and shirts. Very Oddmother wears powdered wig, tutu, leotard, and tights. Cinderella's dress is long enough to cover her stockinged feet with long cardboard sole inserts. Her dress has Velcro glued to places where trim is to be attached.

Properties: Broom, magnifying glass, long scroll, ugly dress wrapped in brown paper, wand, ribbon and flower appliqués backed with Velcro, tape measure, thimble, hand mirror, stack of shoe boxes glued together, pair of clear plastic shoes, evening bag, box of chocolates, small slip of paper, book.

Setting Scenes 1 and 3: Sitting room in Cinderella's house. Door up center leads to outside. Exits left and right lead to rest of house. Off center is small table covered by tablecloth long enough to reach floor, two chairs, throw rug, and clothes rack with 2nd Stepsister's ball gown hanging on it complete room. Scene 2: Ballroom of the Royal Palace. Table is covered with rich cloth, on top of it is a candelabra. Chairs are covered with rich cloth and moved up center to serve as thrones.

Lighting: Blackout in Scene 1.

Sound: Clock chimes as indicated in text.

Hold On!

by Nikki Leigh Mondschein

Can Anna control her nerves when she calls George for a date? . . .

Characters

ANNA
KATE, *her best friend*
GEORGE
SCOTT, *his best friend*

TIME: *The present.*
SETTING: *Divided stage: Anna's bedroom, with twin beds, is left. George's living room, with couch, stool, and table with telephone on it, is right.*
AT RISE: *Lights come up on* ANNA *and* KATE *sitting on beds left.* ANNA *has portable phone on her lap. Right side of stage remains dark.*

ANNA (*Sighing*): I just don't have the nerve!
KATE: There's nothing for you to worry about. I'm sure he likes you. All you have to do is say the magic words. "Will you go out with . . . "
ANNA (*Protesting*): It's not that simple! You know George. He's so shy. I don't want to scare him away. What if something goes wrong?
KATE (*Calmly*): Nothing will go wrong, Anna. I'll be right here to give you moral support, O.K.?
ANNA: O.K. (*Takes a deep breath*) Well, here goes. (*As she dials number, lights come up right.* GEORGE *is on couch, reading magazine. His phone rings.* KATE *leafs through magazine during following exchange.*)
GEORGE (*Answering*): Hello?

99

ANNA (*Tentatively; after a pause*): Hello . . . is . . . is George there?

GEORGE: Yes. (*Continues reading magazine*)

ANNA (*Puzzled*): Yes?

GEORGE: Mm-hmm.

ANNA: May I speak to him, please?

GEORGE (*Suddenly; putting down magazine*): Anna?

ANNA: George!

GEORGE (*Smiling; sitting up*): Hi!

ANNA (*Smiling*): Hi. (*There is a pause.*)

GEORGE: Did you—call for a reason?

ANNA: Oh, I . . . I . . . can you hold on a second?

GEORGE: Sure. (ANNA *puts hand over receiver.* GEORGE *nervously drums fingers on table, runs hand through hair, etc., while he waits.*)

ANNA (*Nervously*): Kate? He . . . he—um. . . .

KATE: What? Just say it, girl!

ANNA: He asked if I called for a reason. I don't know what to tell him!

KATE (*Rolling eyes*): Is that all? Tell him you called to say hello. That's not suspicious. And why don't you start a conversation while you're at it? Talk about the weather or something.

ANNA: Good idea! I'm glad I have your help, Kate.

KATE: It's nothing, really.

ANNA (*Into phone*): Sorry. What were we talking about?

GEORGE: Actually, we weren't . . . yet.

ANNA: I . . . I just called to say hello.

GEORGE: Hello.

ANNA: Hello. (SCOTT *ambles in right, eating chips from large bag he's holding.*)

GEORGE (*Into phone*): Listen, can you hold on a second?

ANNA: Sure. No problem. (GEORGE *puts hand over receiver.* NOTE: *This action is repeated as necessary throughout play. Also, during the dialogue of one set of friends, the other friends ad lib quiet conversation.*)

SCOTT (*Irritated*): You know, you invite me over to your house, George, and then you decide to have a phone conversation. Well, I can see that I'm not wanted . . . (*He begins to exit, then rushes back to* GEORGE.) unless that's Kate, my dearest love, on the phone?

GEORGE (*Shaking head*): Keep dreaming, Scott.

SCOTT (*Pretending to stab himself*): George! You've thwarted my hopes! But that girl will call me soon, I promise you. . . . Who is it?

GEORGE: It's Anna . . . can you believe it? I always talk about asking her out on a date, but I'm never brave enough to go through with it.

SCOTT: And you have to be careful. Anna's so shy. You don't want to scare her away.

GEORGE: What should I do?

SCOTT (*Shrugging*): Play it by ear. Let her make the first move, and follow her lead. If nothing happens, I'll help you out. Unless, of course, you want me to tell you one of my top-secret lines.

GEORGE (*Rolling eyes*): No thanks. (*Into phone*) Hi, Anna. Sorry.

ANNA: That's O.K. So—(*Brightly*) great weather we're having!

GEORGE (*Confused*): Uh—but it's raining outside. In fact, there's a thunderstorm. You'd have to be a fish to like this weather! (*Realizing what he has just said, he slaps palm to his forehead.*)

ANNA *and* GEORGE (*Together*): Hold on!

ANNA: He called me a fish!

KATE: What?

ANNA: And I deserved it, too. Great weather we're having? How could I be so stupid?

KATE: Don't worry about it. I'm sure he still adores you. Just change the subject, quickly.

ANNA: But he called me a fish!

GEORGE: I called her a fish! Follow her lead, huh? I'm perfectly brilliant. She makes a comment about the weather—which, mind you, is horrendous—and I call her a fish. I'll be lucky if she hasn't hung up on me.

SCOTT: Just make a joke about it. How about . . . fish sticks, anyone? I prefer sushi myself.

GEORGE: Very funny, Scott. (ANNA *and* GEORGE *get back on phone.*)

GEORGE *and* ANNA (*Simultaneously; in saccharine voices*): Hello.

ANNA (*Brightly*): Did you see the big game yesterday? It was so . . .

GEORGE: I hate football.

ANNA (*Changing tone*): . . . bad. I can't stand the sport myself.

GEORGE (*Positively*): I found a rare coin yesterday. Coin collecting is . . .

ANNA: How boring. I've never understood how people could think that collecting pieces of metal is fun.

GEORGE (*Negatively*): . . . not the most thrilling thing to do. That's why I do more exciting things, like . . . (*They say the next lines in unison.*)

ANNA: Swimming.

GEORGE: Running. (*Both change their minds and say their next two lines in unison.*)

ANNA: Running.

GEORGE: Swimming.

GEORGE *and* ANNA (*In unison*): Tennis. (*Both smile with relief.*)

ANNA: You know what's great about us, George?

GEORGE: What?

ANNA: We're so much alike.

GEORGE: What would you do if you were stranded on a deserted island?

ANNA: Hm-m-m. I would write S.O.S. in the sand with my toes, make a hammock out of palm leaves, and lie there drinking coconut milk until someone saved me. Why do you ask?

GEORGE: I just wanted to know if you would do the same thing as me.

ANNA: Would I?

GEORGE: Of course.

ANNA: Then we should get stranded on a desert island together more often.

GEORGE *and* ANNA: Hold on!

ANNA: Kate, I'm so embarrassed. I told him I'd like to be stranded on a deserted island with him! What if he thinks it's corny? What if he thinks I'm crazy? What if he laughs at me? What if . . .

GEORGE: Whoa! She wants to be stranded on a deserted island with me. Cool.

SCOTT: I have no idea how this topic came up in the conversation, but you're getting there. I know exactly what you should do now. Make her jealous! Talk about other girls. She'll be begging to go out with you.

GEORGE: I'm not sure. Don't you think that's kind of mean?

SCOTT: If you want to back out of this now, fine. Go ahead. But we've come this far, and I think you should go for it. Besides, all's fair in love and war.

GEORGE: O.K. You've convinced me. Hold on. (*Both get back on phone.*) Hi, Dana. Sorry I took so long.

ANNA: What did you just call me?

GEORGE: Oh, I'm sorry, Kara. You know how things are. I talk to so many girls, I begin to get their names confused.

ANNA: It's Anna.

GEORGE: What?

ANNA (*Annoyed*): Anna. My name is Anna.

GEORGE: Oh, Anna! Forgive me. As if I could ever forget you. Your dazzling smile, your blue-green eyes . . .

ANNA (*Flatly*): My eyes are brown.

GEORGE: Brown? Then who has blue-green eyes?

ANNA (*Irritated*): You tell me.

GEORGE: No matter, Alice. (ANNA *looks horrified, then spiteful.*) As Shakespeare once said, "What's in a name?" (*Laughs uncomfortably*)

ANNA (*Spiritedly*): You are so right, *Gavin*.

GEORGE: What? My name's not . . .

ANNA: When Kate first introduced us, I decided that you were the nicest, most intelligent, blonde boy I'd ever known . . . Gilbert.

GEORGE (*Upset*): It's George! And my hair is . . . wait a minute. Something's wrong here. Hold on. (*To* SCOTT) Thanks a lot! She used my own trick against me. I think I'm jealous!

SCOTT: Well, then, it's time for you to take action. Ask her out to the movies. It's guaranteed not to fail.

GEORGE (*Sarcastically*): Of course not. Has anything else gone wrong in this conversation? (*He gets back on phone.*) Anna, have you seen any good movies lately?

ANNA: Hold on. (*To* KATE) Kate, have I seen any good movies lately?

KATE: No! You're dying to go see any movie that will give you the chance to be alone in a theater with him.

ANNA (*Back on phone*): Well, George, I really haven't had the time to see any movies lately, but I am hoping that I'll have the opportunity to go soon.

GEORGE: Really? That's funny. I was hoping to go soon, too.

GEORGE *and* ANNA: Hold on!

ANNA *and* GEORGE (*In unison, to their friends*): He/She wants to go to a movie!

KATE *and* SCOTT (*In unison*): Ask him/her out!

GEORGE *and* ANNA (*On phone, in unison, after a deep breath*): Will you go out with me? (*Both start laughing.*) Yes!

ANNA: Why couldn't I have just asked you out right at the beginning?

GEORGE: Why couldn't *I* have asked *you* out first?

ANNA: Why did I have to talk about the weather?

GEORGE: Why did I have to call you a fish?

ANNA: I don't know. It's weird the way things get mixed up like this.

GEORGE: I know, but it was worth it. I wish there were some way we could get Scott and Kate to ask each other out.

ANNA (*Slyly*): Are you thinking what I'm thinking?

GEORGE *and* ANNA: Hold on! (*Quick curtain*)

THE END

Production Notes

HOLD ON!

Characters: 2 male; 2 female.
Playing Time: 15 minutes.
Costumes: Modern, casual dress.
Properties: Portable phone; magazine; bag of chips.
Setting: Divided stage: Anna's bedroom, with twin beds, is left. George's living room, with couch, stool, and table with telephone on it, is right.
Lighting: At Rise, right side of stage remains dark; then lights come up full.
Sound: Telephone.

Hairum-Scarum

by Christina Hamlett

Hilarious hairdos at the Fantastic Frills Salon . . .

Characters

OLIVIA, *salon owner*
HILDA, *her assistant*
GOLDILOCKS
RAPUNZEL
CINDERELLA
BRIAR ROSE
ALICE

TIME: *The present.*
SETTING: *Reception area of the Fantastic Frills Salon. Table with phone on it is down left. Three archways leading to "styling booths" are upstage. Main entrance to salon is right. Color scheme is pink and white; photos of different hairstyles adorn the walls. Wig heads, hair spray cans, magazines, etc. round out salon decor.*
AT RISE: OLIVIA *is sitting at table, doing her nails.* HILDA *enters through arch and crosses to* OLIVIA.
OLIVIA (*Sighing heavily*): Hilda, this has to be the slowest day we've ever had!
HILDA: You can say that again!
OLIVIA: I'm almost tempted to close up shop and call it a day.
HILDA: You might as well. The rest of us have styled and re-styled each other's hair so many times, we're bored to tears back there! (*Phone rings.*)
OLIVIA (*Excitedly*): The phone! Things could be looking up. (*Answers phone*) Good morning. Fantastic Frills Salon. . . . An

appointment this afternoon? (*Smiles at* HILDA) Yes, I think
we can fit you in. (*Writing in schedule book*) Name, please?
. . . Helen. . . . Yes, two o'clock would be fine. . . . A special
occasion? (*Nodding*) Your face is going to launch a thousand
ships so you want to look your best? . . . Don't worry, Helen.
We'll send you out in style. O.K., see you at two. (*Hangs up*)
HILDA: Who was that?
OLIVIA: Some woman named Helen. She lives in Troy. She said
something about looking special for Paris.
HILDA (*Pleased*): Wow! Sounds as if there may be a big tip in
it for us.
OLIVIA: Don't count your curlers before they're in. (GOLDI-
LOCKS *runs in right, breathless and looking behind her as if
being pursued.*)
GOLDILOCKS: Is this the Fantastic Frills Salon?
HILDA: You're in the right place. I'm Hilda, and this is Olivia,
the owner.
OLIVIA: What can we do for you, Miss. . . . ?
GOLDILOCKS: Locks. Goldi Locks. And what you can do is get
me out of a lot of hot water!
HILDA: What's the problem?
GOLDILOCKS: Well, there are three bears—a father, a mother,
and a baby bear who whines all the time.
HILDA: What about them?
GOLDILOCKS: It seems they've got a warrant out for my
arrest.
OLIVIA: *Arrest?*
GOLDILOCKS (*In reassuring tones*): Don't worry, it's nothing
serious, really. I wandered into the bears' house by mistake,
and they got in a big huff about it. I tried to explain, but
would they listen? Of course not! In fact, they were downright
grizzly about it, and told the police I broke their chairs and
ate their food, and—
OLIVIA (*Interrupting*): I'm confused. What is it that you want
us to do?
GOLDILOCKS (*Indicating her hair*): Well, see this hair?
HILDA: Yes, it's very pretty.
OLIVIA: Lovely.

GOLDILOCKS: It's also a dead giveaway. They're looking for a girl with golden locks. Until I can get a good lawyer, I need a disguise. Something brunette, maybe. Straight, with feathered bangs.

OLIVIA: Well—

HILDA: She really does seem like a sweet girl, Olivia.

GOLDILOCKS: Will you do it? Please?

OLIVIA: Oh, all right. (*To* HILDA) Take her back to Gladys.

HILDA: Will do.

OLIVIA (*To* GOLDILOCKS): You'll look like a different person after we're through with you.

GOLDILOCKS: Thanks! You're a real lifesaver! (HILDA *and* GOLDILOCKS *exit. Phone rings.*)

OLIVIA (*Into phone*): Good morning. Fantastic Frills Salon. (*Listens in amazement*) What? . . . Why, that's terrible! . . . It completely turned to gold. . . . The brush, too? I've never heard of anything like that happening before! . . . Well, try a good conditioner first, and, if that doesn't work, we'll make an appointment for you. . . . (HILDA *returns*) Good luck. (*Hangs up*)

HILDA: What was that all about?

OLIVIA: It's the most bizarre story I've ever heard. It seems that when this girl's father touched things, they turned to gold, just like that! (*Waves hand*) Anyway, he offered to brush her hair, and as he touched it—zap! Instant gold—and the brush too!

HILDA: That's the weirdest thing I've ever heard.

RAPUNZEL (*Calling from offstage*): Yoo-hoo! Anybody there?

OLIVIA: Come on in—we're open! (RAPUNZEL *enters; she has long hair that drags on the floor.*)

RAPUNZEL: Thank goodness! (*Trips over hair*) I've been tripping all over the street, looking for a salon that's open.

HILDA (*Amazed*): Look at that hair, Olivia!

RAPUNZEL: That's what I'm here for. I want you to cut it.

OLIVIA: But it's absolutely gorgeous! Why on earth would you want to cut it?

RAPUNZEL: You'd want it cut, too, if you knew the trouble it's caused me.

HILDA: Like what?

RAPUNZEL: Like having a witch keep me locked up in a huge tower without an elevator.

OLIVIA: If it doesn't have an elevator, how does anybody get to the top?

RAPUNZEL (*Pointing to hair*): Three guesses and the first two don't count.

HILDA: By climbing up your hair?

RAPUNZEL: Bingo!

OLIVIA: That's incredible!

RAPUNZEL: I mean, here I am, doing my nails or watching the soaps, and all I hear is "Rapunzel, Rapunzel, let down your hair." Day in and day out. I'm sick of it. I want one of those cute short styles.

OLIVIA: Well . . . if you're really sure.

RAPUNZEL: Believe me—I'm sure.

OLIVIA (*To* HILDA): Take her to Loretta—she loves to cut hair.

HILDA: We're on our way. (*Exits with* RAPUNZEL. *Phone rings.* OLIVIA *answers it.*)

OLIVIA (*Into phone*): Good morning. Fantastic Frills Salon. (*Listens*) Yes, that sounds pretty messy. . . . Of course, I'd be startled, too. A spider, you say? . . . Oh, dear. You might try a good shampoo and give us a call if all of it doesn't come out. . . . (HILDA *reenters.*) Certainly, any time. (*Hangs up*)

HILDA: Another customer?

OLIVIA: One of Esther's regulars—that Muffet girl who's into health foods.

HILDA: Remember that stuff she was eating last week—curds and whey? Ick!

OLIVIA: Yes. She said she was outside, eating some of that awful concoction, and a spider scared her so much, she jumped and got a whole bowl of it on her head.

HILDA: Serves her right for eating it in the first place. (CINDERELLA *enters. She wears ragged clothes and one shoe, which appears to be made of glass.*)

CINDERELLA: Pardon me, but can I get an appointment this morning?

OLIVIA: Of course. Come in.

CINDERELLA: Thanks. Listen, I'm in a hurry—my stepmother and stepsisters will be back right after lunch, and I have to get home and clean the fireplace before they get there.

HILDA: Forgive me for staring, but did you know you're wearing only one shoe?

CINDERELLA: Of course! I lost the other one at a discotheque.

OLIVIA: How could you lose a shoe at a discotheque?

CINDERELLA (*Giggling*): Well, at the time, I was preoccupied. There was this really handsome guy who turned out to be a prince or something. And then I had to watch the time or else I'd be stuck with mice and pumpkins out in the parking lot, and no way to get home. (OLIVIA *and* HILDA *exchange looks*.) Anyway, I want to look really fantastic this afternoon, because this guy may be paying me a visit.

HILDA: How nice!

CINDERELLA: Yes, especially if it fits.

OLIVIA: If what fits?

CINDERELLA: The shoe he found—the one I lost. If it does, I can leave this life of drudgery behind and waltz off like a princess.

HILDA: I see.

OLIVIA (*Looking at schedule*): Francine just happens to have an opening. Hilda will show you the way.

CINDERELLA: Terrific. (*Starts to exit*) By the way, if the shoe fits, I'll see that you get an invitation to the wedding.

OLIVIA: Wonderful. (CINDERELLA *and* HILDA *exit. A moment later,* HILDA *reenters, followed by* BRIAR ROSE, *whose hair is a tangled mass, her curls tied in different colored ribbons*.)

BRIAR ROSE: Hi, there!

HILDA (*Gasping*): I can't believe my eyes.

BRIAR ROSE: What's wrong?

HILDA: Your hair. Olivia—look at that!

OLIVIA: I haven't seen a hairstyle like that since—I can't even remember when!

HILDA: Are you here for an appointment?

BRIAR ROSE: Yes, if you have an opening on such short notice . . .

OLIVIA: Forgive me if I seem rude, but where have you been for the last hundred years?

BRIAR ROSE: Actually, I've been asleep.

HILDA: You must be the one they call Sleeping Beauty.

BRIAR ROSE: Yes. You see, the last thing I remember was pricking my finger on a spinning wheel and falling into a deep sleep. Next thing I knew, this strange man I had never seen before gave me a kiss and woke me up.

OLIVIA (*Skeptically*): So you've been asleep for a hundred years?

BRIAR ROSE: Yes. Is something wrong?

OLIVIA (*Soothingly*): Yes, dear, your hairstyle. No one has worn it that way for decades. But don't worry, Hilda's going to take you back to Martha—she's a whiz with restyling. (HILDA *and* BRIAR ROSE *exit.*)

ALICE (*Entering*): Am I late? (*Her blonde hair is quite disheveled.*)

OLIVIA: Late for what?

ALICE: For a very important date.

OLIVIA: Do you have an appointment?

ALICE: Oh, dear, I just can't seem to recall. My life has been rather topsy-turvy lately. And it's all because of that silly rabbit!

OLIVIA: What rabbit?

ALICE: The one with the waistcoat and pocketwatch that I followed down the rabbit hole. It was infinitely more interesting, you see, than having my sister read to me from a book without any pictures. Books without pictures are so boring, you know.

OLIVIA: I suppose. But what about the rabbit?

ALICE: Well, he led me on a wild goose chase . . . or rather, a wild rabbit chase all over the countryside.

OLIVIA: Excuse me, but your hair—

ALICE: I know it's a mess. The way my yesterday went, I'm lucky I still have my head! It was bad enough eating those mushrooms at the tea party, but when the Red Queen started shouting "Off with her head"—well, it was quite a day.

OLIVIA: Yes, I imagine. But back to the subject at hand—

ALICE: Which is?

OLIVIA: The reason you came in here; did you want an appointment?

ALICE: An appointment? Of course not. I'm still trying to catch up with that rabbit. I could have sworn he came in here.

OLIVIA: But where could he have gone?

ALICE: Aha! (*Pointing off left*) There he is . . . and here I go! (*Crossing quickly*)

OLIVIA: Go where?

ALICE: Through the looking glass—where else? (*Exits left. GOLDILOCKS reenters, wearing wig of long, black, straight hair.*)

GOLDILOCKS (*Primping*): You guys are fantastic! I love my hair!

OLIVIA: Are you all set?

GOLDILOCKS (*Checking watch*): Yes, the porridge should have cooled down by now. Thanks! (*Exits; RAPUNZEL reenters, with a short, sleek hairdo.*)

RAPUNZEL: I feel 50 pounds lighter already!

OLIVIA: Would you like some coffee before you leave?

RAPUNZEL (*Romantically*): Thanks, but no. I've got a date with a wonderful guy I met the other day while I was hanging my hair out the window to dry. (*Exits. CINDERELLA enters; she has a new hairdo.*)

CINDERELLA: My fairy godmother was right—you do work miracles here!

OLIVIA: Your hair is beautiful!

CINDERELLA: The folks at home are going to turn absolutely green with envy! (*Exits. BRIAR ROSE enters, wearing multicolored punk-style wig.*)

BRIAR ROSE: How do you like the new me?

OLIVIA (*Startled*): Briar Rose! For a second I didn't recognize you!

BRIAR ROSE: Pretty chic, eh?

OLIVIA: Just don't wait another hundred years! (BRIAR ROSE *laughs and exits. HILDA reenters.*)

HILDA: Where has everyone gone?

OLIVIA: They're off to turn people's heads, I guess.

HILDA: It sure is quiet again.

OLIVIA: Yes, well, you know what they say, Hilda.
HILDA: What's that?
OLIVIA: Hair today, gone tomorrow! (*Curtain*)
                    THE END

Production Notes

HAIRUM-SCARUM

Characters: 7 female.
Playing Time: 15 minutes.
Costumes: Olivia and Hilda wear everyday clothing; others are dressed like the fairy tale characters, with appropriate wigs for changing hairstyles.
Properties: Magazines, hair-care products.
Setting: Reception area of the Fantastic Frills Salon. Table with phone on it is down left. Three archways leading to "styling booths" are upstage. Main entrance to salon is right. Color scheme is pink and white; photos of different hairstyles adorn the walls. Wig heads, hair spray cans, magazines, etc. round out the decor.
Sound and Lighting: No special effects.

Blind Date

by Craig Sodaro

Teenagers thwart plans of international spy. . . .

Characters

ALLISON LEWIS, *high school senior*
EDIE LEWIS, *her sheepish sister*
AUNT ZIZI STARR, *their aunt*
ROSALIE DENTON, *Zizi's matchmaking neighbor*
BORIS KILLBORN, *unlikely intruder*
P.J. PHILLIPS, *postman who doesn't get to ring twice*

SCENE 1

TIME: *The present.*
SETTING: *Living room of Zizi Starr's apartment in Greenwich Village. Exit right leads to hall and street; exit left to kitchen, bedrooms, and back door. French window center opens to small balcony. Couch is right center, with two chairs left center. At right is closet. Left is desk with phone. Posters of Broadway shows are on walls.*
AT RISE: *Stage is empty.* ALLISON *and* EDIE *enter right, each carrying suitcase.* EDIE *also carries briefcase.*
ALLISON (*Excitedly*): I can't believe we're *here!* In New York! Greenwich Village!
EDIE (*Nervously*): Allison, the door was unlocked.
ALLISON: Aunt Zizi always leaves it unlocked. Besides, there's a security guard downstairs.
EDIE (*Ominously; checking room*): Somebody could have sneaked in!

114

ALLISON: Oh, Edie! You're such a worry wart! (ALLISON *sets bags center, her back facing left.*) The way you act, you'd think there's a murderer hiding in every closet! (ROSALIE *enters, holding knife.*)

ROSALIE (*Cheerfully*): Oh, hi! I've been expecting you! (EDIE *gasps.* ALLISON *turns, frightened.*) Oh, I'm so sorry, girls. I didn't mean to startle you. I'm Rosalie Denton. I live down the hall. Your aunt asked me to fix some dinner for you. (AL- LISON *and* EDIE *don't answer.*) You *are* Zizi's nieces, right?

ALLISON (*Embarrassed*): Yes. I'm Allison, and this is my sis- ter Edie.

ROSALIE: Zizi's talked so much about you! I'd really like to spend some time with you, but tonight I've got my body toning class at six and gourmet cooking at eight.

ALLISON (*Smiling*): You take it off and put it back on in one night!

ROSALIE (*Laughing*): Right. I figure they cancel each other out. Now, casserole's in the oven, salad's on the counter, bread's in the box, and your aunt's at the beauty parlor.

EDIE (*Disappointed*): Isn't Aunt Zizi coming home tonight?

ROSALIE: Just to meet her date! (*Confiding*) I fixed her up with a terrific guy. He should be here soon.

ALLISON: Don't tell me Aunt Zizi still goes on blind dates?

ROSALIE (*Dryly*): Girls, your aunt's only middle-aged, not dead. Well, I must be off. See you two tomorrow. (ROSALIE *exits right.*)

ALLISON: Let's find a place to park our suitcases.

EDIE: First I want to make sure I've got all my notes. I can't work on my project without my research. (EDIE *opens brief- case, screams.*)

ALLISON: Now what?

EDIE (*Stunned*): My notes! They're gone! All my research!

ALLISON: Edie, who would want 250 note cards about the life cycle of the sycamore?

EDIE (*Intensely*): Anyone who's trying for the Junior Scientist Summer Scholarship! I know I put my notes in here before we left this morning.

ALLISON: Maybe you grabbed another briefcase by mistake when the driver took the bags out of the bus.

EDIE (*Examining briefcase*): You're right! This isn't mine.

ALLISON: Let's call the bus station. Your briefcase is probably there waiting for you. (ALLISON *goes to phone, looks up number, dials.*)

EDIE (*Tearfully*): This is horrible! There's a worm in every apple! Even the Big Apple.

ALLISON: Edie, you're overreacting again. Just calm down. (*Into phone*) Hi. I just came in on the bus from Kansas, and I left my briefcase at the terminal. Did anyone turn it in? . . Oh. All right. Thank you. (*Hangs up*) Their lost and found is closed for the night. We can check in the morning.

EDIE (*Upset*): Great! What am I supposed to do till then?

ALLISON: You'll just have to try to have fun. After all, this is New York! Maybe we can see a play.

EDIE (*Timidly*): You mean a matinee, right? (ALLISON *looks at* EDIE *in disbelief.*) You mean go out . . . after dark?

ALLISON (*Shaking head*): Edie, I'm sure Aunt Zizi will take care of us. (*Looks around*) Wow, look at all these wonderful posters. Aunt Zizi's had an exciting career in the theater. (ZIZI STARR *sweeps in right, her hair wildly stylish.*)

ZIZI (*Gushing*): Girls! Oh, my dears! You're tiny Allison and teeny Edie? Why, I can hardly believe it!

ALLISON: We're Allison and Edie, all right, but we've dropped the tiny and the teeny.

EDIE: Hi, Aunt Zizi. (*All three embrace.*)

ZIZI: What a thrill to have you here! I have the most wonderful two weeks planned. We'll be so busy!

EDIE *and* ALLISON (*Ad lib*): Great! I can hardly wait. (*Etc.*)

ZIZI: Did Rosalie tell you I have a date tonight? I just couldn't get out of it.

EDIE: I'd be terrified of a blind date in this city.

ZIZI (*Brightly*): Edie, I know judo, karate, tai kwan do, and basic lifesaving. If those fail, there's always my cooking. That's why I asked Rosalie to whip up something for you. I'll try to get back early so we can talk.

ALLISON: I can't wait to hear about your acting career.

ZIZI (*Dreamily*): It has been exciting. Thirty-five shows and I never missed a rehearsal.... Well, I'd better get ready. If there's anything you want, just scream! (ZIZI *exits left.*)

ALLISON: This is going to be so much fun!

EDIE (*Glumly*): Not without my botany notes!

ALLISON (*Rummaging through briefcase*): I wonder whose this is? Well, they sure can't miss what's inside. (*Turns briefcase upside down*) There's nothing in it!

EDIE (*Brightly*): Maybe Aunt Zizi's got a copy of *Willden's Plant and Flora Guide.* (EDIE *and* ALLISON *take suitcases and briefcase, exit left.* BORIS KILLBORN *enters center. He takes gun from pocket, checks room, moves to phone and dials.*)

BORIS (*In stage whisper*): Boris here. I've trailed the agents from the bus depot.... Yes, they have my briefcase. I have theirs.... I tell you, Igor, Agent 48 is getting desperate! These two are teenagers.... Of course I value my head! Don't worry. They won't find anything. I used the old false bottom trick. And I'll get briefcase back. Trust me! (*Hangs up, wipes forehead with handkerchief, then gets down on hands and knees, searches room.* ALLISON *and* EDIE *enter left.*)

EDIE (*To* ALLISON): Look! (*Points to* BORIS)

ALLISON (*Nervously*): Excuse me. Are you looking for my Aunt Zizi?

BORIS (*Rising; nervously*): Yes. Yes, I am.

EDIE (*Sarcastically*): You won't find her on the floor.

BORIS (*Rising; hesitantly*): I was just . . . admiring your carpet.

ALLISON: Do you sell carpet, Mr.—

BORIS: Killborn. Boris Killborn. Yes, I own Lay Down Low Down Carpet Company. Have you heard of it?

EDIE: No.

BORIS: Good.

ALLISON: Well, Aunt Zizi's just getting ready for your date.

BORIS: Date?

ALLISON: Right. Your blind date? Rosalie Denton, your friend, fixed you up?

BORIS (*Quickly*): So I've got Rosalie to thank for this!

ALLISON: We've got some unpacking to do, so make yourself at home. We'll tell Aunt Zizi you're here. (ALLISON *and*

EDIE *exit left.* BORIS *wipes brow again, and is about to exit right.*)

ZIZI (*Offstage*): Yoo-hoo! Mr. Killborn! I'll be ready in just a couple of minutes! There are seaweed nuggets and tuna chips in the dish on the coffee table if you're hungry.

BORIS: Seaweed? Tuna? What does she think I am, a seal? (*Knock at door right.* BORIS *glances right and left.* MR. PHILLIPS *enters right.*)

PHILLIPS (*Shyly*): Good evening. I'm P.J. Phillips. Is this Zizi Starr's apartment?

BORIS (*Nervously*): Come in. You must be her blind date.

PHILLIPS (*Embarrassed*): Yes, you see, we have a mutual friend down the hall. And . . . (*Suddenly*) wait a minute! Who are you?

BORIS (*Confused*): Oh, I . . . I . . . I am Zizi's father.

PHILLIPS: Her father? Hold on! How old is Zizi? (BORIS *drops keys.*)

BORIS: How clumsy of me! (BORIS *opens closet.*)

PHILLIPS (*Bending over to pick up keys*): Something's fishy here! (BORIS *knocks* PHILLIPS *out with gun, pushes him into closet, slams door.* ZIZI *enters left, wearing something a bit more exotic.*)

ZIZI (*Brightly*): Sorry I kept you waiting. (*When she notices* BORIS; *disappointed*) You're my date?

BORIS (*Flustered*): Miss Starr, I am Boris Killborn. (*He kisses her hand.*)

ZIZI: Ooooh! A touch of class!

BORIS: And you, my dear . . . are more beautiful than Venus de Milo!

ZIZI: At least I've got arms. . . . I can't wait to see where you take me. The Four Seasons? The Russian Tea Room?

BORIS: There's a nice Burger Shack on Times Square.

ZIZI: Oh, you're a real comedian!

BORIS: I am when I have to be! Well, get your coat. I promise you an evening you'll never forget! (ZIZI *exits left as* BORIS *dives for phone. He dials frantically.*) Igor! We have problem! . . . I have inherited blind date and cannot search house till it is over. (EDIE *enters left, unseen by* BORIS.) Get rid of her?

... Yes, there is balcony.... Four flights up.... Lure her to balcony.... Give push.... O.K., Igor. I break date soon! (*He hangs up. Terrified,* EDIE *sneaks off left. A moment later,* ZIZI *enters, wearing coat.*)

ZIZI (*Brightly*): O.K., I'm ready. Where are we going?

BORIS (*Grandly*): To sample the finest cuisine in the entire city!

ZIZI: Where's that?

BORIS (*Pointing left*): Your kitchen!

ZIZI (*Stunned*): Boris, I can't cook! The last time I tried to cook in my kitchen, my cat almost died.

BORIS: Nobody said *you* were going to cook. I am a master chef!

ZIZI: But my nieces are all set for a quiet evening at home.

BORIS: All we do is slip downstairs to tiny corner market, pick up a little of this and a little of that, then send girls on their way. They would love a night on the town.

ZIZI (*Considering*): Well, I *did* have a hard day at my dance studio. Did you ever try to teach the tango to retired accountants? (*As* BORIS *leads* ZIZI *off right*) Bye, girls! Back in a little while! (*They exit just as* EDIE *rushes in, followed by* ALLISON.)

EDIE (*Anxiously*): Don't go, Aunt Zizi!

ALLISON: What's wrong with you?

EDIE: I heard him telling someone he's going to try to push Aunt Zizi off the balcony! I'm calling the police. (*Rushes to phone, dials*)

ALLISON: They'll just laugh at you.

EDIE (*On phone*): Hello, 911? This is Edie Lewis.... Well, I don't really know *where* I'm calling from, but my Aunt Zizi lives here, and her blind date is going to try to throw her off the balcony tonight.... Well, I heard him telling some guy named Igor over the phone.... What was that? ... (*Looks at* ALLISON)

ALLISON: What did they say?

EDIE (*Hanging up; embarrassed*): I couldn't understand him because he was laughing so hard.

ALLISON (*Calmly*): I knew it. Now, calm down. Aunt Zizi can take care of herself. I'm dying to look through her clothes. I'll bet she has some great stuff from her days on the stage. (*She opens closet, screams.* EDIE *looks in and screams. They run off left.* PHILLIPS *gets up, rubs his head, and comes into room.*)

PHILLIPS: That's the last time I let Rosalie Denton fix me up with anybody! (*He exits right as curtain falls.*)

* * * * *

SCENE 2

TIME: *Fifteen minutes later.*

SETTING: *Same as Scene 1.*

AT RISE: ALLISON *paces downstage, while* EDIE *stands at window.*

ALLISON: If only I'd listened to you!

EDIE (*Weakly*): Maybe we didn't really see a man in the closet. Maybe it *was* our imagination.

ALLISON: *You* may imagine things, Edie, but I know I saw a man in the closet!

EDIE: Wait! I see Aunt Zizi and Boris! They're walking toward the building.

ALLISON (*Moving to window*): Does he have anything that looks like a weapon?

EDIE: A loaf of French bread.

ALLISON: Let's stay calm. Even if it's hard and crusty, the worst he can do is knock her out.

EDIE: What are we going to do?

ALLISON (*Musing*): We need a plan, and I think I've got one! Here, help me get some costumes from the closet. (ALLISON *opens closet and grabs armful of costumes.* EDIE *does the same.*) Come on! (ALLISON *moves left.*)

EDIE: Where are we going?

ALLISON: The back way to the basement! (ALLISON *and* EDIE *exit left.* ZIZI *and* BORIS *enter right, carrying groceries.*)

BORIS: Nylon pile just will not keep you as warm as wool.

ZIZI (*Bored*): I don't know about you, Boris, but I walk on carpet . . . I don't wear it. (ZIZI *looks around apartment.*) Girls! We're back! Allison? Edie? (*To* BORIS) I wonder where they are?

BORIS: Probably out having a good time. (*Quickly*) You have nice apartment. Mind if I have a look around?

ZIZI: Look, I don't need an estimate on my carpet. I had it done twelve years ago, and this stuff wears for a lifetime. (BORIS *walks to balcony.*)

BORIS: That could be shorter than you think! . . . Why, look at that! (ZIZI *walks over to balcony.*)

ZIZI (*Puzzled*): What? (*Looks out*) Oh, that's Mr. Humpickle, the juggler. He always practices while he goes out for an after-dinner stroll.

BORIS: He's juggling Chihuahuas!

ZIZI (*Amused*): No wonder he's dog-tired every night! (*Just as* BORIS *is about to push* ZIZI *over, knock is heard. He pulls back.*) Now, I wonder who that could be? (*She opens door.* ALLISON *enters, dressed as a hippie, and carrying clipboard.*) Can I . . . help you?

ALLISON: Oh, *I* don't need any help. It's . . . it's . . . (*Suddenly*) the aardvarks! They're almost extinct. Save the aardvarks! Five dollars will buy enough food to save many aardvarks.

BORIS (*Angrily*): How about a loaf of French bread?

ALLISON: Aardvarks eat only ants.

BORIS: The only good ant's a dead ant, in my book! Now, scram, or the aardvarks will have to save you!

ZIZI (*Giving* ALLISON *five dollars*): Here. Make an aardvark happy.

ALLISON: Thanks. Peace and love. (BORIS *pushes* ALLISON *out.*)

ZIZI: Well, where were we?

BORIS (*At window*): Looking over the balcony. (ZIZI *joins him.*)

ZIZI (*Dreamily*): You know what? I still remember how excited I was when I first got off the bus from Kansas. (BORIS *again is about to push* ZIZI *off when knock is heard.*) Coming! (ZIZI *goes to door, opens it to* EDIE, *dressed as a gypsy.*)

EDIE: Good evening! I am Madame Zula, the greatest palm and tea leaf reader this side of Fifth Avenue. I am running a special on fortunes this week, and since I was in the neighborhood, I thought I'd drop in.

BORIS: Then just drop right out. Can't you see that we're having a nice, romantic evening?

EDIE (*Mysteriously*): Aha! I see more than you think!

BORIS: Let me see your credentials. You're no clairvoyant.

EDIE (*Insulted*): I am Madame Zula! Here is proof! (*She takes out a card.*) I received my degree from the palm and tea reading institute in Hoboken. (*Grabs* BORIS' *hand, looks at it*) Oooh! Your lifeline is a long one, but it is very crooked. . . . (BORIS *pulls his hand away.*)

BORIS: Enough of this! Out you go!

EDIE (*To* ZIZI, *nervously*): But I haven't read your palm. If you stay here, I see a long fall! I hear screams and sirens! Get out while you can!

BORIS: Take your own advice, Zulu, and get lost! (*Pushing* EDIE *off*)

EDIE (*Ominously, to* ZIZI): Beware! Beware! (*Exits right*)

ZIZI: Sorry about all these interruptions, Boris. Why don't I just rustle us up a bean sprout salad. If I don't eat soon, I'll faint! (*She exits left.*)

BORIS (*Aside*): That would be convenient! So! No more Mr. Nice Guy! (*He takes out gun, checks it, hides it as* ZIZI *enters left.*)

ZIZI: Boris, do you like wheat germ with your bean sprouts?

BORIS (*Ominously*): I'll just take the briefcase. (*Draws out gun*)

ZIZI (*Terrified*): Is that real?

BORIS: Very real . . . and we must now drop the pretense, Agent 48.

ZIZI: Hey, watch it! I'm only 39!

BORIS: You have stolen the plans for the cold fusion process that I was smuggling out of this country in the bottom of the briefcase. I want them back. I will give you to three. One!

ZIZI: Wait a minute! Look at me! Do I look like the briefcase type?

BORIS (*Counting*): Two!

ZIZI: I don't know anything about cold fusion! I do all my wash in hot water.

BORIS (*Aiming gun*): Two and a half.

ZIZI: I'm glad to see you're willing to compromise! (ALLISON *and* EDIE *enter left, with briefcase.*)

ALLISON: Is this what you're after, Mr. Killborn?

BORIS: Give me that briefcase. Now! (*He advances on them.*)

EDIE: I see a terrible pain in your future! (ALLISON *slugs him with briefcase, and he tumbles to couch.*)

ZIZI: Good one, Ali! (*She grabs the gun.*) Now, hold it!

BORIS: Don't shoot!

EDIE (*Furiously*): You stole my notes on the life cycle of the sycamore, and I want them back!

BORIS: Here's the key to a locker at the bus station. I hid your briefcase there. (*Tosses key on floor. ZIZI goes to pick it up, and he grabs gun. He holds gun on her.*) All right! We're going for a little ride—*with* the briefcase! Hand it over, or this will be your aunt's last date!

ALLISON (*Reluctantly handing over briefcase*): You hurt Aunt Zizi, and we won't rest till you're put away.

BORIS: Enough talk. Igor's dying to meet you, Agent 48. (*Moves right as PHILLIPS and ROSALIE enter*)

PHILLIPS: What are you doing with my date? (*He breaks BORIS from ZIZI, spins BORIS around, and slugs him unconscious.*)

ALLISON (*Shocked*): You're the body in the closet!

ZIZI (*Pointing to PHILLIPS*): So *you're* my blind date?

ROSALIE: Zizi, this is P.J. Phillips, the mailman from the Bronx.

ZIZI: Well, you certainly have a good right hook.

PHILLIPS: After you've handled as many German shepherds as I have, you can tackle anything!

EDIE: Even when they have a gun!

PHILLIPS (*Weakly*): Gun? Did you say . . . gun? (*He faints.*)

ROSALIE: Mr. Phillips! Oh, dear. I'd better retire as a matchmaker.

EDIE: Come on, Allison, we're going to the bus station, to get my notes!

ALLISON: Dressed like this?

EDIE: We're in New York! No one will notice! (*To ZIZI*) You know, Aunt Zizi, I think the next two weeks are going to be fun after all!

ZIZI: Somehow I don't think the Big Apple will ever be the same! (*Curtain*)

THE END

Production Notes

BLIND DATE

Characters: 4 female; 2 male.

Playing Time: 20 minutes.

Costumes: Modern dress. Aunt Zizi wears exotic, colorful clothing. Phillips dresses conservatively. Boris wears ill-fitting suit with dated tie. Allison changes into costume of long, wrap-around skit, beads, sunglasses, and long wig, and Edie changes into flowing robe, headdress, lots of jewelry.

Properties: Suitcases; briefcase; knife; gun; handkerchief; clipboard; bag of groceries with loaf of French bread; certificate; key.

Setting: Aunt Zizi's living room. Exit right leads to hall and street; exit left to kitchen, bedrooms, back door. Up center is open French window showing balcony beyond. Couch is right center. Chairs and tables are left center. Closet at right, near exit. Desk with phone down left. Posters of old Broadway shows are on the walls.

Lighting, Sound: No special effects.

Caveman Blues

by Mark Bruce

When Ogman makes music, he's really playing with fire. . . .

Characters

OONA, *cavewoman*
OGMAN ⎫
ARG ⎭ *cavemen*

SETTING: *Interior of a cave. There are a few large rocks—one flat—and sticks scattered around. Large stone pot with stick to stir it is center.*

AT RISE: OONA *is stirring pot. She sings a traditional "blues" melody.*

> All day long I'm stirring,
> Stirring my blues away.
> All day I'm stirring,
> Stirring my blues away.
> It's just my prehistoric business
> It makes a cavewoman's day.

ARG (*Entering*): Oona? Are you home?

OONA (*Sarcastically*): No, I'm out gathering berries. What does it look like, Arg?

ARG (*Looking around*): Is Ogman here?

OONA: He's at work. Trying to kill a mastodon.

ARG (*Skeptically*): Ogman? Kill a mastodon? I'll believe it when I see it.

OONA (*Sighing*): He's not exactly the Great Hunter, but he tries, poor dear. Well, pull up a rock and sit a spell.

ARG (*Sitting on rock*): Oona, I come on serious business.

OONA: That doesn't sound good.

ARG: We cave people pride ourselves on our inventiveness. It's the only thing that really keeps us one step ahead of the saber-toothed tiger.

OONA: Or the wolf at the door.

ARG: Exactly. We can't afford to be carrying a lot of dead weight.

OONA (*Suspiciously*): So what's your point?

ARG (*Hesitating a bit*): Ahem. Yes. Well, I've been sent to tell you that if Ogman doesn't invent something useful soon, we're going to have to evict you from the village.

OONA (*Alarmed*): You can't do that!

ARG: I don't want to, of course, but the rest of the villagers are impatient.

OONA: But Ogman tries to invent things, Arg.

ARG (*Sarcastically*): Oh, right—like basketball?

OONA (*Defensively*): That was a good idea.

ARG (*In disbelief*): Have you ever tried to bounce a rock? Look, I'm sorry, but you'll have to tell him, Oona. (*Exits.* OONA *stirs vigorously for a moment, then* OGMAN *enters, carrying spear.*)

OGMAN: Honey, I'm home.

OONA: Wipe your feet, Ogman.

OGMAN (*Incredulous*): Wipe my feet? Our floor is made of dirt.

OONA: Our dirt is clean. I sweep our dirt.

OGMAN (*Wiping his feet*): What's for dinner? I had a hard day hunting.

OONA: What did you catch? (OGMAN *sheepishly pulls large cabbage out from under his cloak.* OONA *responds sarcastically.*) My, my, did you kill it with your spear or sneak up on it?

OGMAN: Oona, I'm sorry I couldn't get some fresh meat, but I just can't get the hang of hunting. They keep coming up with these newfangled things like the bow and arrow. I can barely handle a spear.

OONA (*Taking cabbage and throwing it into pot*): Well, then, why don't you invent a hunting weapon of your own?

OGMAN (*Sighing*): You know I've tried.

OONA: That silly idea about mixing powder and setting it on fire so it would throw a small stone?

OGMAN: I call it a bullet.

OONA (*Exasperated*): Whatever. Why can't you invent something practical? Ugson over in the cave by the trees invented the wheel last month. Arg came up with the plow last week. What have *you* come up with? (*Goes to flat rock and spins it around*) "The Lazy Susan." Is this any way to advance civilization?

OGMAN: What about my sticks?

OONA: Oh, I forgot. Your sticks.

OGMAN (*Excitedly*): Oona, anyone can beat two sticks together. (*Picks up sticks*) I'm going to figure out a way to make music by *rubbing* them together. (*Rubs sticks together. OONA shakes her head.*) So—when will dinner be ready?

OONA: Not for a while. It's hard to time meals when I have to do all your cooking over an underground steam.

OGMAN: There *is* a quicker way.

OONA: You mean your crazy idea about fire? No, it's too dangerous. We have no business fooling with it. Besides, you have to wait for lightning to strike in just the right place.

OGMAN (*Pouting*): I'm going to do a little painting before dinner.

OONA: Oh, no! I just scrubbed the last of the mastodon pictures off the bedroom wall. Go paint a pot or something.

OGMAN (*Quizzically*): A pot?

OONA: It would brighten up the cave.

OGMAN (*Scornfully*): Painting pots? It sounds so uncivilized.

ARG (*Reentering*): Ogman, how are you?

OGMAN: Terrible. Oona's stifling my creative talents.

ARG (*To* OONA): Is he on the painting kick again? (OONA nods.) Ogman, your painting was fun in the beginning, a new fad. But you took it too far. Now everywhere we go we see mastodons and stick men.

OGMAN: You just hate art. (*Picks up sticks*) I'm going to play my music. (*Exits*)

ARG (*To* OONA): Well? Did you tell him yet?

OONA: No. I'm working up to it.

ARG (*Sighing*): You'd better do it soon. By the way, there's a saber-toothed tiger that's been hanging around the village. Stay indoors.

OONA: Why don't the hunters just drive it off or kill it?

ARG: There aren't enough hunters for a tiger that big, and he's got a tough hide. Our arrows just bounce right off it. We can't afford to lose any hunters trying to get close enough with the spears. (*Turns to exit*) Tell me when you talk to Ogman. (*Looks off, shakes head*) I'll miss Ogman. He's kooky but amusing. (*Points off*) Look at him, rubbing away at those sticks as if something is really going to happen. (*Horrified*) Oh, no!

OONA: What's wrong? (*Looks off*)

ARG: The saber-toothed tiger is outside, and he's sneaking up on Ogman! (*Yells*) Ogman! Run!

OONA (*Going to cave entrance and shouting*): Ogman! Watch out for the tiger! Put those silly sticks down!

ARG: He can't hear us.

OONA: Go out and get him!

ARG: With that tiger out there? Do you want us both to be eaten?

OONA: Then get the hunters!

ARG: There's no time. (*Amazed*) Look at that!

OONA: Smoke!

ARG: Coming from Ogman's sticks!

OONA: They've caught fire! (*Roar of tiger is heard.*) That's it, honey, put it right in his face!

ARG: The tiger is running away!

OONA: He looks terrified.

ARG: Ogman doesn't look too calm, either. (OGMAN *runs in, with smoking stick in his hand.*)

OGMAN: Did you see that?

OONA (*Embracing* OGMAN): Oggie, you were wonderful!

ARG: Ogman, you've come up with a way to make fire! And just in the nick of time. (*To* OONA) Well, that takes care of our little problem, doesn't it?

OGMAN (*Incredulous*): The tiger? A little problem?

ARG: Among other things. (*Looks knowingly at* OONA) I'd better tell the other villagers about this. They won't believe it. Ogman, you're a real hero! (*Exits*)

OONA (*Hugging* OGMAN): I knew you could invent something useful! (*Looks at him*) Why, Ogman, you look a little sad!

OGMAN: I had hoped my sticks would make music. (*Holds sticks aloft*) But for a while there, I was really hot! (*Curtain*)

THE END

Production Notes

CAVEMAN BLUES

Characters: 1 female; 2 male.

Playing Time: 10 minutes.

Costumes: Caveman style: animal skins, etc.

Properties: Cabbage; spear; smoking stick.

Setting: Cave. There are several large rocks scattered about—including a flat one that spins—and several sticks. A large stone pot with a stick in it is center.

Lighting: No special effects.

Sound: Tiger roar.

Formula for Romance

by Robert Mauro

When friends *don't* know
what's best . . .

Characters

BILL
SUE
PETE
RHONDA

SETTING: *Divided stage. Bill's room is left: Desk, chair, telephone, pencil and paper. A few posters of actresses hang on a blue backdrop. Sue's room is right: Desk, chair, telephone, typewriter, paper and pen. A few posters of actors hang on pink backdrop. Partition separates the rooms. Each room has wastebasket; each desk has large bag of potato chips in drawer.*

AT RISE: BILL *and* SUE *sit at their desks and then get up and pace.*

BILL (*To himself*): You're a man, Bill!

SUE (*To herself*): You're a woman, Sue! (*They stop pacing.*)

BILL (*Sitting at desk*): What'll I do?

SUE (*Sitting at desk*): How do I tell him he's fantastic? Should I call him?

BILL: Maybe I'll call her. (*Picks up phone*)

SUE (*Resolutely*): Yes, I'll call him. (*Picks up phone. After a moment, both hesitate.*)

BILL (*Hanging up*): Then again, maybe I'd better not. (*Stands up*)

SUE: I wouldn't know what to say to him. (*Hangs up*)

BILL: What should I tell her? (*They lean on partition—back to back.*)

SUE: I sense this closeness between us. (*After a pause; suddenly*) I know! I'll send him an anonymous love letter. (*Sits at desk, puts paper into typewriter and stares at it thoughtfully*) What rhymes with spring?

BILL (*Shaking his head*): Why am I so confused? I've read "How to Be a Real Romeo," and I'm still shy. (*He sits at desk. SUE pulls out paper and tears it up, throws it up in air.*)

SUE: This is ridiculous! I've read dozens of articles on how to be a real woman, and I still have no self-confidence!

BILL: Oh, I'll just call her.

SUE: I'll be aggressive! I'll call him. (*They both dial phones and listen.*)

SUE and BILL (*Together*): Great! It's busy! (*They hang up.*)

BILL: She probably has plenty of boyfriends.

SUE: He doesn't need me. He's probably got several girls beating a path to his door.

BILL: Last night I dreamed about her. (*Smiles*)

SUE: I've even dreamed about Bill. (*They both lean their heads in same spot on partition.*)

BILL: What a dream.

SUE: It was perfect.

BILL: We danced—

SUE: Went to dinner. (*Paces; exasperated*) Why don't he and I get together?

BILL: I don't get it.

SUE: I work out. (*Touches toes a few times*)

BILL: I keep in shape (*Does a few sit-ups*)—and I'm still a wreck when it comes to girls. (*They jog in circles around their desks.*)

SUE: I keep to my diet—

BILL: I never eat junk food. (*Each pulls bag of chips out of desk drawer.*)

SUE: Except when I'm down in the dumps. (*They pace and eat chips.*)

BILL (*Suddenly*): I've got it! I'll write her a poem!

SUE: I could write him a poem. (*Both put down chips and pick up pencil and paper.*)

BILL (*Writing*): How do I love thee—no, no. (*Breaks pencil*) That's already been said!

SUE: William . . . William . . . wherefore art thou, William? (*Sighs*) Not very original.

BILL: This is crazy! (*Both crumple up paper and toss into waste-baskets.*) She'll think I'm being pushy.

SUE: He'll think I'm too aggressive. What'll I do? (*Stands on her chair and calls to heaven*) Help! (*Knock on door is heard.*) Who's that?

BILL (*Annoyed*): Who's there?

RHONDA (*From offstage; calling*): It's Rhonda.

PETE (*From offstage; calling*): It's Pete.

SUE: Oh.

BILL: Come on in. (PETE *enters* BILL's *room, and* RHONDA *enters* SUE's *room.*)

RHONDA: Hi, Sue.

SUE (*Dully*): Hi.

PETE: What's happening, Bill? (SUE *and* BILL *plop in chairs.*)

RHONDA (*Cheerfully*): Hey, Sue, it's springtime. Cheer up!

PETE: Don't you realize it's spring? It's beautiful out.

SUE (*Dejectedly*): Bill hasn't called me yet.

BILL: I haven't called Sue.

RHONDA: Why don't you call him? Be aggressive!

PETE: Why not?

SUE: Rhonda, that's not my style.

PETE: She's not very aggressive, is she?

BILL: No. (*Gets up from chair*) And I'm head over heels in love with her.

PETE: That's obvious.

BILL: So what do I do?

SUE: So—what should I do? (*Stands and leans against desk*)

RHONDA (*Panicking*): Don't panic! You're just lovesick.

PETE: Have you tried just telling her you like her?

BILL: Not exactly.

RHONDA (*Pacing*): Listen, you may find this hard to believe, but men like to be told that women like them. (*Waves hands in air*) I know, I know. It's hard, but even aggressive women have to resort to flattery once in a while. So—have you told him?

SUE: Not exactly.

RHONDA: Well, pick up that phone and call him! Ask him something political.

PETE: Call her and tell her you need a . . . political opinion!

BILL: Should I?

RHONDA: Men love to be asked their opinions.

PETE: Certainly.

SUE: If you say so. And, anyway, I really am interested in politics.

BILL (*Skeptically*): Well, I'll give it a try. What have I got to lose? (SUE *and* BILL *pick up phones and dial, then listen.*)

SUE *and* BILL: Still busy! (*They slam phones down.*)

PETE: Bill, this is really getting ridiculous. Just go over there and tell Sue you think she's fantastic, and fabulous!

BILL: Well . . .

RHONDA: Why don't you go over there and tell Bill you need a little softball practice? Men love sports, you know.

SUE: I hate being cunning and manipulative.

RHONDA: Listen, it's better than being bored.

PETE: Come on. I'll go with you. I'll show you how to approach her.

RHONDA: Just remember: Love is war!

SUE: Right.

RHONDA: But never surrender!

BILL: But wait—what will I say to her once I get over there?

RHONDA: Do you have a pencil and paper?

SUE: Yes. (*Gets pencil and paper*)

PETE: Here, let's make a list of do's and don'ts.

BILL: Great idea—(*Skeptically*) I think. (*He gets paper and pencil.*)

RHONDA: We'll make a list of do's and don'ts.

SUE: I'm ready.

BILL: Shoot.

RHONDA: O.K. (RHONDA *stands.*)

PETE: Number one. Always take her to a movie about outer space. Women love macho space jocks. And stay away from foreign films, especially French ones with subtitles, or she'll think you're really weird. (BILL *writes.*)

RHONDA: Ask to go to a French movie, preferably one with subtitles. He'll think you're sophisticated. Oh, and after the movie, insist on eating at a French restaurant. (*Firmly*) No fast food.

SUE: Are you sure? (*Writes*)

RHONDA: Of course! Go absolutely to pieces if he forgets to buy you candy on Valentine's Day!

BILL (*Looking up*): O.K. What's next?

PETE: Never buy her candy on Valentine's Day, or you'll live to regret it.

BILL (*Writing on paper*): Got it. What's next?

PETE: Let's see . . . (*He paces*)

RHONDA: Never offer to pay half if you go to that French restaurant. He's a man—he pays.

SUE (*Surprised*): What?

RHONDA (*Patting* SUE *on back*): It's the law of the jungle. Trust me.

PETE: Aha! Always let her pay half if you take her to an expensive restaurant—or even McDonald's.

RHONDA: Next suggestion. Ready?

SUE: I'm not sure. But go ahead.

PETE: O.K. Important point: *Never* send her poetry. She'll think you're a nerd.

RHONDA: If he ever sends you a romantic little poem—get engaged immediately! He's one in a million!

SUE (*Worried*): Are you sure about all this?

RHONDA: You bet! It's on all the soap operas.

BILL (*Skeptically*): Are you sure about all this?

PETE: Trust me!

RHONDA: All set?

SUE (*Checking her notes*): I guess.

RHONDA: Any questions?

SUE: I have a million of them. (*Stands and paces*)

BILL (*Jumping up*): Wait! I have a question!

PETE: Let's hear it.

BILL (*Hesitating*): Um—what if—I mean, suppose I want to tell her I'd like to buy her flowers and take her out to dinner?

PETE: Hey! Are you nuts? That's against the rules!

SUE (*Skeptically*): Are you sure about all this? I mean, maybe Bill really likes the same things I like.

RHONDA (*With conviction*): Never. Men are our exact opposites. Listen, they barely *like* us.

SUE: I don't know, Rhonda . . . (SUE *and* BILL *look over their lists.*)

RHONDA: Trust me. I know all about this stuff.

PETE: Just memorize these do's and don'ts, and you'll be fine.

BILL (*Hesitating*): O.K.

PETE: Now, let's go meet this girl of your dreams.

RHONDA: Are you ready to meet Bill?

SUE: Ready.

RHONDA: The moment of truth has arrived! (BILL, RHONDA, PETE, *and* SUE *mime walking out front door and toward each other.*)

PETE (*Seeing* RHONDA): Oh, no! (*Pointing to* RHONDA) It's Godzilla!

BILL (*Confused*): Huh?

RHONDA (*Seeing* PETE): You! It's you! (*Points to* PETE) The creature from the black lagoon!

SUE: What?

PETE (*Standing aggressively close to* RHONDA; *pompously*): Aha! So you've slithered back into my life, you phony, self-centered witch. Couldn't stay away, eh?

RHONDA (*Angrily*): I hate your guts, you conceited, chauvinistic creep! (PETE *and* RHONDA *turn their backs on each other and stomp off in a huff.* SUE *and* BILL *look at each other. They crumple up their lists of do's and don'ts and toss them in opposite wings.*)

BILL (*With a shrug and a smile*): Hi.

SUE: Hello. (*They fidget, fold and unfold their arms.*)

BILL: Nice day.

SUE: Wonderful. I love spring. (*She smiles nervously.*)

BILL: So do I. (*Points to audience*) Look! A robin. (*Chirping is heard.*)

SUE (*Looking out into audience*): Oh, yes. And a robiness. (*Smiles at* BILL)

BILL: They look like friends. That's spring for you.

SUE: Smell the hyacinth?

BILL (*Breathing deeply*): Um-m. (*Looks down*) And have you noticed the grass?

SUE (*Looking down*): Right! It's . . . green. (*They look at each other.*)

BILL: Yeah. (*They laugh.*)

SUE (*Seriously*): Bill, I've been meaning to tell you—something. I really like you, and—

BILL: Sue—I've been wanting to go out with you for such a long time, but—

SUE (*Delighted*): Really?

BILL: Yes. But I'll have to be honest. (*Paces with hands in his pockets*) I really like Valentine's Day, and poetry—and I'm not at all crazy about French restaurants or French movies.

SUE: Same here!

BILL (*Surprised*): Really?

SUE: Yes.

BILL: Funny—someone told me girls hated all of that stuff, or most of it.

SUE: That's really ridiculous.

BILL: Something tells me we have a lot in common.

SUE: More than we both think, I'll bet. A whole lot more! Come on! I'll buy you a coffee! (*They laugh again, hold hands and walk off as curtain falls.*)

THE END

Production Notes

FORMULA FOR ROMANCE

Characters: 2 male; 2 female.

Playing Time: 15 minutes.

Costumes: All wear casual clothes. Pete may wear muscle T-shirt and gym shorts.

Setting: Stage is divided. At left is Bill's room, with desk, chair, telephone, wastebasket, pencil and paper. There are also a few posters of actresses hanging on a blue backdrop. At right is Sue's room, with desk, chair, telephone, wastebasket, typewriter, paper and pen. A few posters of actors hang on pink backdrop. In each desk is a large bag of potato chips.

Sound: Knocking on door; bird chirping.

Hassle in the Castle

by *Albert K. Schaaf*

Clever maid holds key to her future. . . .

Characters

MR. FATHERINGHAM, *head of Fatheringham's Medieval
Employment Agency*
MOLLY ⎫ *maids*
MINERVA ⎭
PRINCE CHARMING
KING
QUEEN
PRINCESS
TWO SERVANTS

TIME: *The Middle Ages.*
SETTING: *A castle hallway. Broom leans against wall. Door in
wall, center.*
AT RISE: MR. FATHERINGHAM *and* MOLLY *enter left.*
MOLLY (*Looking around; curiously*): Prithee, Mr. Father-
ingham, pardon my asking, but dost it not strike thee that
this castle is very quiet, and there seems to be no one about?
FATHERINGHAM: Molly, that is indeed true. When thou first
camest to my employment agency, I feared thou mightest turn
down the job if thou knewest about the castle before seeing it.
MOLLY: But, if I am to be employed as a maid here, I ought to
know what is strange about the castle. (*Lowering her voice*)
Is it haunted?
FATHERINGHAM (*Laughing*): No, no.
MOLLY (*Suspiciously*): Are the children messy? Do they track
mud in from the garden?

137

FATHERINGHAM (*Shaking his head*): No.

MOLLY: Do they want me to do windows? (*Firmly*) I do not do windows.

FATHERINGHAM: No. None of those things. It's a minor point, really. You see, all of the family and staff of this castle are asleep.

MOLLY: Asleep? At the hour of two in the afternoon? (*Laughs heartily*) Forsooth, there must have been one fine party here last night!

FATHERINGHAM: No, not at all. They are asleep now, and they are always asleep. They never wake up.

MOLLY: The maids must need to tiptoe around to do their work. (*She tries walking on tiptoes.*) That could be very tiring.

FATHERINGHAM: No, that is not necessary. They doth not wake and cannot be awakened. (MOLLY *looks at him skeptically.*) Many years ago a curse was put upon the beautiful daughter of this castle. An old witch decreed that she would prick her finger with a sewing needle and fall into a deep sleep, never to awaken. And when she did, the entire castle, King and Queen, servants and cooks, maids and all, fell asleep and have slept all these many years.

MOLLY: Then what doth the maid do? Dust off the King and Queen?

FATHERINGHAM (*Haughtily*): Please, Molly. Kings and queens do not collect dust! Except, perhaps, gold dust. (*Laughs*) Hm-m. I should not make jokes.

MOLLY (*Dryly*): Don't worry. Thou didst not.

FATHERINGHAM: Anyway, thy duties, Molly, will be to keep this hall spotlessly clean, the furniture dusted, the metal polished, the windows . . .

MOLLY (*Interrupting him*): I do not do windows.

FATHERINGHAM: Of course. Now, above all, thou must not, under any circumstances, allow any strangers in here; and positively no one may enter that room. (*Indicates door at center*)

MOLLY: Who's in there? The sandman?

FATHERINGHAM: No. In there sleeps the beautiful Princess, and it is thy number-one responsibility to protect her from any intruders.

MOLLY: Mr. Fatheringham.

FATHERINGHAM: Yes, Molly?

MOLLY: If I am to work in this strange place, am I to be all alone? Dost not anyone else work here?

FATHERINGHAM: One other maid. Minerva. She should be here somewhere. (*Calling*) Minerva! Minerva!

MINERVA (*Entering quickly right*): Mr. Fatheringham, please! Stop shouting! Dost thou not know that everyone is asleep?

FATHERINGHAM: Indeed, Minerva, a thunderbolt could not wake anyone in here.

MINERVA: Just the same, I cannot stand loud noise. I'm not used to it.

MOLLY: Thou must have been brought up in a library.

MINERVA: No, but I have worked here for thirty years. (*Indicating* MOLLY) Is this the new maid?

FATHERINGHAM: Yes. Dost thou want the job, Molly?

MOLLY (*Looking around and sighing*): I'm not sure. What be the pay and other working conditions?

MINERVA: Six gold klinkers a week. A quarter-hour nectar break morning and afternoon.

MOLLY: Hast thou sick benefits?

MINERVA: Gold Cross and Gold Shield hospital plan. The very same as the knights have. But the hospital plan doth not cover finger pricks from sewing needles.

MOLLY (*Sighing*): Very well. I shall take the job.

FATHERINGHAM: Fine. I shall fetch the necessary papers which thou canst sign. Canst thou start immediately?

MOLLY: I canst, and I wilst. Wilt. Will. (*Aside*) Verily, I was better in math than in English at school.

FATHERINGHAM: I shall be back soon. (*He exits left.*)

MINERVA: Now, dost thou know what to do, Molly?

MOLLY: I believe so. (*Shakes her head*) This is indeed a strange place. How long have they slept?

MINERVA: I do not know precisely. It must be a hundred years that the sleeping beauty in that room . . .

MOLLY: "The sleeping beauty." That's catchy.

MINERVA: The King and Queen sleep down the hall (*Points right*); the servants sleep in the kitchen and the stables. The horses are asleep, the pigs, the chicken, the geese . . .

MOLLY (*Conspiratorially*): Perhaps if we made a big pot of coffee. . . .

MINERVA (*Firmly*): Do not jest. (*Takes large key from her apron pocket*) Here is the key to the Princess's room. Guard this with thy very life.

MOLLY (*Taking key and putting it into her pocket*): I wilt.

MINERVA (*Handing* MOLLY *broom*): Begin with sweeping the hallway. Then polish the brass and dust the furniture. (*Studying her a moment*) Dost thou do windows?

MOLLY (*Firmly*): I do *not* do windows.

MINERVA (*Relieved*): Good. We must stick together. I do not do windows either. Of course, one can no longer see out the windows in the castle.

MOLLY: No matter. I believe I know what my duties are. Thank you, Minerva.

MINERVA: Thou art quite welcome. If thou needest me, I shall be downstairs. (*She exits right.* MOLLY *begins to sweep floor when suddenly,* PRINCE CHARMING *enters left.*)

MOLLY (*Looking him over*): Gadzooks! Who art thou?

PRINCE: Good morrow, wench. I am Prince Charming.

MOLLY (*Flatly*): Verily.

PRINCE (*Dramatically*): I have come to rescue the Princess.

MOLLY (*Unimpressed*): From what?

PRINCE: From the strange sleep that imprisons her.

MOLLY (*Firmly*): That may be, but it is my duty to see that neither thee nor anyone else disturbs the Princess.

PRINCE: See here, wench. Thou dost not seem to understand. It is my mission to rescue the beautiful Princess, and perhaps to kiss her.

MOLLY (*Staunchly*): Over my dead body! Thou shalt do neither! (*She moves in front of door and folds arms across her chest.*)

PRINCE (*Confused*): But I am destined to marry the Princess and take her away with me.

MOLLY: Thou takest her over the state line and we wilt have thee thrown into the dungeon!

PRINCE (*Pushing* MOLLY *aside*): Out of my way, wench. I must go in and see the Princess. (*He approaches door and tries to open it.*)

MOLLY (*Laughing*): The door be locked and this (*Holds up key*) be the key. Thou shalt not have it!

PRINCE: Ah! Thou hast the key. Give it to me. (*They spar a bit. He reaches for key; she keeps it out of his reach.*) All right. (*He stands back, smooths his clothes and hair.*) I do not wish to harm thee, for I am Prince Charming.

MOLLY: Thou shalt not charm me! (*To audience*) Although, I must admit, I could easily be won over.

PRINCE: I shall merely break down the door with my great strength. (*Throws himself against door several times. His last try is particularly forceful, and he falls down.*)

MOLLY: Thou couldst use some of the elixir made by Lawrence of Geritol.

PRINCE: I am undone. (*Picking himself up*) I cannot outwit thee. Thou winnest.

MOLLY (*Taken aback*): I dost?

PRINCE: Yes, thou dost. (*Hangs his head*) I cannot force myself past such a clever and, indeed, such a beautiful wench as thee.

MOLLY (*Eagerly*): I? A beautiful wench? Didst thou say beautiful?

PRINCE: I sure didst. Thou has a stunning beauty that one does not often see in a serving wench.

MOLLY (*Proudly*): I am a Serving Wench III. Dost thou know what a difficult civil service exam one must take for that position?

PRINCE: I did not know that. (*He moves closer to her. She drops key into her pocket.*)

MOLLY: I make six gold klinkers a week.

PRINCE: Indeed and forsooth, that does not matter to me. I would only look upon thy beauty. (*He is very close to her now.*) Look into my eyes.

MOLLY (*Wilting*): Whatever you say, Your Charmingship.

PRINCE (*Dramatically*): Kiss me! (*She melts into his arms, holding him tightly. He kisses her in a stylized bend-over-backward motion, at the same time taking key from her pocket, in full view of audience. PRINCE releases MOLLY. She stares straight at audience as he moves away from her toward door.*)

MOLLY: Indeed, this job has fringe benefits Mr. Fatheringham did not mention. (PRINCE *opens door with key and goes through doorway.* MOLLY *turns and sees open door. Shocked, she then stares into her pocket.*) The key! He is inside the Princess's room! (*Angrily*) He did not mean anything he said to me! (*To audience*) He's not bad, though. (*Goes to door and looks in*) Gadzooks! The varlet is kissing the Princess! She awakens! She sits up! She rises! (*Calling toward stage right*) Minerva! Minerva! (*All at once* KING *and* QUEEN *enter right,* PRINCE *and* PRINCESS *emerge from room,* TWO SERVANTS *enter left and bow to* KING *and* QUEEN. *Crowing of rooster and other animal sounds are heard offstage.*)

KING: Rejoice, my subjects! We are awake after this long, strange slumber.

QUEEN: And our daughter is awake also, and with her is the handsome Prince of Charming.

PRINCE: How dost thou know my name?

QUEEN: Thou lookest just like thy great-great-grandfather.

KING: Put all that aside, and hear my command. There will be a great wedding and a huge feast. Let the preparations begin. Make the castle come alive again. There will be much rejoicing! (*To* PRINCE *and* PRINCESS) Come, my son and daughter. Thou shalt help us plan thy future.

PRINCE: Thank you, Your Majesty. I am not a proud man. I would be happy to come into the business with thee. (*All exit left, except* MOLLY. *She stands alone for a few seconds, shuffles her feet, looks around uncomfortably.* MINERVA *enters right.* MOLLY *looks at her guiltily.*)

MINERVA: Molly—what happened?

MOLLY (*Uncertain*): I know not whether I shall get a medal or be thrown into the dungeon.

FATHERINGHAM (*Entering*): Oh, there thou art, Molly. This is indeed most unfortunate for you.

MOLLY: Shall I be thrown into the dungeon?

FATHERINGHAM: No, but thou shalt be fired. They need not your services now, nor thine, Minerva.

MINERVA: That's all right with me. I am eligible for ye social security.

FATHERINGHAM: Fear not, Molly. I have yet another job for a Serving Wench III. Fatheringham's Medieval Employment Agency is ever alert!

MINERVA: The most up-to-date medieval service around!

MOLLY (*Anxiously*): Skip the commercial. I shall take the job. What is it, and where is it?

FATHERINGHAM: Across the seven hills in a small cottage. The seven little men who live there need someone to care for their adopted ward, who ate a poisoned apple and fell into a deep sleep.

MOLLY (*Shaking her head*): Again a deep sleep. (*Sighs*) Oh, well. I shall go immediately; and, Mr. Fatheringham, I shall be especially careful. (*Confidently*) No handsome prince shall get past me this time! (*She exits left, as others wave goodbye. Quick curtain*)

THE END

Production Notes

HASSLE IN THE CASTLE

Characters: 3 male; 4 female; 2 male or female for servants.

Playing Time: 10 minutes.

Costumes: Molly and Minerva wear medieval peasant dresses and aprons with big pockets. Mr. Fatheringham wears medieval merchant's attire. Prince wears Elizabethan ruffles and tights; King and Queen wear royal robes and crowns. Princess wears long dress and tiara.

Properties: A large key, an old-fashioned round broom, some papers or a briefcase for Mr. Fatheringham, a scepter for the King.

Setting: A castle hallway. Heavy-looking working door is at center. Broom leans against wall near door. Furniture on either side of door can be heavy chairs or marble benches. Paintings or tapestry may hang on walls; suit of armor could stand at right.

Lighting: No special effects.

Sound: Animal noises are heard off, as indicated.

Avon Calling!

by Lewy Olfson

The play's the thing. . . .

Characters

JERRY GLOBE, *theatrical impresario*
MARVIN, *his assistant*
WILLIAM SHAKESPEARE, *playwright*
FRANCIS BACON, *would-be playwright*

SETTING: *Office of Jerry Globe. Cluttered desk with telephone is left center. Desk chair is behind it. Several chairs are right and left. Doorway is down right.*

AT RISE: JERRY *is at desk. Telephone is ringing.*

JERRY (*Answering phone*): Globe Theater. Jerry Globe speaking. . . . (*Rests phone in crook of neck and shuffles papers during conversation*) Yes, ma'am, this afternoon we have a special matinee: *A Midsummer Night's Dream,* by William Shakespeare. . . . On the same bill, we have three acts of live bear-baiting. Both features are rated PG, parental guidance suggested. . . . Not at all. Thanks for calling the Globe. (*Hangs up.* MARVIN *enters.*)

MARVIN: Good news. Today's matinee is nearly sold out.

JERRY: Terrific! Of course, I'm not surprised. Every time we put on a play by Shakespeare, we sell out.

MARVIN: Yeah, but we can't go on running the same old plays forever. The public's going to get tired of them. When is Shakespeare going to come up with a new one?

JERRY: I wish I knew! I've been begging him for a new play, but so far—nothing.

MARVIN: Well, boss, these artists can't be rushed, you know.

144

JERRY (*In disbelief*): Artist? Shakespeare? Look, that kid's no artist. He's just a hack. That's what makes me so mad. He can grind the stuff out by the mile, if he feels like it.

MARVIN: Shakespeare really is something. *Midsummer Night's Dream* —a sellout. *Julius Caesar*—a sellout. And as for *Macbeth*—we have three road companies doing it.

JERRY: I know. Well (*Checks watch*), our boy wonder is due here any minute. We have an appointment.

MARVIN: Is he bringing a new script?

JERRY (*Shaking his head*): Doubtful. But I have a couple of ideas of my own I hope he won't be able to resist.

MARVIN: I hope he goes for them. We could sure use another smash hit. (*Knock is heard at door.*)

JERRY: Ah, that must be Shakespeare now. Show him in, Marvin. (MARVIN *opens door to admit* WILLIAM SHAKESPEARE, *dressed in black and carrying a skull.*)

MARVIN: Come in, Mr. Shakespeare. We were just talking about you.

SHAKESPEARE (*Glumly*): Good morrow, Marvin.

JERRY (*Jumping up; effusively*): Hey, Willie, baby! Great to see you!

SHAKESPEARE (*Glumly*): Good morrow, Jerry.

JERRY (*Teasingly*): Is that the best you can do? "Good morrow, Jerry"? Where's the old bounce, the old pizzazz?

SHAKESPEARE (*With exaggerated sigh*): Ah, to be or not to be . . . that is the question.

MARVIN (*Blankly*): Huh?

JERRY (*Concerned*): What's with this "To be or not to be" stuff? Is that any way for England's number one up-and-coming playwright to talk? (*Leads* SHAKESPEARE *to chair*) Come and sit down. Tell me what's bothering you. Marvin, go and get Willie a cup of coffee.

MARVIN: Sure, Jerry. How do you take your coffee, Mr. Shakespeare?

SHAKESPEARE (*Staring at skull; sepulchrally*): Black.

MARVIN (*Shaking his head*): Right. (*Exits*)

JERRY: Will, bet I know what's bothering you: girl trouble. That Anne Hathaway you've been going with. She's been giving you a rough time, right? (*Sits on edge of desk*)

SHAKESPEARE (*Dully*): Wrong.

JERRY: Is it money trouble? You want a little advance on your royalties? Just say the word.

SHAKESPEARE (*Scornfully*): What care I for money? Who steals my purse steals trash.

JERRY: Then what is it? What, what, what? You're usually so peppy, so alive! But this (*Gesturing*)—this outfit, this skull, this melancholy pose! This isn't you.

SHAKESPEARE (*With mighty sigh*): Oh, that this too, too solid flesh would melt . . . would thaw . . . resolve itself into a dew. . . .

JERRY (*Shaking his head*): I just don't understand you.

SHAKESPEARE (*Slamming skull down on desk and jumping up, suddenly animated*): You don't understand me, Jerry? Oh, vassal! Miscreant! Rogue and peasant slave! I'm sick of turning out stuff like *A Midsummer Night's Dream* and *Macbeth* and *Julius Caesar!* I want to write poetry, Jerry! I want to create art!

JERRY (*Horrified*): But *A Midsummer Night's Dream* is a sellout!

SHAKESPEARE (*Contemptuously*): It is not worth the dust which the rude wind blows in thy face.

JERRY: *Julius Caesar* made *Variety*'s list of Box Office Top Ten.

SHAKESPEARE (*Scornfully*): Words, words, words! *Julius Caesar* is a tale told by an idiot, full of sound and fury, signifying nothing.

JERRY: *Macbeth,* then! *Macbeth* is going into its third edition in paperback, and we sold the moving portrait rights to Sixteenth-Century Fox. Even Queen Elizabeth thinks it's great.

SHAKESPEARE (*Bitterly*): A dubious honor.

JERRY (*Irritated*): Now look, Shakespeare, I've put up with about as much of this nonsense as I'm going to. You have a twenty-play contract, and I'm going to hold you to it.

SHAKESPEARE (*Dramatically*): Methinks I shall go mad! My wits begin to turn! Don't you understand, Jerry? My brain is drained!

JERRY (*Expansive again*): Is that all that's bothering you? Ideas? Listen, I've got millions of them.

SHAKESPEARE (*Doubtfully*): Well, let me hear one. (*Sits*)

JERRY (*Excitedly*): There's a rich girl named Katharina, see, and she's a real shrew. So even though she's loaded, nobody wants to marry her. Except one guy: Petruchio. He figures he can be twice as mean as Katharina, break her spirit, get her to marry him, and get all her money in the bargain. So he sets out to tame her.

SHAKESPEARE (*Skeptically*): How does he do that?

JERRY (*Airily*): Oh, I don't know. You can figure that out as you go along. The important thing is to keep it funny, funny, funny. You can call it *No, No, Petruchio,* or *Kiss Me, Katharina*—something breezy.

SHAKESPEARE (*Sarcastically*): Why not call it *The Taming of the Shrew?*

JERRY: Because it isn't box office, that's why. Well? Do you like the idea?

SHAKESPEARE (*Angrily*): I hate it.

JERRY (*After a deep breath*): All right, here's one you might like better. There are these two kids, Juliet and Romeo. They fall in love.

SHAKESPEARE (*Sarcastically*): A really original plot!

JERRY: The trouble is, their families hate each other. So Juliet takes this sleeping potion . . . and then Romeo finds her asleep, only he thinks she's dead, so he kills himself . . . and then *she* wakes up and finds *him* dead, so this time she *does* kill herself—

SHAKESPEARE (*Finishing for him*): And we call it *A Comedy of Errors,* and the important thing is to keep it funny, funny, funny. (*Disparagingly*) How do you think up these awful ideas, Jerry?

JERRY: *I* don't think them up. I get them out of a book. Holinshed's *Chronicles.*

SHAKESPEARE (*Pityingly*): Oh, what a noble mind is here o'thrown. (MARVIN *enters with mug, which he hands to* SHAKESPEARE.)

MARVIN: Boss, there's a Francis Bacon here to see you.

JERRY (*In disgust*): Not again! He's been trying to see me for months.

MARVIN: Shall I send him away?

JERRY (*Sighing*): He'll only come back again. Send him in. I'll get rid of him myself. (MARVIN *exits*.) This will just take a minute, Willie. (SHAKESPEARE *nods*. MARVIN *ushers in* FRANCIS BACON.)

BACON (*Eagerly*): Oh, Mr. Globe, I'm so glad you've agreed to see me at last. (MARVIN *exits*.)

JERRY: Well, don't be *too* glad. I agreed to see you only so I could tell you once and for all that your stuff is hopeless and we can't use it.

BACON (*Crushed*): You—you don't think I have any talent?

JERRY: As a philosopher, you're A-number-one. As an essayist, you're tops. But as a playwright (*Makes thumbs-down gesture*)—zero.

BACON: Yet my fondest dream has been to write plays. Who reads philosophy? Who reads essays? Nobody. The only way to be important as a writer nowadays is to write plays that people will come to see.

JERRY: Tell that to *him* (*Indicates* SHAKESPEARE), not me!

BACON: Why? Who's he?

JERRY (*Introducing*): Francis Bacon—William Shakespeare.

SHAKESPEARE (*Shaking hands*): I'm very pleased to meet you.

BACON (*Excitedly*): Not *the* William Shakespeare? (*Fawning*) Oh, Mr. Shakespeare, I admire you more than just about anybody.

SHAKESPEARE: You do? An artist like you admires me? A dry jest, sir! My plays are trifles, light as air. But your writing— such style! Such wit! Such grace! You're just flattering me when you say you like my work.

BACON: Nay, do not think I flatter. For what advancement may I hope from thee, that no revenue hast but thy good spirits?

SHAKESPEARE (*Enraptured*): Beautifully said! (*To* JERRY) *That's* the kind of thing I wish I could write! (*To* BACON) Do you mind if I make a note of that? (*Takes quill pen and paper from pocket and writes*) "Nay, do not think I flatter . . . "

MARVIN (*Rushing in*): Boss! Boss! Emergency down in the theater!

JERRY: What's up?

MARVIN: Walter Raleigh's smoking some of that tobacco he's been importing. The stage manager *told* him there's no smoking allowed—but Raleigh's making a terrible scene.

JERRY (*In disgust*): That Walter Raleigh! Always losing his head! O.K., tell them I'll be right there. (MARVIN *exits*.) Look, Bacon, I hate to be unpleasant, but I'm afraid you're wasting your time. You'll never make it as a playwright. And as for you, Shakespeare—remember our contract! So sit down and start writing! (*Exits*)

BACON: Ah, 'twas ever thus. I want to write plays, and they won't let me. You *don't* want to write plays—and they insist. Ah, I fear I have the green sickness.

SHAKESPEARE: "The green sickness"! A perfect phrase for envy!

BACON: Well, it was a real pleasure meeting you, Mr. Shakespeare.

SHAKESPEARE (*Shaking hands with him*): Oh, call me Will, please.

BACON: Parting is such sweet sorrow that I should say good night till it be morrow.

SHAKESPEARE (*Enchanted*): Oh! "Parting is such sweet sorrow ... " (*Suddenly*) Say, Frank, you really want to write plays, do you?

BACON (*Eagerly*): More than anything!

SHAKESPEARE: Then how would you like to collaborate with me?

BACON (*Overwhelmed*): Do you mean it? You—the great Shakespeare—would work with me? But what about Mr. Globe? I'm sure he'd never agree.

SHAKESPEARE: He doesn't have to know about it. We'll put my name on the finished script. But of course I'll divide all the royalties with you.

BACON: Oh, Will, I'd like nothing better! And I even have an idea for a play that I think might provide the food of sweet and bitter fancy.

SHAKESPEARE (*Overwhelmed*): Ah, wait—let me put that down—"Sweet and bitter fancy." (*Writes*)

BACON: The play is about a melancholy prince in Denmark whose father has been murdered, and whose mother has married the new king—the very man that did the deed.

SHAKESPEARE: Ah! It comes to my ears like a sweet sound. But let's not talk about it—let's start writing.

BACON: Yes! If it were done when 'tis done, then 'twere well it were done quickly.

SHAKESPEARE (*Rushing to desk, piling clutter to one side*): I assume we'll call the play after the prince himself. What's his name?

BACON: I haven't named him yet.

SHAKESPEARE (*Flourishing feather pen*): How about Sam? (BACON *frowns, shakes his head.*) Melvin?

BACON (*Slowly, intensely*): How—about—Hamlet?

SHAKESPEARE (*Trying it out*): Hamlet. Hamlet. (*Decisively*) I like it!

BACON (*With false modesty*): Yes, it does fall trippingly on the tongue, doesn't it?

SHAKESPEARE (*As he writes*): *Hamlet.* Act One. Scene One. (BACON *paces as he dictates.*)

BACON: The Scene: Ramparts of the castle at Elsinore. Time: Midnight. At Rise: Francisco at his post. Enter Bernardo . . . (SHAKESPEARE *smiles happily as he writes.*)

SHAKESPEARE (*Looking up*): Frank, it's wonderful the way the words just roll out off your tongue, as if you're reciting from memory.

BACON: The idea of collaborating with you still overwhelms me!

SHAKESPEARE: Our fortunes shall move upward, and we'll be graced with wreaths of victory! Frank, this above all—to thine own self be true! We will strive with things impossible! The play's the thing! (*Curtain*)

THE END

Production Notes

AVON CALLING!

Characters: 4 male.

Playing Time: 10 minutes.

Costumes: Jerry wears modern business suit and wrist watch. Marvin wears shirt, pants. Shakespeare wears black turtleneck, sports jacket, and tights. In jacket pocket are paper and quill pen. Bacon wears tights, doublet with white ruff.

Properties: Skull, coffee mug.

Setting: Modern office. Cluttered desk is center with telephone and papers on it. Desk chair is behind desk and several other chairs are right and left. Doorway is down right.

Lighting: No special effects.

The Stockbroker and the Fairy Godmother

by Glenda Leznoff

A surprise visitor turns a busy broker into a better father. . . .

Characters

MILTON MILHOUSE, *40-year old stockbroker*
FAIRY GODMOTHER

TIME: *Morning, a busy business day.*
SETTING: *Milton Milhouse's office. On a large desk are two phones, intercom, files, papers, and calendar.*
AT RISE: MILTON *is sitting at his desk, looking through papers.*
MILTON (*Into intercom*): Diane! Get me that financial report on the Farquar/Dewitt takeover. (*Angrily*) I don't want it tomorrow; I want it now! Time is money, Diane. (*One phone rings. MILTON answers.*) Hello. . . . Yeah. . . . Sell! (*Second phone rings. MILTON slams down first phone; picks up second.*) Hello. . . . What?! You're kidding! (*First phone rings.*) Hold on, Harry. (FAIRY GODMOTHER *enters and stands behind* MILTON, *so he does not see her. She hums "When You Wish Upon A Star," gradually humming louder and louder, trying to get his attention.* MILTON *picks up first phone.*) Hello. . . . Hi, sweetheart. I'm on the other line. (*Into second phone*) Harry? . . . A thousand shares? (*Into first phone*) Honey, listen, I'm very busy. (*Into second phone*) Look, sweetheart—I mean, Harry. (FAIRY, *impatient, waves wand.* MILTON *looks puzzled.*) Harry? Are you there? (*Into first phone*) Hello? Sweetheart? (*Into second phone*) Harry? (*Into first*) Sweetheart? (*Hangs up phones; speaks into intercom*) Diane?

FAIRY GODMOTHER: Hello, Milton.

MILTON (*Into intercom*): What? Hello?

FAIRY (*Tapping* MILTON *on shoulder with wand*): Milton, over here.

MILTON (*Jumping*): What? Who are you? (*Into intercom*) Diane! There's some crackpot in my office!

FAIRY: Stop screaming. You're giving me a headache. And anyway, no one can hear you. I disconnected your phone lines.

MILTON (*Frantically; into intercom*): Diane! Diane!

FAIRY: You know, Milty, you've really changed.

MILTON (*Rising*): Get out of my office.

FAIRY (*Pushing papers off desk and sitting on it*): I'm disappointed.

MILTON: I don't know who you are, but—

FAIRY: Oh, how quickly they forget. I liked you better when you were six years old.

MILTON: Look, lady, take a hike.

FAIRY (*Indignantly*): Milton Milhouse! That is no way to talk to your fairy godmother! I ought to wash your mouth out with soap.

MILTON (*Suddenly*): Oh, I get it. This is a joke. Harry sent you, right? I like the costume, and the wig is great.

FAIRY: It's not a wig. (*Primping*) These are natural curls.

MILTON: So do you want a tip?

FAIRY (*To audience*): Isn't this typical. They grow up, become successful, and suddenly they act as if you never existed.

MILTON (*Laughing*): That's very funny.

FAIRY (*Annoyed*): I am your fairy godmother.

MILTON: Sure, sure. And I'm Peter Pan.

FAIRY: Why do I always have to prove myself?

MILTON: There's no such thing as a fairy godmother.

FAIRY: That's not what you said when you were six.

MILTON: Oh, come on.

FAIRY: Remember when you were six years old, and you wanted a pair of skates for your birthday? And you used to say, "Please, please, all I want is a pair of skates!"

MILTON: All kids want skates.

FAIRY: Did you get the skates?

MILTON: Yeah, I got the skates.

FAIRY: Aha!

MILTON: So?

FAIRY: So, who do you think got you the skates? If it weren't for me, your parents would have given you a plaid polyester suit. Boy, was it tacky!

MILTON: I don't believe you.

FAIRY: Milton, trust me. It was one of the ugliest suits I've ever seen.

MILTON: No, no. I don't believe *you*. This getup of yours. Do you think I'm that gullible? Did you really think I'd fall for this fairy godmother stuff?

FAIRY (*Getting angry*): Milton, I'm warning you!

MILTON: Look, I don't have time for this. I'm very busy.

FAIRY: Why do you think your phones went dead?

MILTON: They must be broken.

FAIRY: Wrong.

MILTON (*Approaching her; sneering*): Listen, leave this office, *now!*

FAIRY: Don't threaten me.

MILTON (*Yelling*): Blast off!

FAIRY: You're asking for it.

MILTON: And by the way, tell Harry it's going to take more than an old lady in a princess dress and a tacky wig to get a rise out of me.

FAIRY: That does it! (*She waves wand. MILTON's mouth snaps shut, and he cannot speak. He struggles to open his mouth and makes muffled noises.*) I have had enough! I can't believe how you've changed. And talk about bad manners! You modern guys are all the same. Do this, do that, and then just disappear. You give them skates, and they laugh in your face. Well, how do you think *I* feel? Have you ever once thought about how your poor, overworked fairy godmother feels?

MILTON (*Groaning and pointing to his mouth*): Mm-m . . . m-m-m.

FAIRY: Oh, right. All right, I'll let you speak, but I'm warning you. If you misbehave, I'll turn you into a frog. I mean it.

MILTON: Wow! (*Rubs his jaw*) How did you do that?

FAIRY: I'm not one to trick and tell.

MILTON: Well, what do you know. My fairy godmother! (*Offers her his chair*) Have a seat.

FAIRY (*Sitting*): Recognition at last.

MILTON: Hey, listen, you wouldn't happen to be able to see into the future, would you? (*Shuffles through papers*) There's a stock I'm really interested in buying.

FAIRY: Whoa, Milton. Remember my warning!

MILTON (*Holding hands up*): O.K. O.K. I'll do anything you say.

FAIRY: Fine. Do you know what day it is?

MILTON (*Looking at calendar*): Yes, Thursday, March 9th.

FAIRY: Very good. And what is special about March 9th?

MILTON: Um . . . let's see. . . . Got it! That's the date the anti-trust suit was filed against—

FAIRY (*Interrupting*): Milty, we're not playing Trivial Pursuit here. Let me give you a clue: Megan.

MILTON: What was that?

FAIRY (*Shaking head*): Megan. You know, your daughter, the little girl with the red hair and freckles?

MILTON: Yeah, sure.

FAIRY: So?

MILTON: So, what?

FAIRY: Milton! Think!

MILTON: I *am* thinking.

FAIRY: It's her birthday.

MILTON (*Suddenly*): Oh, it's her birthday! I forgot.

FAIRY: No kidding.

MILTON (*Musing*): So that's why she was staring at me like that at the breakfast table, waiting for me to say something.

FAIRY: You should be ashamed.

MILTON: I know. I'm sorry. I had all these things on my mind. The pressures of work.

FAIRY: Excuses, excuses.

MILTON: How old is she? Seven?

FAIRY: Eight.

MILTON: Wow! They sure grow fast.

FAIRY: And you're missing it all, Milton.

MILTON (*Sheepishly*): You're right.

FAIRY: I know. So what are you going to do about it?

MILTON: Well, I could call my wife and tell her to buy one of those birthday cakes with the pink roses. A lemon cake.

FAIRY: Megan likes chocolate.

MILTON: O.K. Chocolate.

FAIRY: That's not the point. What are *you* going to do?

MILTON: Me? Oh, I get it. I could get her a present. Maybe . . . um . . . a savings bond.

FAIRY: Bonds are boring, Milton.

MILTON: I don't think so.

FAIRY: You are not an eight-year-old girl.

MILTON (*Helplessly*): Look, I don't know what she wants.

FAIRY: That's because you never spend any time with her.

MILTON: A person's got to earn a living.

FAIRY: There's more to life than work, Milty.

MILTON: I know, I know. I feel so guilty. I'll buy her a toy. (FAIRY *shakes her head*.) A dress? A game?

FAIRY: Do you remember when you were eight?

MILTON: Frankly, no.

FAIRY: Try. Your parents gave you a big surprise.

MILTON: A big surprise . . .

FAIRY: A pair of tickets.

MILTON: A pair of tickets . . .

FAIRY (*Annoyed*): Do I have to tell you everything?

MILTON (*Suddenly*): Wait! I know! A pair of tickets to a hockey game!

FAIRY: That's right. Jackpot!

MILTON (*Reminiscing*): Yeah. I remember. The Montreal Canadiens versus the Boston Bruins. Rocket Richard and Bobby Orr. The game was tied at two when Jean Belliveau scored the winning goal. (*Jumps up*) Boy, that was a great game!

FAIRY: Who took you to the game?

MILTON: My dad. He bought me a hot dog and a soda and an ice cream. I cheered so loudly my voice went hoarse. We sure had a good time. I haven't thought about that for years.

FAIRY: Well, Milton, what do you think?

MILTON: You don't suppose Megan might like to go with me to the game tonight? Besides, I'm not sure I could get . . .

FAIRY (*Pulling two tickets out of her pocket*): Tickets?

MILTON (*Taking tickets; amazed*): You knew all along.

FAIRY: It's what she wished for.

MILTON (*Examining tickets*): Front row seats! This really is magic!

FAIRY: So long, Milty! Have fun. And don't work too hard.

MILTON: Thanks a lot. And, fairy godmother . . .

FAIRY: Yes?

MILTON: Thanks for the skates, too.

FAIRY: You're welcome. Oh, this job is so rewarding when things work out happily. Well, now, who's next? (*She takes out a list.*) A girl named Rapunzel. Hm-m-m. Looks like she needs a hair cut. (FAIRY *exits. Phones start to ring, but* MILTON *ignores them, sits back, and smiles. Curtain*)

THE END

Production Notes

THE STOCKBROKER AND THE FAIRY GODMOTHER

Characters: 1 male; 1 female.

Playing Time: 15 minutes.

Costumes: Milton wears a suit. Fairy Godmother wears a flouncy but faded fairy dress and carries a wand with a tacky-looking star on its tip.

Properties: Two tickets.

Setting: Milton's office. On a large desk are two phones, an intercom, heaps of papers and files, and a calendar.

Lighting and Sound: No special effects.

Broadway Hit

by Val R. Cheatham

Everybody's a star in this uproarious comedy about the New York theatre world . . . .

Characters

MOSS ROSENHART, *director preparing Broadway show opening*
CAROL CREED, *cleaning woman who belongs to union*
IRMA DILSAVER, *small-town girl who wants to be a star*
OSCAR ROGERS, *lyricist who says music should fit words*
IRVING COHAN, *composer who says lyrics should fit music*
HAROLD KING, *Texas oil man with money to invest*
MARYETHYLL STARBRIGHT, *tardy and conceited star*
SIR JOHN ALFRED, *vain and hammy star*

SCENE 1

SETTING: *Backstage in a Broadway theater. Exit at left leads to stage. There are two dressing room doors upstage marked with stars and names* SIR JOHN *and* MARYETHYLL.

AT RISE: CAROL CREED, *with mop and bucket, is cleaning floor.*

MOSS (*From offstage*): Dancers, that was terrible! (*Enters left, still addressing unseen dancers, offstage*) Now, go through it again. And, do it right.

CAROL (*Heatedly*): Hey! Mr. Rosenhart! I'm mopping here. How do you expect me to keep these floors clean with you walking all over them? You can't do that. I belong to the union, you know.

158

MOSS (*Bored*): Yes, I know. (*Strongly*) How I know! Listen, Carol: I'm expecting an oil man from Texas who is interested in putting big money into our show. And, believe me, we need more money if we plan on opening. If he comes in here, send him on through. If it's anybody else, they'll want money. I don't care where you send them. I'll be on stage.

CAROL: O.K. But, remember, if he comes while I'm mopping, he won't be able to come *through* here, he'll have to go *around* here. I belong to the union, you know. (*Resumes mopping*)

MOSS: I know, I know! (*Shakes head and exits left*)

KING (*Entering right and walking over mopped floor*): Say, miss. I'm looking for someone.

CAROL: Well, now, who's this clown, traipsing all over my clean floor? You a bill collector?

KING: Oh, sorry, little lady.

CAROL: "Sorry" just won't do it, buster. When I report this to my union, they'll probably send a picket line down here!

KING: Well, I'm only hankerin' to know if I'm in the right place.

CAROL: What is wrong with you? You're standing on my clean floor! Does that look like the right place?

KING: I apologize, ma'am. (*Moves*) What I meant was, is this the Palace Theater? (MOSS *enters.*) You see, I'm Harold King—from Texas.

MOSS (*Going up to* KING): Mr. King, I'm Moss Rosenhart, the director. Welcome to the Palace Theater, home of the next great Broadway hit, "Robinson Crusoe and Friends." (CAROL *exits.*)

KING (*Extending hand*): Right pleased to meet you. I'm up here in New York from Texas to maybe invest some cash money in a little ole show.

MOSS: You have certainly come to the right place! (*Takes contract from pocket*) If you'll just sign right here.

KING (*Ignoring contract*): From what I hear, this here show biz is easier than pumpin' oil. You just rent a theater, hire a few hands, paste up a little scenery, then sit back and watch the greenbacks roll in.

MOSS: That might be just a little oversimplified. (*Holds out contract*) Here . . . just sign on the bottom line.

KING (*Still ignoring contract*): This story you're a-doin'—what is it? Robinson Crusoe? If I recollect what Miss Tillson said—Miss Tillson was my English teacher back at Alamo High—she said Robinson Crusoe lived on this little island all alone, except for some guy who came on Fridays. Why, it ought to be plumb easy to act that story!

MOSS: That was only the book story. For Broadway we have to change it a little—give it panache. (*Calls off*) Hey, Irving, Oscar! Come in here and tell Mr. King—the oil man from Texas—what our musical is all about. (OSCAR *and* IRVING *enter*.) Mr. King, this is Irving Cohan, the composer, and Oscar Rogers, the lyricist, who have teamed up to write some of America's favorite songs.

OSCAR: Robinson Crusoe is a story which I have completely rewritten for the stage.

IRVING: And for which I have composed songs that will become classics in our lifetime.

OSCAR: Only because my lyrics are poetry—sheer poetry!

IRVING (*In disbelief*): Poetry! If you didn't own a rhyming dictionary, you couldn't match "June" with "moon"!

IRMA (*Entering with a suitcase and looking about, gawking and gaping*): Pardon me!

OSCAR (*Ignoring* IRMA): Say what you like. I will not change a single word. You are supposed to compose melodies to fit my lyrics!

IRVING: Oh no! That's where you have it all wrong! Words are supposed to be written to fit melodies.

OSCAR: Just listen a minute. It would work just fine if you had the melody go this way. (*Hums simple tune*)

IRVING: For your information, that (*Mimics hum*) is not a melody. It's more like the mating cry of a Norwegian mongoose!

IRMA: Pardon me. I'm looking for (*Stops*)—Golle-ee! (*Thrilled*) Irving Cohan and Oscar Rogers! You wrote my favorite song, "I Spoon by the Moon in June"! (*Hums different tune*)

IRVING: The melody you remember so well is mine. The limpid lyrics (*Scornfully*)—who remembers words?—are someone else's.

OSCAR: Just for that, I'll never write another song with you, no matter what!

IRVING: Good! That suits me just fine! Why I ever chose you to write with me in the first place, I'll never know! (*Exits*)

OSCAR (*Indignantly*): *You* chose me? Ha! I'm the one who did the choosing, and I readily admit it was a mistake! (*Exits behind* IRVING) A big mistake!

IRMA: Are they always like that?

KING: Little lady, all I know is that they were supposed to talk songs, but it sounded more like sows feeding at the slop bucket.

MOSS: Pay no attention to their bickering. They're close friends—inseparable, really.

KING (*Surprised*): Friends? Why, back in Texas, we'd practice our punches on a friend that talked like that.

MOSS: I'll tell you what. Maybe you'd understand more if you took a seat out in front and watched some of the rehearsal. (*Moves toward exit with* KING)

KING: Thankee, I'll do just that. (*Exits*)

MOSS (*Seeing* IRMA *following him*): What do you want?

IRMA: I'm here for tryouts.

MOSS: Tryouts are over.

IRMA: They can't be! The paper said today was the final day. (*Takes clipping from handbag*)

MOSS: I know, but we had a long waiting list, and we've already hired all we needed.

IRMA: But, I came all the way from Kansas to try out for this show. I planned to start in the chorus and end up as the lead! This was my big chance! I'm going to be a big star!

MISS STARBRIGHT (*Entering from first dressing room, stopping to pose at every step*): Big star? Did I hear someone call for the big star?

MOSS (*Sarcastically*): Well, well. Rise up, everybody, and bow low to our great "star." (IRMA *bows*) We are most fortunate today that she has decided to honor us by coming to rehearsal.

IRMA: Golle-e-e! Is that really Miss Maryethyll Starbright?

MOSS: But, of course. One does not open on Broadway without a big star, (*In scolding tone*) no matter how late she comes to rehearsal.

MISS STARBRIGHT (*Fanning herself*): Oh, Moss, darling—
don't scold me as if I were a naughty schoolgirl. You know
I'm never late for rehearsal unless there is a perfectly good
reason.

MOSS: Oh, yes, how thoughtless of me. Let's see . . . last week
you had your watch on upside down and you thought it was
nine o'clock at three-thirty.

KING (*Reentering*): Hey, did I hear y'all say that Miss Starbright was here? (*Goes up to her, shakes her hand vigorously*)
This is a real barn-raising honor, ma'am. (*She starts to pull
away.*)

MOSS: Miss Starbright, this is Harold J. King, an oil man from
Texas. He is planning on putting some money into our show.

MISS STARBRIGHT: Hello! (*Sidles up to* KING *and smiles*) An
oil producer—and from Texas, my favorite state.

KING: Miss Starbright, with you in this little ole show, I don't
see any reason at all why I can't invest a little cash money
in it. (MOSS *takes contract out of pocket, but* KING *again
ignores it.*) But one thing has me a mite puzzled. If I recollect
right, Robinson Crusoe was about a *man* on an island—and
you're a woman.

MISS STARBRIGHT: I certainly hope so, darling. You see, I
play Friday, the girl who finds and helps Robbie. After all,
who would come to see a Broadway play about two *men* on
an island?

KING: Now, that's what we call bull's-eye true in Texas.

SIR JOHN (*Entering from second dressing room*): What is all
this racket disturbing my sleep? (*Indicating* MISS STAR-
BRIGHT; *with disdain*) I see. It's Maryethyll Starbright—
that spoiled, self-centered snip.

IRMA: Gosh, it's Sir John Alfred!

SIR JOHN: Yes, it is I, Sir John Alfred, the star who will tran-
scend this mass of middling mediocrity into a smash Broadway hit.

MISS STARBRIGHT (*Peevishly*): Why, it is John, isn't it? I
hardly recognized him. He looks so much *older* in person.

SIR JOHN: Why, Maryethyll, I'm surprised you could see at
all—without your bifocals.

MISS STARBRIGHT: I can tell when you are around. All one has to do is smell—*ham*—half-baked! (*Exits*)

SIR JOHN: How can one of my stature work with such an insufferable egomaniac? It certainly taps all my more than ample talents. I shall retire to my dressing room. Ring me up when all is ready. (*Exits*)

IRVING (*Reentering with* OSCAR): Hey, Moss!

OSCAR: One of the dancers just sprained her ankle.

IRVING: I was going to tell him!

OSCAR: I'm the lyricist. I should tell him. (*Exits with* IRVING)

MOSS: O.K., I'll take care of it. (*To* IRMA) Can you dance?

IRMA: Can I dance? (*Begins dance routine*) I've had ballet since I was three, started tap dancing at ten—you name it.

MOSS: You're hired. Get in there and learn the routines.

IRMA: This is just like the movies! Today the chorus—tomorrow the star. (*Dances off*)

MOSS: And now, Mr. King, if you will just sign this contract. (*Holds out paper*)

KING: Yeah, the contract. I was wondering if you were ever going to get it out. (*Signs*) There . . . my ole "Sam Houston" makes it all nice and legal.

MOSS (*Pocketing contract; mimicking* KING): Now all we have to do is to sit back and watch the greenbacks roll in. (*Curtain*)

* * * * *

SCENE 2

TIME: *Later that day.*

SETTING: *Same as Scene 1.*

AT RISE: CAROL *is slowly mopping floor.*

IRMA (*Entering*): Just think, opening night, and I'll be dancing on Broadway!

CAROL: Opening, closing . . . it's all the same to me. Somebody is always walking on my mopped floor!

IRMA (*Looking down*): I'm sorry. (*Takes mop*) Here, let me get it.

CAROL (*Grabbing back mop*): Oh, no, you don't! I belong to the union! And we have our rules. You're paid to sing and dance— I'm paid to mop floors. I'm a specialist!

MOSS (*Entering*): Say, did either of you see Maryethyll or Sir John?

IRMA: Why, no.

MOSS: It's time they were dressed. (*Walks across mopped floor*)

CAROL: Here we go again! Walking on my clean floor. (*Picks up bucket and moves toward exit*) Why didn't I join the army like my mother? (*Exits*)

IRVING (*Entering with* OSCAR): I heard you tell the band to change that C sharp to a B flat. Did you really think I wouldn't hear the difference?

OSCAR: As tone deaf as you are, you wouldn't recognize "The Star Spangled Banner"!

MOSS: Irving, Oscar. Will one of you step into Sir John's dressing room and see if he's awake?

OSCAR: I will. (*Moving toward dressing room door*)

IRVING: I will. (*Also moving toward door*) I'm the composer.

OSCAR: He asked me. (*Both try to exit together.*)

IRVING: He said, "One of you," and he was looking directly at me. (*They exit together.*)

OSCAR (*From off*): Oh, no! He can't do this!

IRVING (*Reentering with note in hand*): This was taped to his mirror.

OSCAR (*Entering and grabbing note*): It says, "Could not resist my eager heart another minute."

IRVING (*Grabbing note and continuing*): "Have eloped to be married."

OSCAR (*Reading together with* IRVING): "To Maryethyll Starbright."

IRMA: My goodness.

MOSS: What? (*Grabs note*) They can't do this. This is opening night! Tell me this isn't happening!

OSCAR (*Taking note*): Say, I like that. (*Reads*) "Could not resist my eager heart another minute." It would make a great lyric!

IRVING: Say, you're right! The tune could be . . . (*Hums*)

OSCAR: Yes! Perfect! You're a genius! Let's go work it out. (*Exits arm in arm with* IRVING)

KING (*Entering*): Say, Moss, the stage manager said to call you. Says we got us a problem.

MOSS: A problem! Now that's got to be the year's biggest understatement. What is the problem?

KING: It seems as how the horses you have back there for the big escape scene broke out of that little corral and trotted all over the stage.

MOSS: All the horses?

KING: Yep, all twelve of them.

MOSS: Tell him to get some help and get them back into the stable.

KING: I already helped him do that. That's not the problem.

MOSS: Then what *is* the problem?

KING: Well, you see . . . (*Peers off*) The horses trotted through the dressing room and left a trail of oats and straw behind them.

MOSS (*Calling*): Carol, come here! (CAROL *enters with mop and bucket.*) Take that mop and clean up the dressing rooms. (*She moves toward exit.*) Some horses got loose.

CAROL (*Stopping*): Horses? Did you say horses? (*Turns and moves toward opposite exit*) My union doesn't say I have to clean up after horses. No siree! It's bad enough, people—horses, no!

MOSS (*Commandingly*): Now, wait just a minute! (*She stops.*) Your union is the Amalgamated Federation of United Custodial Sanitizers, right?

CAROL (*Standing straighter*): Yes.

MOSS: And your credo is, "You Can't Beat Neat," right?

CAROL (*Dropping bucket and shouldering mop*): Yes, sir!

MOSS (*Dramatically*): Why, your famous founding father, Samuel Moppers, inspired the world with his epitaph, "We made the world safe for actors"—right?

CAROL (*Turning to face* MOSS): Yes, yes!

MOSS: Then your time has come! Bucket, up! Forward, march! Hut, 2-3-4! Hut, 2-3-4! Hut, 2-3-4! (CAROL *exits, marching in time. To* IRMA) You—come here!

IRMA: Yes, sir?

MOSS: Maryethyll's part—do you know it?

IRMA: Oh, yes! Yes! Every word! Every gesture!

MOSS: Then, get her costumes! You're taking her place!

IRMA: Golle-e-e-e! It worked! It came true! Chorus girl becomes star! I thought it only happened in the movies. (*Exits*)

MOSS: And now, Sir John's part . . . there's only one other person that could possibly know all his lines, all his moves, all his songs. Only one person could step in at the last minute and pull off a great performance: me! The director! (*Moves toward exit*) Come on, gang, it's curtain time for another great Broadway hit! (*Curtain*)

THE END

Production Notes

BROADWAY HIT

Characters: 5 male, 3 female.

Playing Time: 15 to 20 minutes.

Costumes: Moss, sport clothes; Carol, baggy dress, army boots, head covering, sweatshirt; Irma, cotton print dress for Scene 1, dancing shorts, Scene 2; Oscar and Irving, sports clothes; King, western hat, boots, etc.; Maryethyll, long, tight, sparkly dress, much jewelry; Sir John, elegant, sequined dressing gown.

Properties: Mop; bucket; contract; pen; suitcase.

Setting: Backstage in Broadway theater. Two doors upstage are marked with large stars and names SIR JOHN and MARYETHYLL. Stage is cluttered with ropes, ladders, and discarded pieces of scenery. Exit at left leads to stage.

Lighting: No special effects.

A Perfect Match

by Ron Charles, Jr.

True love finds a way . . . .

Characters

LIZ MASON, *26-year-old advertising designer*
ALICE, *her friend and colleague*
JOHN, *a figment of Liz's imagination*

TIME: *The present.*
SETTING: *An office. Desk and chair are center; two chairs are in front of desk. Telephone and intercom are on desk, which is covered with papers.*
AT RISE: LIZ MASON *is seated behind desk, talking to* ALICE.
ALICE (*Looking at her watch*): I have only a few minutes before my meeting, Liz, but something is obviously bothering you, and I wish you'd tell me what it is.
LIZ: Robert just called to tell me that he lost his job again.
ALICE: Oh, no. He didn't!
LIZ: Yes, and I hung up on him.
ALICE: Oh, no. You didn't!
LIZ: Alice, he's got to be the worst salesman in the world.
ALICE: Oh, no, he isn't.
LIZ: He couldn't sell a pound of gold for ten dollars. He's a great person, and I love him, but everything he touches seems to go wrong.
ALICE: Oh, no, it doesn't.
LIZ: Basically, he's the sweetest guy I've ever known, and he's always doing things to make me happy. But I'm beginning to think that I might need someone who has more in common with me. Do you know what I mean, Alice?
ALICE: Oh, no, I don't. I mean, yes, of course, I do.

LIZ: Maybe I should call Robert back and tell him I'm sorry. But I'm not sorry. I meant what I said. And maybe it's time we went our separate ways.

ALICE: Oh, no. It isn't!

LIZ: You don't think so?

ALICE: Oh, no, I don't. I don't think you should do anything until you've considered what I've told you.

LIZ (*Gratefully*): You've been such a help, Alice. I'd be lost if I couldn't talk things over with you.

ALICE: Oh, no, you wouldn't. Now just relax and think this thing through. (*Looks at watch*) I wish I could stay and talk, Liz, but I've got to go.

LIZ: Of course, you go ahead. I'll be all right. Thanks again.

ALICE: We can talk some more later, O.K.? (ALICE *exits.*)

LIZ (*To herself*): I just wish I knew what to do. Sometimes I think I'm in love with him, and then other times I can't imagine what I ever saw in him. (*Pause*) We have a great time together. (*Smiles*) How can I not like someone who pasted hearts all over my front door on Valentine's Day? But I'm beginning to wonder how I could possibly spend the rest of my life with him. (*Sighs and shakes her head*) I wish I weren't so confused . . . (LIZ *stares off into space, lost in thought.* JOHN, *carrying briefcase, enters right. He walks up to* LIZ's *desk and taps on corner.*)

JOHN: Hello.

LIZ (*Startled*): Oh! Where did you come from?

JOHN: Would you marry me?

LIZ: How did you get in here?

JOHN: Why, can't you get out?

LIZ: Listen, Mr. . . . .

JOHN: Oh, please, Liz, call me John.

LIZ: You'd better go . . . (*Suddenly*) How do you know my name?

JOHN: I waited until the planet Jupiter was lined up with Saturn in the constellation of Aquarius. Then I sat in the lotus position in front of the large oak in Central Park.

LIZ (*Sarcastically*): A tree told you my name?

JOHN: No, I read the nameplate on your door.

LIZ (*Trying to coax him out*): John, you don't seem to understand. It's very nice meeting you, but I've got lots of work to do, and I'm afraid I'm going to have to cut our visit short.

JOHN: First, tell me "yes."

LIZ (*Confused*): Yes?

JOHN (*Thrilled*): You've made me the happiest man in the world! Thank you, thank you, thank you. (*He grabs her hand and puts a ring on it.*) The invitations are already out.

LIZ: Invitations? Wait a minute. You've got this all wrong. You have to take this ring back and leave.

JOHN: How could you change your mind already?

LIZ: Change my mind? I hadn't made it up!

JOHN (*Angrily*): There's someone else, isn't there? I knew it! I've known it all along, but I wasn't sure. Well, nobody's going to take you away from me. We've been together too long for that.

LIZ (*Bewildered*): What is going on here?

JOHN: You tell me; you're the one who's been cheating.

LIZ (*In disbelief*): Cheating?

JOHN: Ah-hah! A confession!

LIZ: Listen, I am trying to be reasonable with you. Now, please tell me what you're doing here and why you're harassing me like this.

JOHN: *I'm* harassing *you?*

LIZ (*Mockingly*): Ah-hah! A confession!

JOHN (*In disbelief*): That's good.

LIZ (*Pleased*): Thanks. (*Infuriated*) What am I doing? Thanking you? Who are you? What do you want from me?

JOHN: Your hand.

LIZ: Is this a soap commercial?

JOHN: Your hand in marriage.

LIZ: You want to marry me?

JOHN: Now, why couldn't I put it that way?

LIZ: That's absurd!

JOHN: Lots of people are doing it, you know.

LIZ: Listen, John . . . (*Trying to compose herself*) If someone put you up to this, I don't think it's the least bit funny. I don't want to talk to you. I don't want to see you. I don't ever want you to come back, O.K.? Now, please leave me alone.

JOHN: I suppose this means the engagement is off.

LIZ (*Yelling*): *Get out!*

JOHN: Don't I even get the ring back?

LIZ (*Trying to get ring off*): How did you get this on my finger? I can't seem to get it off.

JOHN: It looks great on you.

LIZ: Would you mind? (*She extends her hand to him.*)

JOHN: A pleasure. (*He kisses her hand.*)

LIZ: The ring.

JOHN: Yes, it's beautiful, isn't it?

LIZ: I'm beginning to lose my patience.

JOHN: Don't worry. I'll keep an eye on it.

LIZ: Look, mister, I've had all of this I can take.

JOHN (*Reciting, as if he doesn't hear her*): "Let me not to the marriage of true minds admit impediments."

LIZ: If you aren't out of here immediately . . .

JOHN (*Continuing*): "Love is not love which alters when it alteration finds."

LIZ: I'm going to call the police.

JOHN (*Continuing*): "Or bends with the remover to remove."

LIZ (*Amazed*): You know Shakespeare?

JOHN: Not personally.

LIZ: That's beautiful poetry.

JOHN: Next to you it's plain.

LIZ (*Flattered*): That's very kind. Thank you.

JOHN: Look, Liz, I can tell you're under a lot of pressure.

LIZ: Yes, I am.

JOHN: You still haven't finished that advertising campaign, have you?

LIZ: No, and it's due at three o'clock, and . . . How did you know that?

JOHN: Well, I was in the middle of a large field, when suddenly this huge cucumber-shaped object shot over the horizon and hovered over me.

LIZ: An outer space pickle told you I was behind in my work?

JOHN: No. Actually, your secretary told me.

LIZ: What about this thing from the cosmic delicatessen?

JOHN: She didn't say anything about it. Besides, how can you think about all that when you've got a big project due in three hours?

LIZ: I don't understand any of this.

JOHN: Let's see what you've got so far. (*He starts looking through papers on her desk.*) Ah, good. Very good. (*Looks up*) But you'll never finish in time.

LIZ: I won't if you keep bothering me.

JOHN: All right, all right. (*He picks up briefcase and pulls out several pages.*) Here.

LIZ: Here what?

JOHN: Your advertising campaign. It's finished.

LIZ: What?

JOHN (*Loudly*): Your advertising campaign is finished!

LIZ: I heard you . . . I can't—I don't believe it. (*She looks through the pages.*) How did you know I was working on this account?

JOHN: I was swimming down the Amazon River, when suddenly . . .

LIZ: Skip it.

JOHN: Your secretary told me.

LIZ: Why would my secretary tell you all these things?

JOHN: You know how friends are. Everybody wants to help out people in love.

LIZ: We are not in love. I have never seen you before.

JOHN: We're perfect for each other.

LIZ: We're strangers.

JOHN: Ah, something in common already!

LIZ: I don't know anything about you.

JOHN: Of course you do. I'm everything you've always wanted.

LIZ: I have never, even momentarily, wanted some kook to come running into my office and make me lose my job.

JOHN: Our favorite food is Chinese food.

LIZ: There are a billion people on this planet who eat Chinese food at every meal. Go bother one of them.

JOHN: Your favorite color is light blue.

LIZ: I'm beginning to see red.

JOHN: You love to ski.

LIZ: I'll have lots of opportunities to ski when I lose my job.

JOHN: Your favorite author is F. Scott Fitzgerald, and you love poetry, especially Shakespeare. They're my favorites, too.

LIZ: So we both have good taste in books. So what?

JOHN: Our favorite fruit is watermelon.

LIZ (*Sarcastically*): A match made in heaven.

JOHN: I thought so.

LIZ: Well, I don't. I think this is crazy, your waltzing in here professing you're in love with me.

JOHN: We both hate lima beans.

LIZ (*Ignoring him*): I've tried to be as polite about this as I can.

JOHN: We prefer linoleum over tile, and we love antiques.

LIZ: I don't know what is going on here!

JOHN: We want a small family.

LIZ (*Holding up hands*): Please stop. Right now.

JOHN: We'd rather live in the country than in the city.

LIZ: Stop! Stop! Stop! (*Pause*) Now, listen to me. You must leave. I must finish this account. Do you hear me? These two events must take place in that order, beginning immediately.

JOHN: But I've already finished your account for you.

LIZ: I can't use that.

JOHN: Why not? You need the account finished. I just handed you a finished copy, photos and all. Isn't it good enough?

LIZ: Well, no, that's not it. It's just that I need to do my own work. (*Looks at papers*) Actually . . .

JOHN: What?

LIZ (*Amazed*): This is exactly what I'd planned on doing myself, if I'd only had the time.

JOHN: Well, I had the time.

LIZ: No one knew what I was working on—I mean, not the specific ideas I was thinking of. How could you . . .?

JOHN: We're perfect for each other, Liz. Forget this salesman Robert and come with me.

LIZ: Robert?

JOHN: You remember Robert. He's shorter than I am, brown hair, unemployed.

LIZ: This can't be happening. Things like this just don't happen.

JOHN: People don't fall in love?

LIZ: I'm not in . . .

JOHN: We're perfect for each other. I knew it the moment I met you.

LIZ: When did you meet me?

JOHN: Don't you remember? It was just a few minutes ago.

LIZ: I mean, before that. When did we meet before that?

JOHN: It's love, don't you see? We're a cliché come true. We're absolutely right. Just be glad we found each other.

LIZ (*Bewildered*): Somehow . . . I *am* glad. But it doesn't make any sense.

JOHN: It doesn't have to make sense. We're talking about love, not a math problem.

LIZ: But how can I possibly love you?

JOHN: How can you help it? Your life's been a mess. You've been spending so much time running interference for Robert that you've been missing your deadlines month after month. Let's face it, that salesman-boyfriend of yours couldn't sell a banana to a monkey. (*Pauses*) Come with me.

LIZ (*Defensively*): Wait a minute! You don't have to be so mean! Robert and I have had some good times together—and he'll be a good salesman someday, I know. He just needs time.

JOHN: Maybe someday his mother will need a car, and Robert will manage to sell her one.

LIZ: He needs me, you know. And he really cares about me.

JOHN: Liz, ten minutes ago you told Alice you weren't sure you could marry someone like Robert.

LIZ: He loves me very much.

JOHN: But you and I have everything in common.

LIZ (*Slowly*): When you first came in, somewhere in the back of my mind, even though I thought you were crazy, I knew there was something very special about you. (*Pause*) We like the same things. We're interested in the same things. But there's something more about you . . . I can't quite put my finger on it.

JOHN: We're a perfect match.

LIZ: Is that it?

JOHN: You believe me, don't you?

LIZ: I believe that with you I would have absolutely everything
I ever wanted.

JOHN: That's what everybody's after: happiness, satisfaction.

LIZ: And would you have everything you ever wanted?

JOHN: Everything.

LIZ: It sounds marvelous, doesn't it? Two people absolutely, instantly happy. Never a disagreement, never a difference to
cause any problems.

JOHN: No aggravating little habits, no interests that don't interest you.

LIZ: Nothing to have to work out between us. Nothing to give
up.

JOHN: That's right. (*Telephone rings.* LIZ *answers it.*)

LIZ: Hello, Liz Mason . . . Yes, hello, Robert.

JOHN: Tell him now, Liz. Tell him now.

LIZ (*Pleased*): You got your job back? Oh that's fantastic, Robert.
I'm so glad. (*Pause*) I know you'll do better this time. I believe
in you. (*Pause*) Robert? I'm sorry I hung up on you before. I
was aggravated about something here at work. I didn't mean
to. It's just that for a minute I didn't think that . . . Well, I
just didn't think, that's all, and I'm sorry.

JOHN: Liz, tell him.

LIZ: Oh, that's just a client here in the office. No, it's all right.
I'm glad you called. I was worried about you . . . Dinner tonight? Well . . . O.K. Bye, Robert. (*She hangs up.*)

JOHN: How could you do that?

LIZ: Do what?

JOHN: Lead him on like that.

LIZ: You don't understand. I wasn't leading him on.

JOHN: What about us?

LIZ: That man is my best friend. I can't leave him.

JOHN: That doesn't make any sense.

LIZ: Remember, this is love, not a math problem. (*Pause*) At my
last birthday, Robert spent the entire night before filling my
office with red balloons.

JOHN: But your favorite color is blue.

LIZ: Last month when I had a cold, he stayed with me round
the clock for three days because he didn't want me to be alone
in case I needed anything.

JOHN: So? Maybe he always wanted to be a doctor.

LIZ: During the subway strike, he came down here every after-noon, spending hours in traffic, just so he could drive me home.

JOHN: So what?

LIZ: I suppose it isn't much.

JOHN: No, it isn't.

LIZ: But there are other things. Years of things—sacrifices, and gifts, and silly inside jokes—things we've done because we cared about each other regardless of the little arguments and differences that come up now and then.

JOHN: But you don't have anything in common with him.

LIZ: I love him and he loves me. That's a lot to have in common.

JOHN: I'm perfect for you.

LIZ: I'm perfect for someone who needs me. You don't.

JOHN: But . . .

LIZ: Please. (*Pause*) Go. And don't come back. (*Takes ring off finger, hands it to him*)

JOHN: Do you mean that?

LIZ: It's not easy, but yes, I do mean it.

JOHN (*Relieved*): Good. (*He takes his papers back and puts them in his briefcase.*)

LIZ: What?

JOHN: I'm through here.

LIZ: I don't get it. What really made you come through that door?

JOHN: I thought I heard someone in trouble.

LIZ: You did all this for me?

JOHN: He was wrong, you know.

LIZ: Who?

JOHN: Parting isn't such *sweet* sorrow.

LIZ (*Smiling*): You knew all along it would end like this, didn't you?

JOHN: I hoped it would. (LIZ *looks away for a moment, as* JOHN *exits.*)

LIZ (*To herself*): I've got to call Robert back and tell him all about this. He'll never believe that a total stranger helped me realize how much I love him. (*She turns to speak to* JOHN *who has already left.*) Maybe you could ... Thank you, Whoever-You-Were. (*She laughs quietly as she picks up phone. Curtain*)

THE END

Production Notes

A PERFECT MATCH

Characters: 2 female; 1 male.
Playing Time: 15 minutes.
Costumes: Everyday clothing. Alice wears watch.
Properties: Briefcase filled with papers; ring.
Setting: Office. Desk, covered with papers, is center. Telephone and intercom are on desk. One chair is placed behind desk and two chairs are arranged in front of it.
Lighting and Sound: No special effects.

Madcap Monster Inn

by Frank V. Priore

Dracula terrifies guests at Hotel Transylvania . . . .

Characters

MR. GARDNER
MRS. GARDNER
HOTEL MANAGER
BELLBOY
DRACULA
CHILD
WITCH

TIME: *The present.*

SETTING: *Main lobby of Hotel Transylvania. Front desk is up center. Papers, ledger, register, bell, and phone are on desk. Two chairs are along the downstage left wall. A doorway up left leads to upstairs rooms. Exit outside is along the right wall. Sign over front desk reads,* HOTEL TRANSYLVANIA.

AT RISE: HOTEL MANAGER *is standing behind desk, shuffling through some papers. Crash of thunder is heard, followed by flash of lightning. MR. and MRS. GARDNER enter right, quickly. They wear raincoats and carry open umbrellas, which they close as they move toward desk.*

MR. GARDNER (*Shuddering*): This weather is ghastly!

MANAGER (*Looking up, smiling*): Yes, lovely, isn't it?

MRS. GARDNER: To each his own. We were just passing through Transylvania. We didn't intend to stop over, but this storm has washed out the only bridge.

MR. GARDNER: We'd like to take a room for the night.

MRS. GARDNER: I do hope you have something available. Our only alternative is to sleep in the car.

MANAGER: I see. (*He looks through ledger book, then looks up.*) I do have one vacancy, but I'm not sure if the room is ready yet. (*He rings bell on desk, then calls out.*) Bellboy! (BELLBOY *enters left. He is wearing a baseball uniform, and carries two baseballs.*)

MR. GARDNER (*In disbelief*): *That's* a bellboy?

MANAGER (*Sighing*): Yes. Our regular bellboy is sick. We called the agency for a temporary replacement, but unfortunately, on such short notice, the best they could do was to send a *ball*-boy. (*To* BELLBOY, *angrily*) Put those baseballs away!

BELLBOY: Yes, sir. (*He puts baseballs into his pockets.*)

MANAGER: Now, then, is room 31 ready?

BELLBOY: Not quite, sir. The plumbers and electricians have finished, but the plasterers are still at work.

MR. GARDNER (*To* MANAGER): Electricians and plasterers? Just to get a room ready?

MANAGER: You see, the Wolfman was using that room last night, and he forgot to report to his cage before the full moon rose. (MR. *and* MRS. GARDNER *exchange nervous glances.* MANAGER *addresses* BELLBOY.) By the way, how are they coming with the mattress and the drapes?

BELLBOY: Quite well, sir. They've almost finished sewing up the gashes. You can hardly tell that they've been clawed.

MRS. GARDNER (*To* MANAGER; *horrified*): Do you mean to say a real werewolf lives here?

MANAGER: Not all the time. His wife sends him here only when there's a full moon. She says it cuts down on her household insurance claims.

MRS. GARDNER: Heavens! Is it safe to stay here with a werewolf roaming the halls?

MANAGER: Perfectly, madam. We have a cage in the basement for him. (*To* BELLBOY) He's there now, isn't he?

BELLBOY: Oh, yes, sir. He's been there all day. He's not feeling too well, I'm afraid. He says it must have been something he ate.

MANAGER: Undoubtedly. The rug was missing this morning. You'd better send for the doctor.

BELLBOY (*Looking at his wristwatch; hesitating*): Ah—sir, the moon will be up in half an hour.

MANAGER (*Nodding*): True. Forget the doctor—send for the vet.

BELLBOY: Right, sir. (*He turns and exits left. Phone on desk rings. MANAGER answers it.*)

MANAGER (*Into phone*): Hotel Transylvania . . . Oh, hello, Frankie. How are you? . . . You did? Congratulations! . . . Oh, of course. I'll reserve it for you right now. Goodbye, and give my best to the little lady . . . What? . . . She's not very little. I see. Give her my regards, anyway. Goodbye. (*He hangs up, speaks to* MR. *and* MRS. GARDNER) That was Frankenstein. His bride has finally been brought to life. They were married today. They're going to be honeymooning right here at the hotel, in our bridal crypt. Isn't that nice?

MRS. GARDNER (*To* MR. GARDNER; *nervously*): Perhaps we'd better leave, dear. This place is making me very nervous.

MR. GARDNER (*Boldly*): Nonsense! I'll admit it sounds a bit weird, but it's better than spending the night in our car. (*To* MANAGER) I'll register now. We can wait here in the lobby until our room is ready. (*To* MRS. GARDNER, *as he registers*) Why don't you sit down and relax, dear? (MRS. GARDNER *sits in one of the chairs down left.*)

MANAGER (*Looking at register*): Mr. and Mrs. Gardner. (*To* MR. GARDNER) Have a seat, Mr. Gardner. Your room will be ready soon. (MR. GARDNER *moves toward chair down left, and sits.* DRACULA *enters up left, wearing traditional costume, and holding a lunch box.* MANAGER *addresses him good-naturedly.*) Hi, Drac. Off to work?

DRACULA: Yes. And the sun doesn't rise until six tomorrow morning. It's going to be another nine-to-five night for me. (*He sees* MR. *and* MRS. GARDNER, *crosses to them.*) Ah! New guests?

MR. GARDNER (*Stammering*): Ah, yes. We'll just be here for the night.

DRACULA: Too bad. It would be nice to see a little new blood in the neighborhood.

MRS. GARDNER (*Moving her hand to her throat*): Are you really the famous Count Dracula?

DRACULA (*Bowing*): At your service, my dear lady. And may I ask your name?

MRS. GARDNER: Mrs. Gardner. This is my husband. (*Indicating* MR. GARDNER)

DRACULA: Gardner—a nice, earthy name.

MRS. GARDNER: May I ask you something? Did you say you were going out to work?

DRACULA: Quite right.

MRS. GARDNER: Then why are you carrying a lunch box? Don't you—um—catch a snack or two on the job?

DRACULA: That is quite true. This lunch box is not for me. It belongs to my good friend, Renfield. He left in a hurry and forgot it.

MANAGER: Renfield! Did he leave those spiders crawling around the refrigerator again?

DRACULA (*Delighted*): Yes! (*Patting lunch box*) There are a few nice ones in here. Would you like to see them? (*He starts to open lunch box.*)

MRS. GARDNER (*Quickly*): No, thank you. That's quite all right.

DRACULA (*Stopping*): Very well. I must be leaving now. A vampire's work is never done. Charmed to meet you both. (*Bows and heads for exit right*)

MR. GARDNER (*Calling after him*): The bridge is out, you know, Dracula.

DRACULA: That does not bother me, my friend. I provide my own transportation. (*He spreads out his arms, flaring out the cape, laughs maniacally, and runs out right. After a moment* CHILD *enters left.*)

CHILD (*Whimpering*): Where's my mummy? I want my mummy!

MANAGER (*Crossing to* CHILD; *comforting him*): Don't cry. Your mummy will be back soon, dear. She just went out to get a new wrap. Go upstairs, and wait in your room. I'm sure she'll be back any minute. (CHILD *turns and exits left*. MRS. GARDNER *rises, and moves to* MANAGER.)

MRS. GARDNER: That poor dear! What sort of mother would leave her child alone to go buy a new coat?

MANAGER (*Confused*): I beg your pardon?

MRS. GARDNER: Didn't you just tell that child that his mother went out to get a new wrap?

MANAGER: I'm afraid you're mistaken, Mrs. Gardner. In the first place, the child is not looking for his *mommy;* he's looking for his *mummy*. His mummy went out to buy some new bandages. She needs to be rewrapped every century or so.

MRS. GARDNER: I see. I guess we all have different ways of giving ourselves a new lease on life. (WITCH *enters right, wearing traditional costume. She carries a full grocery bag.*)

WITCH (*To* MANAGER): Whew! What a night! That was some bumpy ride. But I managed to get everything I needed. (*She looks into bag.*) Bat wings, buzzard beaks, rat tails—the works! Can I have the key, please? I want to put my buggy away for the night.

MANAGER: Certainly. (*He hands her a key.*) There you go.

WITCH (*Taking the key*): Thank you. (*She exits up left.*)

MR. GARDNER (*Rising and moving to desk*): I didn't know this hotel had a garage. Perhaps I can park my car there, too.

MANAGER: I'm sorry sir. We don't have a garage.

MR. GARDNER: But didn't you just give her the key to the garage? She said she wanted to put her buggy away.

MANAGER: True. But she doesn't need a garage for that. I just gave her the key to the broom closet. (*He looks at his wristwatch.*) Aha! Nine o'clock. It's time for me to go off duty. The bellboy will let you know when your room is ready. Good night. (*He moves right.*)

MR. GARDNER: Just a moment. (MANAGER *stops and turns toward* MR. GARDNER.) I'd like to know something before you leave. How can you work in a crazy place like this with all the weird guests who stay here? Doesn't it drive you batty?

MANAGER: Batty? (*He laughs.*) Yes, indeed. That's exactly what it does! (*Laughing, he turns and exits right.* MR. *and* MRS. GARDNER *follow him to doorway, then stare out after him.* MANAGER *yells from offstage.)* Bye, now! (MR. *and* MRS. GARDNER *continue to stare after him, gradually tilting their heads back as if they are watching* MANAGER *"fly" away.)*

MRS. GARDNER (*Waving*): Goodbye.

MR. GARDNER: I guess this place really does drive you batty! (BELLBOY *enters left.*)

BELLBOY: Your room is ready, sir. (MR. GARDNER *looks at* MRS. GARDNER, *who shakes her head.*

MR. GARDNER *addresses* BELLBOY.) Why don't you take it? (*He takes money from pocket and puts it on desk.*) It's on me. Come on, dear. (*Takes* MRS. GARDNER's *arm; they both head right.*)

BELLBOY: Where are you going? There's no other hotel in town.

MR. GARDNER: We're going to spend the night in our nice, cozy car!

MRS. GARDNER: With the doors locked! (*They exit right.*)

BELLBOY (*Looking after them and shaking his head*): What weirdos! (*He takes off hat, revealing horns, then turns and exits, as curtain falls.*)

THE END

Production Notes

MADCAP MONSTER INN

Characters: 4 male; 2 female; 1 male or female for Child.

Playing Time: 10 minutes.

Costumes: Mr. and Mrs. Gardner wear everyday dress and raincoats; Witch and Dracula, traditional costumes. Manager wears dark suit; Bellboy, baseball uniform and baseball cap, which covers horns. Manager and Bellboy also wear wristwatches.

Properties: Two umbrellas; 2 baseballs; lunchbox; bag of groceries; key; paper money.

Setting: Main lobby of Hotel Transylvania. Front desk is up center. Papers, ledger, bell, and phone are on desk. Two chairs are along downstage left wall. Doorway left leads to upstairs rooms. Exit outside is along the right wall. Sign over front desk reads, HOTEL TRANSYLVANIA.

Lighting: Lightning flash.

Sound: Thunder clap, phone ringing.

A Dog's Best Friend

by *Claire Boiko*

A dog's guide to choosing a playmate . . .

Characters

WOOFINGTON T. BOWSER
MADAME FIDEAUX
FIFI FIDEAUX
NANCY
EMILY OGLEBY VON BLUESTOCKING
MAJOR BEAGLE
BILL
MR. ROVER
MRS. ROVER
SPORTY ROVER
HUNTER
BOXER
GREYHOUND DRIVER
HUSKY BOY

SETTING: *Woofington T. Bowser's People Shop. Counter with telephone on it is up center. Signs on curtain read:* PEDIGREED PEOPLE SOLD HERE; A DOG'S BEST FRIEND IS A PERSON; THIS IS BE-KIND-TO-PEOPLE WEEK.

AT RISE: WOOFINGTON T. BOWSER *is at counter, writing an order form. Telephone rings.*

BOWSER (*Answering phone*): Hello. Woofington T. Bowser's People Shop. Our people are guaranteed free from fleas. May I help you? . . . You say your pet is listless, pale, and won't eat? . . . What kind of pet, and how old is it, please? . . . A teenage boy? I see. What have you been feeding him, ma'am?

183

. . . Hamburgers three times a day? You'll have to stop that, ma'am. That's too much hamburger, even for a teenage boy. Try hot dogs for the next week or two—and be sure to use mustard. Human beings need lots of mustard . . . . Thank you, ma'am. (*He hangs up, shaking his head.*) Honestly, dogs are so careless about people these days! (MADAME FIDEAUX *and* FIFI, *who holds* NANCY *by the collar of her dress, enter from right.* NANCY *carries a jump rope.*) Ah, Madame Fideaux and little Fifi. What brings you back to my shop so soon?

MADAME (*With French accent*): Monsieur Bowser, this little girl you sold us—she will not do. When Fifi first saw her in your window, playing with all the other little girls, she thought this girl was perfect.

FIFI (*Also with French accent*): But she's not. She's spoiled. She's too, too dull. She doesn't know how to play with me. I want her to chase balls on the lawn, and dig for bones in the garden with me. But this girl—all she wants to do is stand on her silly hind legs and jump over that silly rope she has. (NANCY *jumps rope.*) See? What kind of a companion is that?

BOWSER: Down, Nancy. Good girl. (NANCY *stops jumping.*) Why, she's just a child. It takes time and patience to teach a human being to dig for bones. Some never learn.

FIFI: Take her back. I want a smarter human being.

BOWSER: All right, all right. Back to your kennel, Nancy. There's a good little person. (NANCY *exits left.*)

MADAME: I myself would like someone much showier. Someone with a pedigree that we could enter in the People Show. Have you anyone like that, perhaps?

BOWSER (*Bowing*): Of course, Madame. (*Calling off left*) Emily! Here, Emily! (EMILY *enters left, wearing a party dress and bow in hair. She walks over to* BOWSER.)

FIFI (*Impressed*): Well, that's more like it.

BOWSER: This is Emily Ogleby Von Bluestocking, a direct descendant of the Bluestockings who came over on the *Mayflower* with the English bulls. A pedigreed poodle would never be ashamed to walk down the street with Emily.

MADAME: Has she had obedience training?

BOWSER: The best. Let me demonstrate. (*He fastens the clip end of a leash to his collar, and places end of leash in* EMILY's *hand. Then he leads her down right. She walks in a haughty fashion.*) Heel, Emily. (*She trips daintily beside him.*) Sit, Emily. (EMILY *sits in a chair. She folds her hands in her lap and crosses her ankles.* BOWSER *unfastens leash from his collar.*)

FIFI: Does she do tricks?

BOWSER: Of course. Speak, Emily.

EMILY (*In a cultured voice*) How do you do? I am delighted to make your acquaintance.

MADAME: *Charmante!* A real blue-blood. We'll take her. Just charge her to my account and send along a diamond-studded leash for her. Come, Fifi. *Au revoir,* monsieur. (BOWSER *clips* EMILY's *leash to* FIFI's *collar.* FIFI *and* EMILY *walk haughtily off right, followed by* MADAME.)

BOWSER (*Calling off right*): Goodbye, Madame Fideaux. I hope she works out for you. (*To audience*) That's the fourth child in a month. Those poodles are never satisfied. It seems that dogs don't want human beings for friendship any more. (MAJOR BEAGLE *storms in right, dragging* BILL *by the arm.* BILL *is crying.*) Why, it's Major Beagle, and Bill. What's the matter, Major?

MAJOR (*Sputtering*): What is the matter? False representation, that's what! When you sold me this miserable boy yesterday, you assured me he was in perfect shape—intelligent, reliable—

BOWSER: He is. At least he was . . .

MAJOR: Then why can't he hunt ducks, tell me that? He can't point. He can't retrieve. He just sits and looks at me.

BOWSER: But I thought you wanted a friend—somebody to sit by your side.

MAJOR: Fiddle-faddle. I want a hunting boy, sir, someone I can treat like a well-oiled machine. I don't need a friend. I need a hunter.

BOWSER: All right. All right. (*He pats* BILL *on the head, and feels his brow.*) Hm-m. Your head is hot. Emotionally upset, that's what you are. Never mind, Bill, we'll find a good home for you. (BILL *sits in chair down right.*) Here, Major, I'll call a hunter for you. (*Takes a whistle from his pocket and pretends to blow it*) Did you hear that whistle?

MAJOR: No, sir, I heard nothing.

BOWSER: It's a new low-intensity whistle. Only people can hear it. (HUNTER, *wearing pith helmet, a toy gun slung on his back, runs on left.*) There you are, Major Beagle. A real hunter.

MAJOR: Does he point? That's the important thing.

BOWSER: Point, boy, point. (HUNTER *shades his eyes, looks off right, and slowly extends his arm, pointing his finger toward the ceiling.*)

MAJOR: Splendid. That's just what I want. Sold! (*He whistles.*) Come along, boy. (*They exit right.*)

BOWSER (*Shaking his head*): A well-oiled machine! That's all a human being means to him. Sometimes I think I ought to close up shop and go back to being a bloodhound. Dogs are never satisfied. Why, dogs are going to the people these days! (MR. *and* MRS. ROVER *and* SPORTY *enter right.*)

MR. ROVER: Good afternoon. We're looking for a person for our pup, Sporty.

SPORTY: Every pup on the block has a person, and I want one, too.

BOWSER: Right you are, tail-wagger. Nothing like a boy or girl to teach a pup responsibility. I'll show you a few of my best people. (*He blows whistle.* BOXER, *wearing trunks and boxing gloves, enters left. He shadowboxes to center and holds a pose.*) There you are, folks, my very best watchman and protector. A boxer.

MRS. ROVER: Oh, we aren't looking for protection. (SPORTY *goes to* BILL, *who is still sitting in chair, and pats his head.* BILL *perks up and smiles at him.* BOXER *exits left, still shadowboxing.*)

BOWSER: Well, then, how about a really speedy fellow? You can enter this one in the races. (*He blows whistle.* GREYHOUND DRIVER, *wearing bus driver's uniform and carrying an auto horn, enters left. He pantomimes driving to center stage.*)

GREYHOUND: . . . and leave the driving to us!

BOWSER: How do you like that one? A genuine Greyhound!

MR. ROVER: Oh, we don't want to race our boy. We want some-body—more friendly. (SPORTY *pats* BILL *again, as* GREY-HOUND *exits left.*)

BOWSER: Then how about a good work person? Somebody to help around the yard. (*He blows whistle.* HUSKY BOY *enters left, wearing a sweatshirt stuffed with "muscles," and dunga-rees. He carries large barbells. He groans as he carries barbells across stage. He pauses center stage, lifts them above his head, and holds them there.*) There he is. He'll pull, push, shovel and carry. A genuine Alaskan Husky!

SPORTY: I don't want a boy just for working. I want a pal. A two-legged pal. Like this fellow right here. (*He pats* BILL*'s head.*) He has a nice head of hair, and understanding eyes. (BILL *nods and smiles.*) See? He likes me, too.

BOWSER (*Pleased*): Well, well, young tail-wagger, you've re-stored my faith in the canine race. But before I let you take this boy, you have to repeat the oath of allegiance to people. Are you ready? (SPORTY *nods.*) Do you, Sporty Rover, take Bill to be your best friend? Will you see that he gets sunshine and fresh air, and plenty of romping in the fields? Will you feed him three square meals a day, not forgetting his orange juice? Will you give him a friendly bark from time to time and wag your tail to let him know you're pleased with him? Will you give him a place of his own by the fire, and once in a while give him a chocolate bar for good behavior?

SPORTY (*Solemnly*): I will.

BOWSER (*Handing end of leash to* BILL, *and fastening the clip to* SPORTY*'s collar*): Then, I now pronounce you dog and boy! (*Smiling*) You know, maybe I won't go back to being a blood-hound after all. If there's anything that encourages a People Shop owner like me, it's getting the right dog and the right person together! (SPORTY *barks and* BILL *cheers as cur-tains close.*)

THE END

Production Notes

A DOG'S BEST FRIEND

Characters: 6 male; 5 female; 3 male or female for Boxer, Hunter, Greyhound Driver.

Playing Time: 15 minutes.

Costumes: All dog characters wear beanies with ears. Bowser wears white jacket, collar, and spectacle. Madame Fideaux and Fifi, tutus and leotards, ankle frills, curly hair, jeweled collars. Major Beagle, hunting jacket and high boots. Mr. Rover, business suit, tie and collar. Mrs. Rover, dress and collar. Sporty, jeans, T-shirt and collar. Nancy, simple dress. Emily, fancy party dress, bow in hair. Hunter, pith helmet, safari jacket, toy gun over shoulder. Boxer, boxing trunks, T-shirt, sneakers. Greyhound, bus driver's uniform. Husky Boy, sweatshirt padded with "muscles," jeans.

Properties: Pad and pencil, jump rope, two leashes, whistle, auto horn, toy barbells.

Setting: Woofington T. Bowser's People Shop. Counter with telephone, leashes, collars, and other pet store items is up center. Signs on backdrop read, PEDIGREED PEOPLE SOLD HERE; A DOG'S BEST FRIEND IS A PERSON; THIS IS BE KIND TO PEOPLE WEEK. Chair is down right. Exit at left leads to back of shop, exit right leads outside.

Sound: Telephone, as indicated.

Super Dooper Man

by *Thomas J. Hatton*

Rousing pep skit, featuring Superman's counterpart . . .

Characters

SUPER DOOPER MAN
LOLA LARK, *girl reporter*
BARRY BLACK, *editor*
KRYPTONITE KID
ANNOUNCER

TIME: *The present.*

SETTING: *Newsroom of the* Daily Asteroid. *There are two desks with typewriters. Newspapers litter the floor.*

AT RISE: SUPER DOOPER MAN, *posing as Bart Bent, and* LOLA LARK *are sitting at desks, typing.* ANNOUNCER *enters.*

ANNOUNCER: Faster than a speeding paper wad! Able to leap medium-sized potholes at a single bound! Now, Central High School (*Insert name of your school here and in other places throughout the script*) brings you the adventures of that great hero, Super Dooper Man! As today's adventure opens, we find Super Dooper Man in his disguise as Bart Bent, mild-mannered reporter for the (*Insert name of home town*) *Daily Asteroid,* hard at work in the newsroom. With him is Lola Lark, girl reporter. (ANNOUNCER *exits.*)

SUPER: Well, so much for that story. Say, Lola Lark, girl reporter, I . . . ah . . . I don't suppose you'd like to go to the big Central High game with me tonight, would you?

LOLA (*Pleased*): Why, yes, I'd like that very much, Bart.

SUPER (*Ignoring her comment*): Naw, I don't imagine you would.

LOLA: But I'd really like to.

SUPER: You're probably going to be busy. I won't bother you.

LOLA (*Insistently*): Really, Bart, I'm not doing a thing tonight.

SUPER (*To himself; dejectedly*): I don't see why I bother trying to get a date with that girl. I'll never get anywhere. If only she knew my real identity. (BARRY BLACK *enters*.)

BARRY: Bart, we've just received a flash report that the Kryptonite Kid is on his way here, looking for Super Dooper Man. He's boasted that he has a secret weapon that will make Super Dooper Man weaker than a kitten.

SUPER (*Excitedly*): He's probably going to find out Central High's secret plays for tonight's game. He's always had it in for Super Dooper Man, and he knows the only way to get to him is to make sure (*Insert name of rival school here and in other places throughout script*) beats Central—Super Dooper Man's beloved alma mater! (*Puts hand to chest*)

BARRY: If the Kryptonite Kid gets Super Dooper Man out of his way, nothing can stop him. Bart, you know that Super Dooper Man shows up here a lot. A fight between him and the Kryptonite Kid would be the story of the century. I want you and Lola to hide here and see what happens.

SUPER: Right, Chief.

LOLA: Check, Chief. (BARRY BLACK *exits*.)

SUPER: Uh, Lola—suppose you keep watch somewhere else, like the circulation room, or . . . uh . . . how about the janitor's closet?

LOLA: All right, Bart. You never can tell where the Kryptonite Kid is going to turn up. I'll check back with you later. (LOLA *exits*.)

SUPER (*To himself*): Thank goodness I was able to get rid of Lola. When the Kryptonite Kid is around, that's a job for Super Dooper Man. Too bad my costume is at the laundry today, but luckily, I'm always prepared. (*Pulls small black mask out of his pocket and puts it on*) There—this ought to do it. (LOLA *reenters*.)

LOLA: Bart! Bart! The Kryptonite Kid is coming! (*Looks at him closely*) Oh! Who are you?

SUPER: What's the matter with you? Don't you recognize Super Dooper Man?

LOLA: But where's your costume?

SUPER: Laundry trouble. Did you say the Kryptonite Kid is coming?

LOLA: Yes. (*Looks off; nervously*) And here he is now! (KRYPTONITE KID *enters.*)

KID: Ah, there you are—Super Dooper Man, my greatest enemy. I've been trying to find you. Prepare to meet your doom.

SUPER: That's what you think. I'll knock you so far you'll have to come back by dog sled. (*Winds up to strike him*)

KID: Not so fast, Super. (*Holds up a rock*) You know what this is, don't you?

SUPER (*Frightened*): I sure do! It's a piece of kryptonite.

KID: Right. And what happens when you're near kryptonite?

SUPER (*Weakly*): I get weak, and weaker . . . (*Falls to floor*)

LOLA (*Concerned*): Super Dooper Man!

KID: It's no use, Ms. Lark. Super Dooper Man is too weak to move a muscle. Isn't that right, Super? (*Laughs evilly*)

SUPER (*Weakly*): Right.

KID: I'll just leave this little rock right here. (*Puts it on desk*) There are no windows in this room, and I'll lock the door, so you can't get out. I'm off now to steal the secret plays for Central High's game tonight, and there's no way you can stop me. (KID *exits, laughing maliciously.*)

SUPER: Quick, Ms. Lark, get rid of the kryptonite.

LOLA: I can't. There's no place to throw it. (*Tries to move rock*) I can't even move it!

SUPER (*Discouraged*): Then we're done for. The Kryptonite Kid has won.

LOLA (*After a pause*): Not quite yet, Super Dooper Man. I've been keeping something from you. I'm not really Lola Lark, girl reporter. I took this job and this name, because I thought I might enjoy a career change. In reality, all I have to do is say the magic word, and I become (*Strikes pose*) Mary Wonderful, Girl Crime Fighter!

SUPER (*Delighted*): Mary Wonderful! It's wonderful! We're saved! Quick, say the magic words.

LOLA: All right. Here I go. (*Closes eyes, deep in thought*) Um—ah—

SUPER: What's the matter?

LOLA: I can't seem to remember them.

SUPER: How about, "Shazam"?

LOLA: No, that was last week's magic word. Darn! I had it on the tip of my tongue a minute ago.

SUPER (*Desperately*): Think! Think!

LOLA: Let's see . . . Is it hocus pocus? Open sesame? Hm-m. I wonder if it's bigger than a bread box. (KID *returns, waving papers.*)

KID (*Menacingly*): Now, Ms. Lark, you come along with me.

LOLA (*As* KID *pulls her offstage*): Alakazam? Antidisestablishmentarianism? Scooby doo? (*Exits with* KID)

SUPER: All is lost. (*Looks at newspapers on floor*) Wait a minute. What does this story in yesterday's sports section say? (*Reads*) "School spirit expected to influence tomorrow night's game." Could it be? (*Yells*) Lola—er, Mary—can you still hear me?

LOLA (*Offstage*): I hear you, Super.

SUPER: I think I know your magic words. They're "school spirit"!

LOLA: You're a genius! That's it, of course! School spirit! (*Crash of thunder or drum roll is heard.* LOLA *reenters, in cape and mask.*) Thanks, Super. I've taken care of the Kryptonite Kid, and this will take care of the kryptonite. (*She throws rock offstage. Crash is heard.*)

SUPER (*Looking off, in disbelief*): Wow! It went right through the wall! (*Leaps to his feet*) Thanks, Mary. Did you get the secret plans back?

LOLA (*Holding up papers*): Right here, Super. With the secret plans back in the right hands, Central High will be a cinch to win the game tonight.

SUPER: That's right. Especially if they remember the magic words.

LOLA: Right. All it takes is school spirit.

SUPER: Say, Mary, now that everything's back to normal, I guess I'll give you a break and take you to that game tonight.
LOLA: Oh, I'm sorry, Super, but I'm going with Bart Bent, if I can get him to ask me. (*Dreamily*) I think he's something else! (SUPER *looks at audience in disbelief; quick curtain*)

THE END

Production Notes

SUPER DOOPER MAN

Characters: 3 male; 1 female; 1 male or female.
Playing Time: 10 minutes.
Costumes: Announcer, Super Dooper Man, Barry Black, and Lola Lark, modern, everyday dress. Later, Super adds mask, Lola adds cape and mask. Kryptonite Kid wears silver costume.
Properties: Rock, sheets of paper.
Setting: Newsroom, with two desks and typewriters. Several pages of newspaper litter the floor.
Lighting: No special effects.
Sound: Drum roll; crash.

The Numbers Game

by Juliet Garver

What would the world be like without love? . . .

Characters

32075, *a female*
19386, *a male*
OFFICER, *a government official*

TIME: *The future.*
SETTING: *Outpatient clinic of a hospital. There are a few straight chairs, in three rows, facing audience, a small table at right, and signs on backdrop reading,* NUCLEAR MEDICINE CLINIC: MONDAY, WEDNESDAY, FRIDAY, NUMBERS 1,000–50,000, TUESDAY, THURSDAY, SATURDAY, NUMBERS 60,000–100,000.
AT RISE: 32075 *and* 19386 *are sitting side by side. He is staring straight ahead.*
32075 (*In friendly manner*): Hello. My name's Helen.
19386 (*Coldly*): No one has a name here. It's against the rules. My number is 19386.
32075: All right. I'm 32075. But I like to think of myself as Helen. Like Helen of Troy, whose face launched a thousand ships.
19386 (*Looking around; scared*): Sh-h! Someone will hear you and report you. You know you're not allowed to read anything except the daily statistics. 4,000,000 new jobs in computer technology. 16,000 babies born yesterday.
32075 (*Sadly*): All with brand-new numbers.
19386: Of course. It's the law of our society.
32075: Laws are cold, unromantic. (*Pauses*) Do you live alone?
19386: No. I live with my mother. All 19,000's live with a parent.

194

32075: That's right. I forgot. All people in the 32,000's live alone. I don't like that. It's cold. Lonely. Unromantic.

19386 (*Shocked*): Now, that's dangerous talk.

32075 (*Matter-of-factly; in mechanical tone*): Of course, I have my computer clock print-out, and the TV wall system announces the daily statistics three times a day—births, marriages, jobs, accidents, special awards, deaths.

19386 (*Approvingly*): Yes. We have a very ordered society. A place for every number, and every number in its place.

32075: Cold. Unromantic.

19386: Exactly. Statistical serenity. Statistical security.

32075 (*Looking at him closely; surprised*): You really like it!

19386: Of course. Every human being is like a well-run computer. But, sometimes the human machinery has to be repaired. That's why I'm here. I seem to have a touch of stomach trouble. (*Holds stomach, winces*)

32075: I have heart trouble.

19386: Then you're here for a nuclear heart profile and computer hematology.

32075: No. Not that kind of heart trouble. I'd like to know what it's like to love someone.

19386: An unnecessary emotion in our society. Fear, yes. Fear is a safety factor. People who are afraid are cautious. But love? No. Outdated, outmoded, obsolete. Out.

32075 (*Sighing*): Why is it against the law to love someone?

19386: It isn't exactly against the law. It's just a superfluous emotion. Statistically unimportant.

32075: It didn't used to be. The world was different once. There was love and . . .

19386 (*Interrupting*): War. Don't forget that. We don't have wars anymore. It must have been a terrible world. People killing each other right and left.

32075: It wasn't perfect, I know, yet it must have been a wonderful world with love all around, and people living in families and loving each other.

19386: The government takes care of families today. A much more practical arrangement. Children are housed in government dormitories. They're well fed, clothed, housed and educated.

32075: But not loved.

19386: It seems like a sensible arrangement. And there are no more starving children.

32075 (*Suddenly*): Do you think you ever could love someone like me?

19386 (*Startled*): What?

32075: Love is a very nice feeling, like warming your hands in front of a fire, like seeing a child smile. (*After a pause*) I think I could love a man like you.

19386 (*Worriedly*): If you keep on talking like this, I'll have to report you to the authorities.

32075 (*Ignoring him*): When people love each other, they're never lonely.

19386: Now, look here . . .

32075: Why aren't you married?

19386: I'm not supposed to get married till next year. I live exactly the way a person in my number group is supposed to live.

32075: Have you ever wanted to break the rules?

19386 (*Firmly*): All right. Now I understand. You've been sent by the government to check up on me. Well, you can take back a report that I am a loyal, statistic-loving, law-abiding citizen.

32075 (*Giggling*): Don't be ridiculous. Nobody sent me. I'm not a government spy.

19386: Well, you certainly have a strange way of talking.

32075: I feel strange, too. I keep thinking about love and marriage. You know, I wouldn't want to marry a man I didn't love.

19386: The law doesn't force you to get married.

32075: No, but there are special bonuses and tax exemptions if you get married before you're 25.

19386: I fully intend to take advantage of the tax exemption.

32075: Is that how you're going to propose to some woman? (*Dramatically*) Will you be my tax exemption?

19386: No one proposes anymore. You just go to City Hall and both parties sign a marriage contract. It's easier than buying a solar house or an electric car.

32075: And then you change your I.D. number and live happily ever after in the complex for married people.

19386: Yes. The government provides the housing. Of course, my mother will go to a middle-aged complex. It's all part of the plan.

32075: Do you think there are any married people who really love each other?

19386: It's not at all necessary.

32075: Sometimes I think we're all a bunch of human robots.

19386 (*Looking around nervously*): Will you please be quiet? You'll be sent to the dissenters' dormitory if you keep this up.

32075: Would it bother you if that happened to me?

19386: Bother *me*? Why should it?

32075 (*Disappointed*): I was hoping you'd say yes.

19386: Why should I do that?

32075: Don't you ever do anything you're not supposed to or anything that isn't part of the plan?

19386: I do my best to live up to the requirements of our society.

32075: Do you ever get angry? Do you ever laugh for no reason at all, just because it feels good to laugh?

19386: No. Never.

32075: Do you ever feel like doing something absolutely crazy?

19386: Of course not. Now, look here, number . . . uh . . .

32075: Helen. Call me Helen.

19386 (*Shaking his head*): You're a disconcerting, aggravating female. (OFFICER *enters, unnoticed, and watches them.*)

32075 (*Pleased*): I am?

19386: Yes. I should report you. I don't know where you get your ideas.

32075: But aren't you curious to know what love would be like?

19386: No.

32075: I don't believe you. And I know why you have stomach trouble. You're tense, all tied in knots. What you need is someone to love with all your heart. People who love each other build a wonderful world of their own.

19386: Now I really will have to report you. (*Stands*)

32075: Go ahead. (*Points to* OFFICER) There's an officer over there. Call him.

19386: I will.

32075: He's been watching us. I'll tell him that you've been annoying me, that you said you fell madly in love with me the minute you saw me.

19386 (*Alarmed*): But that's not true!

32075: There'll be an investigation, but I don't mind. Go on. Call him over.

19386: I still think you're a spy, and this is some kind of a test.

32075 (*Smiling*): No, don't worry. I'm not a spy.

19386: I think I'd better go and sit on the other side of the room until they call my number. (*He starts to cross stage.*)

OFFICER (*Crossing over to them*): What seems to be the problem here?

32075: Go on. Tell him.

19386 (*Quickly*): No problem at all, Officer.

OFFICER: Your I.D.'s, please. (*They take out I.D. cards and show them.*) Hm-m. For two people on a different number level, you were doing a lot of talking. Looked like arguing to me.

32075: It's all my fault, Officer. I initiated the conversation.

OFFICER: Then I'll have to ask you to come along with me. (*She stands.*)

32075: I don't mind. I'm tired of sitting here anyway. (*She starts to walk off with* OFFICER, *who is holding her arm.*)

19386 (*Following them, putting his arm on* OFFICER's *arm*): One moment, Officer. There's no law against talking.

OFFICER: There is against dangerous talk.

19386: Conversation with a purpose is allowed, according to government bulletin 284-736-092.

OFFICER: Yes. What was your purpose?

19386: People in my number group are supposed to get married next year.

OFFICER (*Impatiently*): Young man, what is your point?

19386: We were discussing the economics and statistics of this procedure. I work as a statistician, and my life is dedicated to statistical serenity and statistical security.

OFFICER: Very commendable. Do you vouch for this young lady?

19386: I certainly do.

OFFICER: In that case, I'll let her go. (*Releases* 32075 *and exits*)

32075: You didn't have to do that.

19386 (*Abruptly*): I know. Come on, let's go for a walk.

32075: What about your stomach?

19386 (*Smiling*): It feels much better. Come on, Helen.

32075 (*Pleased*): You called me Helen!

19386: Yes. Let's go.

32075: Then you *were* listening to me.

19386: Of course.

32075: Did you mean what you said about getting married?

19386: Well, there is the special bonus and tax exemption.

32075 (*Disappointed*): I'm sure you can find many girls who'd be happy to be your tax exemption.

19386: I'm sure, too, but there's only one whose name is Helen. (*Takes her hand*) Let's go.

32075: You really surprise me.

19386 (*Smiling*): I surprise myself. (*Curtain*)

THE END

Production Notes

THE NUMBERS GAME

Characters: 2 male; 1 female.

Playing Time: 10 minutes.

Costumes: All wear white shirts, black pants. Officer also has huge silver star on shirt pocket, and may wear dark cap.

Properties: Large, cardboard I.D. cards.

Setting: Outpatient clinic, with straight chairs facing audience, a small table at right, and signs reading, NUCLEAR MEDICINE CLINIC: MONDAY, WEDNESDAY, FRIDAY, NUMBERS 1,000–50,000; TUESDAY, THURSDAY, SATURDAY, NUMBERS 60,000–100,000.

Lighting and Sound: No special effects.

Car Crazy

by Mark Bruce

Heather competes with a glamorous rival for Jack's attention. . . .

Characters

JACK, *a teenage boy*
HEATHER, *his girlfriend*

TIME: *The present.*
SETTING: *Stage is empty, except for two chairs, center, which
    represent Jack's car.*
AT RISE: JACK, *cloth in hand, pantomimes polishing the side
    of the car.* HEATHER *enters from stage left.* JACK *doesn't
    notice her.*
JACK (*Singing*): She's wonderful, she's marvelous, and she be-
    longs to me!
HEATHER (*Standing behind* JACK; *pleased*): Well, thank you.
JACK: Oh, I wasn't singing to you, Heather. I was singing to
    Elizabeth.
HEATHER (*Suspiciously*): Elizabeth?
JACK (*Gesturing toward car*): My new car. (*Polishes "hood"*)
HEATHER: Oh, the new car. (*Walks back and forth in front of
    "car," examining it*) So, this is the replacement for the rust-
    mobile. It's very nice.
JACK: It's more than nice—it's beautiful.
HEATHER: O.K. It's beautiful.
JACK: It's perfect—a work of art, worthy of Michelangelo.
HEATHER: That's good, because when you were finished with
    your last car, it looked like something worthy of Picasso.
JACK: You liked the way it looked wrapped around that tree,
    did you?

200

HEATHER (*Kissing* JACK's *forehead*): As long as you weren't in it. (*Frowns*) I forget exactly how that happened.

JACK: I'd parked on a hill so that I could start it without using jumper cables—remember?

HEATHER: Ah, yes. Then the emergency brake gave out.

JACK (*Shrugging*): I'd forgotten it was worn out.

HEATHER: Well, those are the breaks. I'm sure the rust-mobile is much happier where it is now. It's best to have it out of its misery—not to mention ours. (*Looks again at "car"*) This new car has brakes, I presume.

JACK: The greatest! When I hit the brake pedal, she grabs hold of the road and hangs on for dear life.

HEATHER: That's usually what I do with the dashboard when you're driving.

JACK (*Ignoring* HEATHER's *remark*): Did you notice her sleek, glistening body? (*Rubs side of car*)

HEATHER: Yes, I did. Fiberglass, isn't it? (*Touches the hood*)

JACK (*Quickly rubbing with his cloth where* HEATHER *touched*): The latest design.

HEATHER: Isn't glass a bit too fragile to use for a car body?

JACK: Are you kidding? It'll withstand the elements as metal never could. And because it's all one piece, it's more aerodynamically advanced than metal, with a stronger inherent structure.

HEATHER (*Sarcastically*): Yes, but if somebody hits a high C note, the whole body will shatter like a champagne glass.

JACK: I don't intend to take this car to the opera.

HEATHER: How about the movies?

JACK (*Without looking up from his work*): The movies?

HEATHER: Yes, the movies. There's a new science fiction film over at the Bijou. (*Looks at her watch*) If we hurry we can catch the first show.

JACK (*Nervously*): Hurry?

HEATHER: I'll tell you what, Jack. The movie is my treat.

JACK (*Hesitantly*): I don't know, Heather.

HEATHER: Why not? You don't intend to keep this car in the driveway forever, do you?

JACK: No, but I'm not sure I want Elizabeth out on the roads at this time of night. There are a lot of nuts driving around out there, you know.

HEATHER (*Sarcastically*): Look who's talking! The man who used to break the sound barrier on the freeway!

JACK: Yes, but that was before I bought Elizabeth.

HEATHER: And now you've reformed?

JACK: A good car can do that.

HEATHER (*Pantomiming reaching for door handle*): Silly me. All along I've been thinking *I* could do that.

JACK: Wait, Heather! Please—allow me. (*Opens "door"*)

HEATHER: Well! You're quite the gentleman, all of a sudden!

JACK: Thanks, but really, I didn't want you to get your finger-prints on the door.

HEATHER: Jack, you sure do know how to sweet-talk a girl. (*Starts to sit*)

JACK: Hold it! (*She stops, rises. JACK takes a handkerchief out of his pocket and lays it gently on the chair.*)

HEATHER: Jack, you don't have to do that. I'm sure there's nothing on the seat that will get my pants dirty.

JACK: I want to keep the seat clean.

HEATHER: Well! Why not dip me in boiling water before we go?

JACK: Don't be silly. That would take too much time. (*HEATHER looks at him in disbelief, then sits in chair. JACK goes to "driver's side" and lays another handkerchief on his seat.*)

HEATHER (*Shaking head*): I don't believe this. (*JACK takes a pair of gloves out of his back pocket, sits in "driver's seat," and puts the gloves on carefully. HEATHER looks on in disbelief.*) Are you going to drive or operate, doctor?

JACK: I don't want to smudge the vinyl on the steering wheel.

HEATHER: Jack, aren't you being a little ridiculous?

JACK: I don't think so. I'm going to take care of this car. I'm going to pamper it. (*Rubs "dashboard"*) Aren't I, Lizzy-poo?

HEATHER: What do you do when you fill the gas tank? Hold it over your shoulder and burp it?

JACK (*Pantomiming starting car*): Well, here we go! (*HEATHER braces herself against the seat and squeezes her eyes shut. JACK looks at her, pats her knee.*) Hey, relax.

HEATHER: I can't. I've been out driving with you before.

JACK: I'm not that bad, am I?

HEATHER: Every time you get behind the wheel I think you're trying to reach warp speed.

JACK: Elizabeth could probably do it, if she wanted to. (*Pantomimes shifting gear.* HEATHER *grabs her seat.*)

HEATHER: Pry me loose when it's over. (JACK *"accelerates."* HEATHER *stays frozen in place for a moment, then relaxes, looks over at* JACK.) Say, this is smooth. It feels as if we're only going ten miles an hour!

JACK: We are.

HEATHER: We are? (*Looks at "speedometer," reads*) Ten miles an hour. (*Looks at* JACK) What's wrong?

JACK: Nothing's wrong. She's handling very nicely.

HEATHER: But you're only going ten miles an hour!

JACK: Why take chances?

HEATHER (*Worried*): Jack, are you feeling O.K.?

JACK (*Smiling*): Never felt better. Whoops! Stop sign. (*They lurch forward slightly, as if car has stopped.* JACK *looks both ways—once, twice, three times.*)

HEATHER (*Folding arms*): The road's clear, Jack. (JACK *continues looking*) Jack, there's not another car in sight.

JACK: I just want to be sure. You never know when another car will come out of nowhere.

HEATHER: Do you want me to get out and put my ear to the ground?

JACK: I guess it's clear.

HEATHER: Brilliant deduction. (*They start again. After a few moments,* HEATHER *looks at speedometer again.*) You're going ten miles an hour again.

JACK: Yes, I am. It's a nice safe speed.

HEATHER: How about being reckless and pushing it up to fifteen?

JACK: Heather, I can't figure you out. You used to complain that I drove too fast. Now you complain because I drive too slowly.

HEATHER: What we're aiming for here is a happy medium. If we drive any slower, we'll get a parking ticket.

JACK: That's easy for you to say. It's not *your* new car!

HEATHER (*Looking at watch*): Listen, Jack, it's seven o'clock. The movie starts in a few minutes. Do you think we could throw caution to the wind and drive at the speed limit to the Bijou? I'm sure Elizabeth wouldn't mind.

JACK: Mind? She'd probably enjoy it. But I don't think we'll go to the Bijou.

HEATHER (*Dismayed*): What do you mean?

JACK: Because we'd have to leave Elizabeth outside in the parking lot.

HEATHER: True. She probably wouldn't fit into one of the seats.

JACK: There's no telling what might happen to her if I left her outside all by herself.

HEATHER: Do you mean she might run away?

JACK: No, the emergency brake works fine on this car. I'm talking about what some other driver might do.

HEATHER: Oh, you mean (*Claps hands*)—crunch!

JACK (*Flinching*): Don't say that, Heather! Not even in fun!

HEATHER: Don't say what? You mean (*Claps hands*)—crunch?

JACK (*Upset*): That's a horrible thought! (*Pats dashboard*) Don't you listen, Lizzie, honey.

HEATHER (*Throwing up hands*): So what? She gets a dent—big deal. You can get it ironed out.

JACK: You don't understand. This car's body is made out of fiberglass.

HEATHER: Ah, yes, how silly of me to forget.

JACK: It's all one piece. If the body gets hit . . .

HEATHER: Don't tell me. You'll be left with a ton of fiberglass cornflakes.

JACK (*Shuddering*): Exactly.

HEATHER: If we're not going to the Bijou, where are we going?

JACK: I was thinking about the drive-in.

HEATHER: The drive-in? Jack, all they ever play are monster movies!

JACK (*With enthusiasm*): I know. This week it's a triple bill: "The Beast From Mars," "The Horror From Venus," and "The Monster From Mercury!"

HEATHER: A classic, every one of them. I notice they kept it in the solar system.

JACK: Well, it would take too long for a space ship to reach us from another star. I guess they wanted it to be realistic.

HEATHER: Seriously, Jack, I'd rather see something else.

JACK: And miss "The Horror from Venus"? Besides, if we go to the drive-in, Elizabeth will be able to see the movie, too.

HEATHER (*In utter disbelief*): Elizabeth will be able to. That's it, Jack. Stop the car and let me out.

JACK (*Puzzled*): What?

HEATHER: You've gone over the deep end. You've flipped. You're not, as they say, running on all your cylinders.

JACK: Are you trying to tell me I'm crazy?

HEATHER: That's a nice way of putting it. I'm being nice about it.

JACK: Heather, this is uncalled-for!

HEATHER: Uncalled-for! Jack, you're treating this car as if it's a baby! You're trying to give a personality to a bunch of nuts and bolts with a fiberglass body! This is just a machine, Jack, a sack of rods and pistons, and axles and gears and gaskets and hose, filled with oil and gas—not flesh and blood! This is a mechanical object, not a human being. (*Sounds of sputtering, then dying engine, are heard.*)

JACK (*Dismayed*): *Now* look what you've done!

HEATHER: What I've done?

JACK: You hurt her feelings.

HEATHER: And she's pouting, right?

JACK: Wouldn't you?

HEATHER (*Getting out of car*): Jack, the car probably stalled because you were going too slowly up this hill. That's not good for a new engine (*To "car"*)—is it, Elizabeth? (*Sputtering sound is heard.*) See? Even the car agreed with me.

JACK: (*Getting out*): I'd better look under the hood to be sure.

HEATHER (*Walking down right*): Go ahead. I'll see you later.

JACK: Heather, where are you going?

HEATHER: I'm going to the Bijou. You and your new love can go watch the monster from Mercury. I certainly don't want to intrude.

JACK (*Crossing to her*): Heather, don't be unreasonable. (*She stops.* NOTE: *At this point, spotlight goes out on "car," up on* JACK *and* HEATHER. *Stagehands remove chairs from stage.*)

HEATHER (*Laughing*): I've been the soul of reason, Jack.

JACK: If it's the drive-in that's bothering you, we'll do something else.

HEATHER: What? Take Elizabeth to a car wash and watch her get polished? I'm sorry, Jack, but I'm not going to compete with that car for your attention.

JACK: You're jealous! You're jealous of my new car!

HEATHER: That's right, I am.

JACK: I suppose you're going to want me to choose between you and her. (HEATHER *shrugs, looks over* JACK's *shoulder, as if at car.*) I think that's pretty immature of you, Heather.

HEATHER: Jack . . .

JACK: Imagine, a grown person like you jealous of a car.

HEATHER (*Insistently*): Jack . . .

JACK: It just goes to show how inconsiderate you are, how unmindful of my welfare, how unobservant of the car's obvious qualities . . .

HEATHER (*In loud voice*): Jack, your car stalled on a hill. Did you remember to put the emergency brake on?

JACK: Of course not, I . . . (*Suddenly, in realization*) Oh, no! (*Turns around. He and* HEATHER *run off left.* JACK *is shouting.*) Stop that car! Elizabeth, come back! (*After a pause, the sound of a crash, and glass breaking, is heard. After another pause,* HEATHER *and* JACK *reenter from left.* JACK *has glazed expression on his face.*)

HEATHER (*Consolingly*): There, there, Jack. It isn't the end of the world.

JACK: My car—my beautiful car!

HEATHER: Just look on the bright side, Jack. You haven't lost a car, you've gained a ton of fiberglass cornflakes! (*Quick curtain*)

THE END

Production Notes

CAR CRAZY

Characters: 1 male; 1 female.
Playing Time: 15 minutes.
Costumes: Jack and Heather wear jeans and T-shirts.
Properties: Rubbing cloth; two handkerchiefs; pair of gloves.
Setting: Bare stage, with two chairs, center.
Lighting: Dimming of spotlight on "car," as indicated in text.
Sound: Sputtering engine, crash and glass breaking, as indicated in text.

Once Upon a Taxi

by *Christina Hamlett*

Hard-boiled cabbie receives unusual proposal from mysterious woman. . . .

Characters

NEW YORK CABBIE
LADY

TIME: *Evening.*
SETTING: *A taxi in New York. Taxi may be represented by two chairs on stage, one behind the other. Cardboard cutout of taxi may be used to conceal chairs.*
AT RISE: CABBIE, *sitting in front chair, pantomimes driving. LADY, elegantly dressed, sits in "back seat," admiring the view. In her lap are small evening bag and bouquet of flowers.*
CABBIE (*After a moment, calling over his shoulder*): Say, lady?
LADY (*Pleasantly*): Yes?
CABBIE: You've run up $8.40 on my meter, and you still haven't told me where it is you're going.
LADY (*With a nonchalant shrug*): Oh, anywhere. (CABBIE *shakes his head in disbelief, pantomimes pulling cab to curb and stopping.*) Why are we stopping?
CABBIE (*Turning off ignition, and turning to look at* LADY): Look, lady, you don't just say (*Imitating her*), "Oh, anywhere," to a cabbie. I mean, that's not too smart.
LADY (*Pondering a moment, then brightly*): Then how about California?
CABBIE (*Suspiciously*): Don't you know how far away California is?
LADY (*Shaking her head*): No.

CABBIE: Let me put it this way. You'd run up more on that meter than I make in a year.

LADY (*Amazed*): That far, hm-m-m?

CABBIE: Uh-huh.

LADY (*Brightly*): Is it worth it?

CABBIE: You've never been there, right?

LADY (*Shaking her head*): No. I'd never been to New York, either—until the day before yesterday.

CABBIE: You're a foreigner, aren't you?

LADY (*Amused*): You say it as if I've got a disease that can't be cured.

CABBIE (*Chuckling*): Sorry. Where are you from?

LADY (*Smiling*): Saturnicus Mellaglovia.

CABBIE: How's that again?

LADY: Saturnicus Mellaglovia.

CABBIE (*Nodding*): It *does* sound like a disease.

LADY (*Surprised*): Do you mean you've never heard of it?

CABBIE: Can't say that I have.

LADY (*Shaking her head*): How strange. (*Quickly*) We even have an office at the U.N.

CABBIE: No kidding.

LADY: Right now it's behind the oil burner in the basement, but that's only temporary.

CABBIE: I see.

LADY (*Proudly*): My father's the king.

CABBIE (*Impressed*): Really?

LADY: Of course. While we're in the United States he doesn't use his title, but back in Saturnicus Mellaglovia, he's king. King Arlen. (*After a pause*) Well, actually, his name's *Richard* Arlen—you know, after the movie star. (CABBIE *smiles, nods.*) You see, his mother went to lots of movies. Everybody calls him Richard except me—I call him "Dad"—and my grandmother calls him Arlen. Besides, there already was a King Richard—like Richard the Lionhearted, right? (*Smiles with satisfaction*) And so that's why.

CABBIE (*Bewildered*): That's why what?

LADY: That's why he goes by King Arlen.

CABBIE (*Skeptically*): Oh, I see.

LADY: And you'll never guess who my mother was!

CABBIE (*Tentatively*): *Mrs.* Arlen?

LADY (*Shaking head*): She was the Lofty-lite Cold Cream Lady.
She used to do commercials in Burbank.

CABBIE: How did she meet your father?

LADY (*Shrugging*): He saw her on TV while he was here on a
visit, called the studio and asked her for a date.

CABBIE: And I take it that she accepted.

LADY: Not at first. I mean—would *you* go out with some totally
strange person who called you up from out of nowhere and
said, "I want to take you to the most expensive restaurant
and lavish wealth upon you for the rest of your life"?

CABBIE (*Nodding*): Granted, it's not one of my typical, everyday phone calls.

LADY: Anyway, after he told her that if she didn't go out with
him, he was going to abdicate the throne and join the Foreign
Legion, she finally agreed.

CABBIE (*Chuckling*): What a line! And she fell for it?

LADY (*Nodding*): She became Princess Gertrude. *Queen* Gertrude when my father became King.

CABBIE: And they lived happily ever after, right?

LADY (*Sadly*): I think they would have, if the country hadn't
suffered a depression. (*Shaking head*) I don't think my father's ever recovered. And as for me, I'm lucky I can buy one
new dress a year.

CABBIE (*Indicating her dress*): Does everyone in your kingdom
dress up like that?

LADY (*Laughing*): Heavens, no! (*Explains*) You see, I'm dressed
this way because I've just come from my wedding.

CABBIE (*Puzzled*): Your wedding! Uh—didn't you forget
someone?

LADY: Who?

CABBIE: Your husband. (*Shrugs*) It's a quaint American cus-
tom we have—the bride and groom usually spend some time
together.

LADY (*Aghast*): I wouldn't spend five minutes with *him* at . . .
opposite ends of the Waldorf Astoria!

CABBIE (*Scratching his head*): So why did you marry him?

LADY: I didn't. You happened along at exactly the right moment.

CABBIE: Lady, I didn't *happen along*—you called a cab, remember? And I'm the one who came to pick you up.

LADY: Thank goodness for that! Do you realize if you'd been late, I'd be married to the Duke of Dragonmede?

CABBIE: Is that good or bad?

LADY: It's absolutely *awful!* Have you ever met the Duke of Dragonmede?

CABBIE (*Wryly*): I think we travel in different circles.

LADY: Oh, he's the most dreadful bore I have ever met in my entire life! I'm only thankful I escaped!

CABBIE: Do you mean he was holding you prisoner?

LADY: Yes. Can you believe it? And he actually dragged in all these musicians and caterers and told me we were getting married!

CABBIE: You could have refused.

LADY (*Shocked*): What? And make my father pay the ransom?

CABBIE: There was a ransom involved? (*She nods emphatically.*) Wouldn't your father pay it?

LADY: If he could have. Saturnicus Mellaglovia just isn't a very wealthy kingdom anymore. That's why we're in the United States. We're applying for foreign aid.

CABBIE: I see. (*Gesturing*) This duke of whatever—if he kidnapped you, how come he let you use the phone to call a cab?

LADY (*Pleased*): I told him that I simply *had* to have my hair done, and asked if I could call the beauty parlor. You see, he was standing right there listening to my side of the conversation, but he didn't know that I dialed the cab company. I simply gave the address and said, "Could you send someone over right away? I'm really in a hurry." As soon as I saw your cab pull up, I slipped out the door, and here I am!

CABBIE: You sure lead an exciting life, lady. Tell me, did all this happen to you since the day before yesterday?

LADY (*Shaking head*): Just since last night at the embassy party. Three hundred people all dressed to the teeth, and enough caviar and champagne to gag an elephant. Didn't you read about it? It was one of *the* social events of the year.

CABBIE (*Shrugging*): I must have missed it.

LADY: Anyway, this strange little man decided to kidnap me and hold me for some exorbitant ransom. (*Puts hand on* CABBIE's *shoulder*) I'm eternally grateful you saved me.

CABBIE: Not to mention all the money I saved your father—money that he didn't have anyway.

LADY: You performed a deed that won't go unrewarded.

CABBIE (*Hopefully*): Do you think he'll give me half his kingdom?

LADY (*Pondering*): Well, since you can drive from one end of it to the other in 20 minutes, I rather doubt it. (*Pause*) He might name a sidewalk after you ... but don't hold your breath for half a kingdom.

CABBIE: So what's my reward?

LADY (*After a moment, snapping her fingers*): I have it! Did you ever read fairy tales?

CABBIE (*Sardonically*): Lady, I grew up in a tough neighborhood. We didn't read a whole lot—and when we did, it wasn't fairy tales. Why do you ask?

LADY: Because in fairy tales, when the princess was saved from the ugly dragon, her father always gave her hand in marriage to her rescuer. (*Smiling*) How about it?

CABBIE: Sorry. I'm already spoken for.

LADY: Oh, you're married?

CABBIE: Engaged. Have been for four years.

LADY: Isn't that an awfully long engagement?

CABBIE: Yes, but that's part of the deal. I told my girlfriend I wouldn't marry her until she graduated.

LADY: Oh. What's her major?

CABBIE: Filing. She goes nights to Daisy Mae Business School. I have it all figured—in another two or three years, she'll get a job with the state, I'll buy my own cab, and we'll settle down.

LADY: How would you like to settle down in Saturnicus Mellaglovia?

CABBIE: That'd be a tough commute, wouldn't it?

LADY: But if you married me, you wouldn't *have* to commute! You wouldn't even have to be a cab driver.

CABBIE (*With a smirk*): Yeah, in a country that small, I'll bet everybody *walks*. (*Smiles*) No, thanks, lady.

LADY (*Disgruntled*): It hardly seems fair.

CABBIE: What?

LADY: You're doing everything wrong.

CABBIE: What am I supposed to do?

LADY: Can't you see? I was a princess held captive, and you rode up on your white horse—

CABBIE (*Pointing out her error*): It's a yellow taxi.

LADY (*Exasperated*): Whatever! And you carried me to safety!

CABBIE: It's my job, lady!

LADY: The least you could do is propose.

CABBIE (*Suspiciously*): But what if you said, "yes"?

LADY: Then my father would give his blessing, and we'd live happily ever after.

CABBIE: There's a hitch, though.

LADY: What?

CABBIE: I wouldn't be happy.

LADY: Why on earth not?

CABBIE: In the first place, I don't know you. In the second place, there's Angela. And in the third . . . I'm just not cut out to live in a castle.

LADY (*Protesting*): We don't live in a castle! We live in a duplex—my father rents the other side to my grandmother.

CABBIE: All the same, New York's my home. I don't want to leave.

LADY: So what if *I* lived in New York?

CABBIE: You wouldn't like it.

LADY: Why not?

CABBIE: Just picture this—an overpriced third-floor walk-up, flies in the summer, no heat in the winter . . . (*Shrugs*) A couple of years down the road, we have some kids. You have to take in ironing and scrub floors to make ends meet. I forget your birthday and our anniversary. I never buy you flowers. And by the time you hit 35, you can't stand me. (*Pauses*) Is that "happily every after"?

LADY (*Sighing*): I'm beginning to see your point.

CABBIE (*Looking at his watch*): Listen, lady, I've enjoyed this little chit chat, but I have to get back to work. And since you haven't made up your mind—

LADY (*Holding up her hand*): You're absolutely right. I've taken enough of your time. (*Puts hand on his arm*) Thanks.

CABBIE: For what?

LADY (*Shrugging*): The memory? It was nice while it lasted.

CABBIE (*Smiling, then turning to start ignition*): So—where to?

LADY (*Looking out window*): Oh, it's not that far. I think I'll walk.

CABBIE (*Looking at her*): Are you serious?

LADY: It's a nice night. (*Points up*) Ah, the wishing star. (*Looks at CABBIE*) Make a wish. (*After a pause*) Do you have one?

CABBIE: Yeah. I hope it turns out O.K. for you, lady.

LADY: That's sweet of you. I thank you again.

CABBIE: What did you wish?

LADY (*Thinking a moment, then giving him a kiss*): How much do I owe you?

CABBIE: For the kiss?

LADY (*With a smirk*): For the ride. (*Opens purse*)

CABBIE (*Shaking head*): This one's on me, Princess.

LADY: Are you sure? (*Closes purse*)

CABBIE: Sure! It's not every day I get a proposal to marry a king's daughter. You're not one of those people I'm gonna forget, you know?

LADY (*As she rises*): I won't forget you, either. (*She starts to walk off.*)

CABBIE (*Suddenly*): Hey—uh—(*She turns.*) If things don't work out with me and Angela . . .

LADY (*Smiling*): Give me a call. (*Realizes she's still carrying bouquet; she tosses it to him and exits as he stares at it.*)

CABBIE: You know, it's funny—here I am, just a cab driver and all, but (*Shakes his head*) I don't even know your first name. (*He looks up and sees that LADY is gone. He is exasperated.*) Well, you really blew that one, didn't you? The lady flat-out proposed and you let her walk right out of your life! What a dummy! . . . I could have asked her out for coffee, or something. (*Shrugs*) Of course, she might have said no. (*Scratches his head)* Then again, she already asked me to share her life, so why would she say no to sharing a sandwich and a cup of coffee? (*Shakes his head*) Crazy. Boy, would I ever catch it from Angela, marrying some king's daughter I never met before tonight! (*Pauses, then throws hands up in disgust*) Oh, forget it—she's gone and you're never going to see her again. (*Pantomimes turning on radio; music is heard*) Just forget you ever saw her. (*Music plays a moment, then is interrupted by announcement.*)

ANNOUNCER: We interrupt this program for a special bulletin. The New York City Police Department has issued an APB for a young woman believed to be responsible for the robbery tonight at the wedding of Senator Robert Lavette's niece. According to witnesses, the suspect—unknown to both bride and groom—caught the wedding bouquet, pulled a gun from her purse, and demanded that the envelopes containing wedding money be placed on the table. (CABBIE *looks quizzically at the bouquet.*) Then the woman stole their money and vanished. Inspector Ralph Monegan of NYPD has asked—(CABBIE *turns off radio.*)

CABBIE (*Shrugging*): Well, *I* never believed her for a second! Ha! (*Tosses bouquet out "window"; pantomimes putting cab into gear, but pauses a second, and looks offstage, where* LADY *exited. As curtain falls, he has a wistful look on his face, and speaks quietly.*) Still, I wonder . . .

THE END

Production Notes

ONCE UPON A TAXI

Characters: 1 male; 1 female.

Playing Time: 10 minutes.

Costumes: Cabbie wears T-shirt and pants. Lady is elegantly dressed in long gown; she carries small evening bag and bouquet of flowers.

Setting: A taxi in New York. Taxi may be represented simply by having two chairs on stage, one behind the other. If desired, cardboard cutout of taxi may conceal chairs.

Lighting: No special effects.

Sound: No special effects.

Heart to Heart

by *Barbara Tutt*

Can the Knave of Hearts
redeem himself? . . .

Characters

QUEEN OF HEARTS
QUEEN OF CLUBS
KNAVE OF HEARTS
FOUR OF HEARTS
FIVE OF HEARTS
TEN OF HEARTS
SEVEN OF HEARTS
THREE OF HEARTS

TIME: *Valentine's Day.*
SETTING: *Courtyard of the Queen of Hearts' palace. Two chairs are center; there is a small table in front of chairs.*
AT RISE: KNAVE OF HEARTS *enters left, carrying paper bag full of tarts, and looking around fearfully. Suddenly, he looks off right, as if he's heard something, and looks frantically around for a place to hide. He crouches down left as* FOUR OF HEARTS *and* FIVE OF HEARTS *enter right, carrying a sign, which they tape or pin to backstage wall.*
FOUR OF HEARTS (*Reading sign*): "Wanted: Male or female to be the new Knave of Hearts. Must be kindhearted, healthy and hearty. Above all, must be honest and trustworthy. See me here today for interview. Signed, the Queen of Hearts."
FIVE OF HEARTS: What happened to the old Knave of Hearts?
FOUR OF HEARTS: Didn't you hear? Vanished without a trace last summer. The Queen of Hearts, she made some tarts, all

217

on a summer's day. The Knave of Hearts, he stole the tarts, and took them clean away.

FIVE: No kidding!

FOUR: And he never came back.

FIVE: Not only a thief, but a coward as well. Pitiful.

KNAVE (*Jumping up*): Now, just a minute! I—that is, he—isn't such a bad guy. I like him.

FOUR: Then why did he steal the tarts?

KNAVE: Maybe he was hungry.

FIVE: No excuse. Why did he run away?

KNAVE: Maybe he was afraid.

FOUR: He'd better hurry back if he wants to keep his job. The Queen is tired of waiting for him. (FOUR *and* FIVE *exit right.*)

KNAVE (*Sadly*): She's going to replace me. She didn't even tell me I was fired! Well, how could she tell me—I've been away for so long. Let me see. (*Counts on fingers*) August, September, October, November, December, January, February. Seven months ago I stole those tarts and ran away. And look at me now. Four and Five didn't even recognize me. I used to wear nice clothes and live in a castle. Now I've got no food, no money, no home (*Gestures toward sign*), and no job! (QUEEN OF CLUBS *enters left.*)

QUEEN OF CLUBS: No job? Well, you can have mine! I had no idea what I was getting into. Sure, I'll be the Queen of Clubs, I said. Bring on the jewels, and the feasting, and all that other good stuff that queens get to have. But do I have time for banquets and royal balls? No way! I've got to run the country club and the supper club. I'm president of every club there is! There's the garden club, the bird-watcher's club, the photography club—

KNAVE: I get the picture.

QUEEN OF CLUBS (*Indignantly*): How dare you make fun of me!

KNAVE: Sorry. It's just that I haven't had much fun lately. In fact, since I stole the tarts I haven't had much fun at all.

QUEEN OF CLUBS: Stole the tarts! You?

KNAVE: Yes, but I'm awfully sorry I did it. Oh, you can't imagine how sorry I am!

QUEEN OF CLUBS: Then you must be that good-for-nothing Knave of Hearts!

KNAVE: I'm good for something. I'm good at apologizing, if the Queen of Hearts would only listen. She was always so nice to me, and I let her down. I feel terrible about what I did.

QUEEN OF CLUBS: You've been gone since last summer. Why did you come back today?

KNAVE: Because today is Valentine's Day. You see, I was so ashamed, I was afraid to come back before. But since this is the Queen's favorite holiday, I thought this would be the perfect day.

QUEEN OF CLUBS: Not a chance. She'll be here any minute to interview people for your job.

KNAVE: I even brought back the tarts. (*Lifts bag and shakes it; shrugs apologetically*) They're a little stale.

QUEEN OF CLUBS: You mean you went to all the trouble of stealing them, and you didn't even eat them?

KNAVE: I had a couple. But just between you and me, the Queen of Hearts is a terrible cook. I did her a favor, getting these things out of the way before somebody broke a tooth on them.

QUEEN OF CLUBS: Tell you what. Wear this mask (*Hands him a black mask from her pocket*), and apply for the job. If you make a good impression on the Queen, by the time you take off the mask and she realizes who you are, she'll let bygones be bygones.

KNAVE: Do you really think so?

QUEEN OF CLUBS: I'll bet my golf clubs on it! (*Looks off right*) Oh, here she comes. Go to the end of the line, and good luck! (KNAVE *exits left.* QUEEN OF HEARTS *enters right.*)

QUEEN OF HEARTS: Dear Queen of Clubs! You're all heart, helping me with these interviews.

QUEEN OF CLUBS: I had to cancel a club meeting to be here, you know.

QUEEN OF HEARTS: You have my heart-felt thanks. To think that it's come to this! I've been heartbroken over that ungrateful Knave. I trusted him, and he let me down. Well, I can't wait forever for an apology. I must have a new assistant, but I doubt that I'll find anyone suitable.

QUEEN OF CLUBS: You might. Let's get on with it, shall we? (QUEENS *sit in chairs; calling*) Interviews for Knave of Hearts will now begin. Enter, first applicant! (TEN OF HEARTS *enters left.*)

QUEEN OF HEARTS: Ah, Ten of Hearts! Why do you want this position?

TEN: I'm stuck in a dead-end job. I mean, there's no eleven of hearts, is there? I want a promotion! I want to move up in life! I'll step on anybody to get this job!

QUEEN OF HEARTS (*Shaking head*): Tsk, tsk. Heartless ambition. (*Waves him off*) Next! (TEN *storms off left, almost knocking over* SEVEN OF HEARTS, *who enters timidly.*)

SEVEN (*Barely audible*): Well, I . . . that is, if you don't mind . . .

QUEEN OF CLUBS: Speak up, Seven!

SEVEN: I really don't know if I should be here, but I . . . well, that is I . . . what I mean to say is, I . . .

QUEEN OF HEARTS: I'm afraid you're too faint-hearted for this job. (SEVEN *exits left, dejected.*)

QUEEN OF CLUBS: Next! (THREE OF HEARTS *enters left, carrying handkerchief.*)

THREE: Please, Your Majesty, I'm just a poor little three. Nobody cares about me. I'm just a number and I want to be somebody! (*Cries*)

QUEEN OF CLUBS: How sad!

QUEEN OF HEARTS: Heart-breaking! But you're young and inexperienced. I'm sorry. (THREE *runs off left in tears.*) It's so disheartening! I had my heart set on finding someone today. (*Sighs*)

QUEEN OF CLUBS (*Looking off left*): I believe there's one more applicant.

QUEEN OF HEARTS: Who is it?

QUEEN OF CLUBS: I don't know. He's wearing a mask. (*Calling*) Enter! (KNAVE *enters left.*)

QUEEN OF HEARTS: Come here, young fellow, and we'll have a heart-to-heart chat. You realize, of course, that this is a very demanding job. Do you like tarts?

KNAVE: I . . . uh . . . don't eat much anymore.

QUEEN OF HEARTS: It does my heart good to hear you say that. The last person on this job was overly fond of tarts, which led to quite a scandal last summer. My heart still flutters when I think of it. I do a lot of baking, you see. And I made a nice batch of tarts all on a summer's day. The knave of hearts, he—

QUEEN OF CLUBS: Stole the tarts!

KNAVE: And took them clean away. Yes, yes, the word got around. How dreadful for you.

QUEEN OF HEARTS: Haven't I heard your voice somewhere before? Well, never mind. Let's go to the heart of the matter. Are you hard-working?

KNAVE: Yes.

QUEEN OF HEARTS: Conscientious?

KNAVE: Yes.

QUEEN OF HEARTS: Ever been arrested for a crime?

KNAVE: No, they never caught me.

QUEEN OF HEARTS: Very well, I'm willing to give you a try. You're hired!

KNAVE (*Taking off mask*): Hurray!

QUEEN OF HEARTS (*Gasping*): It's you! (*Furiously*) Oh, you hard-hearted Knave! Where have you been? Where are my tarts?

KNAVE (*Shaking tarts from bag on to table*): I brought them back. Well, most of them. To tell you the truth, they gave me heartburn. (QUEEN OF CLUBS *chuckles.*)

QUEEN OF HEARTS: You're a heartless Knave! Queen of Clubs, stop laughing, and go fetch the King of Hearts. Tell him to come here at once and punish this criminal!

QUEEN OF CLUBS (*Shrugging*): If you insist. (QUEEN OF CLUBS *exits right.*)

QUEEN OF HEARTS (*Rising from chair*): Look at these tarts— hard as stone. (*Walks next to* KNAVE) Just like your heart! And to think that I trusted you.

KNAVE: I'm really not so bad at heart. It was more of a joke.

QUEEN OF HEARTS: We already have a joker in the deck, thank you!

KNAVE: Call it overwhelming temptation, then. Those tarts looked so delicious! Of course, looks can be deceiving.

QUEEN OF HEARTS: The King will give you a good thrashing.

KNAVE: I know I deserve to be punished, but I hope you'll forgive me. I've learned my lesson. Believe me, I've been miserable. I know now that crime does not pay.

QUEEN OF HEARTS (*Beginning to soften*): But I've been sick at heart over those tarts!

KNAVE: Better than being sick to your stomach! (QUEEN OF CLUBS *enters right*.)

QUEEN OF HEARTS: Where's the King of Hearts?

QUEEN OF CLUBS: He says he doesn't have the heart to try the prisoner.

KNAVE: But I'm not a prisoner! I came back of my own free will. Doesn't that prove my heart's in the right place?

QUEEN OF HEARTS: Well . . .

QUEEN OF CLUBS: Come on—give the poor fellow a break.

QUEEN OF HEARTS (*After a pause; to* KNAVE): Are you really sorry?

KNAVE: With all my heart.

QUEEN OF HEARTS: Promise never to do it again?

KNAVE: I promise!

QUEEN OF HEARTS (*Beaming*): Then all is forgiven!

KNAVE: Thanks, Queen! You have a heart of gold.

QUEEN OF CLUBS: Let's celebrate this happy ending. Lunch at my country club.

KNAVE: You don't have tarts on the menu, do you?

QUEEN OF CLUBS: No. We serve club sandwiches, of course. But, I could ask the chef to make an exception in your case and serve artichoke hearts.

QUEEN OF HEARTS: Lovely! We'll eat to our hearts' content! (*All exit. Curtain*)

THE END

Production Notes

HEART TO HEART

Characters: 2 female; 1 male; 5 male or female.

Playing Time: About 15 minutes.

Costumes: Queen of Hearts wears crown and red cape; Queen of Clubs, crown and black cape. Knave is dressed very shabbily, and wears a black mask at his second entrance. The remaining characters wear sandwich boards with their respective numbers on them.

Properties: Knave carries paper sack holding small, round, hard objects resembling tarts—these could be made of hardened clay. Four and Five carry a large, heart-shaped sign with the Queen's ad printed on it (audience does not need to be able to read the sign). Queen of Clubs has black mask in pocket. Three carries a handkerchief.

Setting: Courtyard of Queen of Hearts' palace. Two chairs are center stage, and a small table stands in front of the chairs.

Spooks on Strike!

by *Frank V. Priore*

Ghosts demand new dress code . . . .

Characters

RECEPTIONIST, *with a haunting personality*
HIGH TIDE
LITTLE SQUIRT
CLANK, *the noisiest ghost in the world*
MAC GREGOR, *resident ghost of a Scottish castle*
GHOST OF A CHANCE, *an unlucky spirit*
GHOSTESS WITH THE MOSTESS, *a party-loving spirit*
GHOSTMASTER GENERAL, *the boss*

SCENE 1

SETTING: *The lobby of Spook Central, the source of all hauntings. Exit right leads outside. Door in left wall leads to the Ghostmaster's office. There are four folding chairs along right wall below door. On desk up center are phone, large appointment book, typewriter, and various scattered papers. Large sign on upstage wall reads:* SPOOK CENTRAL—GHOSTS AVAILABLE FOR ALL OCCASIONS—HOUSES HAUNTED TO ORDER—REASONABLE RATES—GROUP DISCOUNT FOR CONDOS.
AT RISE: RECEPTIONIST *sits at desk, wearing traditional ghost sheet, with holes for her arms. Her arms and hands are covered with white makeup. Phone rings.*
RECEPTIONIST (*Answering phone*): Spook Central. A scary good morning to you . . . . How much do we charge to haunt a house? How many rooms do you have? . . . I see. Is that one or two stories? . . . Attic? . . . O.K. . . . Oh, you've had other houses haunted by us? You may qualify for our frequent

haunters discount. In fact, we're running a two-for-one special this week. Have one house haunted at the regular rate, and we'll throw in a summer home, camper or two-car garage at no additional cost . . . . You'll sign up? Excellent. We can have a ghost on the job by midnight. (*Hangs up.* HIGH TIDE *and* LITTLE SQUIRT *enter.* HIGH TIDE *is twice the size of* LITTLE SQUIRT. *They both wear white sheets.*) Well, well. It's the ghosts of the Rivers brothers, High Tide and Little Squirt. What can I do for you?

HIGH TIDE (*Annoyed*): We're bored!

LITTLE SQUIRT: I'll say! Day in, day out, it's the same old thing—haunt this house, haunt that house, shout "Boo!," scare people. *Bo-ring!*

RECEPTIONIST: Oh, I wouldn't say that. I get a kick out of being scary. In fact, I'm having such a good time, I can't imagine what I ever liked about being alive.

HIGH TIDE: Sure, it's all great fun now, but wait until you've been a ghost for a couple of centuries like us.

LITTLE SQUIRT: Then it'll start to get on your nerves. Tell me, do you like new clothes?

RECEPTIONIST: Sure, doesn't everybody?

LITTLE SQUIRT: Well, you can forget about them. Over the years, clothing styles will be changing constantly, but you'll be stuck wearing the same old thing—a sheet!

HIGH TIDE: A white sheet, at that! Not even a nice pastel or print.

LITTLE SQUIRT (*Sighing*): What I wouldn't give for a sheet with Mickey Mouse on it.

RECEPTIONIST: I don't think the boss will ever approve of that costume change.

HIGH TIDE (*Angrily*): Well, you can just tell him that we're not going out to haunt any more houses until we get designer sheets!

LITTLE SQUIRT: Yeah! I want one that has a pocket with a little alligator on it.

RECEPTIONIST (*Uneasily*): Er, why don't you two have a seat. The boss will be in soon. You can take it up with him.

HIGH TIDE: We will! (*They sit on folding chairs. A loud clanking noise is heard.*)

LITTLE SQUIRT: What's that?

RECEPTIONIST: Nothing to be alarmed at. It's just Clank reporting in. He's the noisiest ghost in the world—the best chain rattler in the business. (*CLANK enters. He also wears a white sheet, but is wrapped in several long chains that drag noisily on the ground.*) Hi, Clank. How are you doing?

CLANK (*Annoyed*): Terribly! I'm sick and tired of rattling these ridiculous chains!

RECEPTIONIST: But I thought you liked making noise.

CLANK: I do. I love it. But why do I have to use chains?

RECEPTIONIST: Chains are traditional. Besides, nothing makes more noise than a good set of chains.

CLANK: Want to bet? I found something ten times as noisy. I have it right outside. (*Steps out, then reenters with huge "boom box" radio*) A teenager I scared dropped it. Do you think the boss will let me trade in my chains for this?

RECEPTIONIST (*Skeptically*): You can ask him, but I wouldn't hold out too much hope.

CLANK (*Annoyed*): Well, he'd *better* let me! I've rattled my last chain! (*Slips chains off and lets them fall to floor*)

RECEPTIONIST (*Startled*): Oh, dear! (*Indicating chairs*) Why don't you have a seat. He should be here any minute. (*CLANK sits. Suddenly MAC GREGOR enters, wearing a white sheet and highlander's cap, and carrying bagpipes. RECEPTIONIST spots him.*) Mac Gregor! What brings you here? You're supposed to be haunting a castle in Glasgow.

MAC GREGOR: And don't I know it! There'll be no more hauntings by this ghost, lassie, until they put central heating in that castle! Drafty old thing; it's a good thing I'm a ghost, or I would have caught my death of cold by now!

RECEPTIONIST: That sounds like a serious problem. Why don't you talk to the boss about it? He'll be here soon. Have a seat. (*MAC GREGOR sits. GHOST OF A CHANCE enters. His sheet has pockets filled with raffle books. He walks quickly to seated ghosts.*)

CHANCE: Hi there, fellow ghosts. Anybody want to take a chance? (*Takes out fistful of raffle books and waves them*) I've got turkey raffles, ham raffles, baffle raffles, door prizes, store prizes, pick-'em-off-the-floor prizes . . .

HIGH TIDE (*To other ghosts*): Any of you know this dude?

LITTLE SQUIRT: Never seen him before in my life—or after it.

MAC GREGOR: I don't think I'd want to know him, laddie. He appears to be a wee bit daft, if ye know what I mean.

RECEPTIONIST: I'm surprised you don't recognize him. He's the Ghost of a Chance you hear so much about.

CLANK: Is he, now? (*Suddenly offstage, sound of several party noisemakers is heard.*)

LITTLE SQUIRT (*Alarmed*): What's that racket?

CLANK: I don't know, but I love it. It's so noisy! (GHOSTESS WITH THE MOSTESS *enters right. She wears a polka-dot sheet draped with streamers. She has a horn in her mouth and several noisemakers in each hand. She blows horn and rattles noisemakers.*

GHOSTESS: (*Taking horn from her mouth*): I demand to see the Ghostmaster right now!

HIGH TIDE: Who are you, and what are you doing with all those party horns and noisemakers?

GHOSTESS: I'm the Ghostess with the Mostess, and these are the tools of my trade. I'm the official party thrower for all of spookdom.

RECEPTIONIST: What are you doing here, Ghostess? (*Consults appointment book*) I have you scheduled for a "Come As You Died" party in New York.

GHOSTESS: I know. It was a big flop. Ever since Spook Central started booking hauntings, all the ghosts have been too busy to attend my parties. That's why I'm here. (*Angrily*) I want to register a complaint with the boss! He's got to give everybody more time off so they can come to my parties.

CHANCE: Wait a minute! I have nothing *but* time off. That's what I came here to complain about.

LITTLE SQUIRT (*To* CHANCE): You don't have enough work?

CHANCE: I don't have *any* work. People keep saying that they "don't have a ghost of a chance." So, I'm always out of work.

HIGH TIDE (*Sympathetically*): That's too bad.

CHANCE (*Angrily*): Well, I'm not going to stand for it anymore! (*Takes chance books out of his pockets and flings them on ground on top of chains*) I'm through with all these foolish chance books!

GHOSTESS: And I'm through with throwing parties that nobody attends. (*Throws noisemakers onto pile*)

RECEPTIONIST: Er, why don't all of you tell your problems to the boss when he comes in? I'm sure he can work something out. Just take a seat.

GHOSTESS (*Seeing that all chairs are occupied*): Where? All the chairs are taken.

CLANK (*Rising*): Well, somebody can have my seat. I'm tired of sitting around here. I'm going to take some action!

MAC GREGOR: (*Rising*): Same here.

HIGH TIDE (*Rising*): I'm with you. It's about time something was done!

LITTLE SQUIRT: Yeah! After all, ghosts are people too—sort of. (*All except* RECEPTIONIST *exit right. A few seconds later they return, carrying signs reading:* SPOOKS ON STRIKE! UNFAIR TO GHOSTS! HAUNT YOUR OWN HOUSES! *etc.* MAC GREGOR's *sign reads:* NO HEAT, NO HAUNT! *They march around in a circle, waving their signs. Suddenly, booming voice is heard. It reverberates throughout the room. [*NOTE: *Use PA system, if possible.] Ghosts halt in their tracks, alarmed.*) What was that?

CLANK: I don't know, but it sounded good. I love loud noises.

GHOSTESS: Maybe the heating pipes are knocking.

MAC GREGOR: I dinna think it's the heating pipes, lassie. Although, I certainly wish it were. It's a wee bit chilly in here.

RECEPTIONIST: I guess you've all been away from here longer than I thought. That sound means the boss has arrived in his office.

CHANCE: The boss? You mean . . .

RECEPTIONIST: Yes, the Ghostmaster General! (*Door left flies open, and* GHOSTMASTER GENERAL *enters. He wears a sheet, army officer's hat and military bars on his shoulders. A row of ribbons and medals is pinned to his chest.*)

GHOSTMASTER (*Angrily*): What is all this nonsense? (*Points to chains, etc. on floor.*) And why is all this junk on the floor?

RECEPTIONIST: Well, sir, it seems that some of your spooks are on strike.

GHOSTMASTER (*Laughing heartily*): On strike? Why, that's ridiculous. (*To ghosts*) If you stopped haunting houses, what else would you do?

HIGH TIDE: I never thought of that.

GHOSTMASTER (*Sarcastically*): Perhaps you'd like to work in a fast food shop—selling quarter pound haunt burgers with french frights on the side. I'm sure you could scare up a lot of business! (*Laughs loudly*)

CHANCE (*Angrily*): This may all be a big joke to you, but our problems are serious!

CLANK: We're not going back on the job until they're resolved.

HIGH TIDE: And we're going to call all our fellow spooks. I'm sure they'll join us. There will be no more hauntings until our demands are met! We're walking off the job! (*To other ghosts*) Come on, let's get out of here. (*They exit right. Quick curtain*)

* * * * *

SCENE 2

TIME: *Two weeks later—the day before Halloween.*

SETTING: *Same. Chains and other debris have been removed from floor.*

AT RISE: RECEPTIONIST *is sitting at her desk. Phone rings.*

RECEPTIONIST (*Answering phone*): Spook Central . . . . No, I'm sorry. We have no ghosts available. They're all on strike. (*Hangs up.* GHOSTMASTER *enters from his office.*)

GHOSTMASTER (*Furiously*): This is ridiculous! The day before Halloween, and not a spook on the job! If this strike doesn't end immediately, we'll have to cancel Halloween!

RECEPTIONIST (*Thoughtfully*): Hm-m-m, I think I may have a solution to the problem. (*Rises, walks over to* GHOSTMASTER) What do you think about this? (*Whispers in his ear*)

GHOSTMASTER (*Cheering up as he listens*): Mm hm-m . . . Say, that may just do the trick. Call the ghosts in immediately!
RECEPTIONIST: Yes, sir.
GHOSTMASTER (*Going to door of office, turning*): If this works, I'll see that you get a big promotion. (*Exits*)
RECEPTIONIST (*Sighing*): I think I'd settle for one of those designer sheets. (*Picks up phone. Blackout*)

* * * * *

SCENE 3

TIME: *Several hours later.*
SETTING: *Same as Scene 2.*
AT RISE: *Ghosts enter, carrying strike signs.*
HIGH TIDE (*To* RECEPTIONIST): Well, we're all here. The Ghostmaster's offer had better be good.
RECEPTIONIST: Oh, I'm sure you'll find it more than satisfactory. (*Picks up phone, speaks into it*) They're all here, sir. (*Puts phone down.* GHOSTMASTER *enters from office.*)
LITTLE SQUIRT (*To* GHOSTMASTER): Are you ready to give us what we want?
GHOSTMASTER: I believe so. Now, as I recall, you River brothers want fancier sheets. (*To* MAC GREGOR) And you, Mac Gregor—you're tired of haunting drafty Scottish castles. (*They nod.*) Very well. Come with me. (*They follow him to his office, where he turns and stops them.*) I'm going to switch your assignments. Mac Gregor, from now on you're going to haunt the condo that the Rivers brothers used to haunt.
MAC GREGOR: Does it have central heating?
LITTLE SQUIRT: It doesn't need it. It's in Florida.
MAC GREGOR: Hoot mon! I've always wanted to see Disneyworld!
GHOSTMASTER (*To* HIGH TIDE *and* LITTLE SQUIRT): And you two are assigned to Mac Gregor's castle in Glasgow.
HIGH TIDE: But how does that get us fancier sheets?
GHOSTMASTER: Oh, didn't I tell you? (*Reaches in through his office door, pulls out two colorful plaid sheets with eye holes in them, hands them to ghosts*) These go with the job.

LITTLE SQUIRT (*Excited as he looks over his new sheet*): Wow! It's got a little alligator on the pocket.

GHOSTMASTER: Actually, it's a Loch Ness monster.

MAC GREGOR: Can I bring my bagpipes with me to Florida?

GHOSTMASTER: Certainly.

MAC GREGOR: Good! There's nothing like the sound of a good set of pipes to send shivers through people. When I play those pipes, it'll be the scariest sounds they've ever heard.

GHOSTMASTER (*To* CLANK): I understand you want to trade in your chains for that boom-box you found. Well, I'm going to give you an opportunity to work with the Ghostess. (*He reaches into pocket in his sheet, and takes out several audio cassettes.*) You can supply the music for her parties. (*To* GHOSTESS) You see, the ghosts weren't avoiding your parties because they were too busy. It's just that without music, those parties were boring.

GHOSTESS: I never thought of that!

CLANK (*Looking at tapes*): These are great! (*Reads a label*) "Music To Drive You Batty," by Count Dracula and Friends. And here's one by King Tut's rock group: "Songs My Mummy Taught Me."

GHOSTESS: Is there anything there by Dr. Frankenstein? His music always gives you a jolt.

CLANK: Here's one by him. "Sounds to Raise The Dead."

GHOSTESS: That'll certainly liven up my parties.

CHANCE (*To* GHOSTMASTER): Hey, what about me? Have you found a job to keep me busy?

GHOSTMASTER: I certainly have. You're going to work with the Ghostess, too, but no more of those silly raffle books. I've got some better games of chance for you. (*Goes into his office, and brings out some game boxes, hands them to* CHANCE)

CHANCE: Wow! Party games! (*Reads titles*) "Pin The Tail On The Werewolf." "Musical Coffins." "Horrible Pursuit."

GHOSTMASTER: (*To ghosts*): I hope everyone is happy now.

GHOSTS (*Ad lib*): It's great. Sure. You bet. Terrific. (*Etc.*)

GHOSTMASTER: All right, then—everybody back on the job. (*They exit right.* RECEPTIONIST *clears her throat loudly.* GHOSTMASTER *turns to her.*)

RECEPTIONIST: Excuse me, sir, but not quite everybody is happy.

GHOSTMASTER: Oh, yes. This was all your idea, wasn't it? I promised you a promotion.

RECEPTIONIST: I don't need a promotion, sir. I'm happy doing just what I'm doing. But the River brothers are right—fashions will be coming and going, but I'll still be wearing this same old sheet.

GHOSTMASTER: You know, you're absolutely right. It's not fair for some of my ghosts to be decked out in fancy sheets while others are still wearing the old-fashioned white ones. (*Smacks his fist into his other hand for emphasis*) And by golly, I'm going to do something about it! Call the sheet manufacturers. I want designer sheets for the whole crew. All the top labels, too, like Scario Valenti and Gorier Vanderbilt.

RECEPTIONIST (*Delighted*): That's terrific, boss. I'll get on it right away. (*She picks up phone, quickly dials and speaks quietly into it.*)

GHOSTMASTER (*Proudly*): Oh, yes. I'm going to make sure every one of my ghosts is happy. I'll see to it that the celebration of Halloween is never in danger of being canceled again!

RECEPTIONIST (*Covering receiver with her hand as she speaks to* GHOSTMASTER): Sir, we can't get our designer sheets.

GHOSTMASTER: What! Why not?

RECEPTIONIST: All the sheetmakers are on strike!

GHOSTMASTER (*Putting his hand on his forehead*) Oh no! (*Curtain*)

THE END

Production Notes

SPOOKS ON STRIKE!

Characters: 6 male; 2 female.

Playing Time: 20 minutes.

Costumes: All wear sheets with eyeholes and armholes cut into them. Mac Gregor wears highlander's cap and carries bagpipes. Clank has several long chains wrapped around him. Chance's sheet has several pockets filled with raffle books. Ghostess with the Mostess is covered with streamers and confetti. She has a horn and several noisemakers. Ghostmaster has army officer's hat, military ribbons and medals pinned to his sheet. All use white makeup on hands and arms.

Properties: Two plaid sheets, audio cassettes, raffle books, bagpipes, horn, noisemakers, signs reading SPOOKS ON STRIKE, UNFAIR TO GHOSTS! HAUNT YOUR OWN HOUSES! NO HEAT, NO HAUNT!, game boxes, "boom-box" radio.

Setting: The lobby of Spook Central. A door in right wall leads to outside world. Door in left wall leads to Ghostmaster's office. Four folding chairs are lined up along right wall below door. A desk is up center, angled slightly toward right wall. Phone, appointment book, typewriter, and various scattered papers on the desk. A large sign on upstage wall reads, SPOOK CENTRAL—GHOSTS AVAILABLE FOR ALL OCCASIONS—HOUSES HAUNTED TO ORDER—REASONABLE RATES—GROUP DISCOUNT FOR CONDOS.

Lighting and Sound: No special lighting effects. PA system useful, but not essential.

Old MacDonald's Farmyard Follies

by Lu Sampson

Charming spoof of
old-time favorite . . .

Characters

OLD MACDONALD
MRS. MACDONALD, *his wife*
LITTLE BOY BLUE
FOUR SHEEP
FOUR COWS
MISTRESS MARY
OLD WOMAN WHO LIVED IN A SHOE
EIGHT CHILDREN

TIME: *The present.*
SETTING: *Old MacDonald's farmyard. Large haystack is at right (could be painted on backdrop). Painting of farmhouse is on backdrop, left. Sign reading,* HELP WANTED, *is leaning against wall. Bench stands left.*
AT RISE: OLD MACDONALD *is raking, stopping often to wipe his brow with large red bandana. He faces audience, and leans on rake.*
OLD MACDONALD (*Singing to tune of "Old MacDonald Had a Farm"*):
Old MacDonald is my name
What a busy life!
On this farm I live and work
With my loving wife.
With hard work here (*Gestures left*)

And hard work there (*Gestures right*)

Here some work (*Gestures left*), there some work (*Gestures right*),

Everywhere some work, work.

Times are tough down on the farm,

Too much toil and strife.

(*Does a little dance step, tips hat, and bows low. Offstage, sounds of mooing cows and bleating sheep are heard.*)

MRS. MACDONALD (*Shouting off left*): Get out of there! Away from the corn! Out, out, I say! (MRS. MACDONALD *runs in, goes to* OLD MACDONALD.) Paw, come as quickly as you can! Those sheep of yours are getting into the meadow, and those pesky cows are on their way to the cornfield. You must chase them back where they belong! (OLD MACDONALD *shakes head, rolls up sleeves, and runs off left, as more bleating and mooing sounds are heard.* MRS. MACDONALD *faces audience and sings to tune of "Old MacDonald."*)

I am Old MacDonald's wife.

I am busy, too.

On this farm I live and work,

Sometimes feeling blue.

With hard work here (*Gestures left*)

And hard work there. (*Gestures right*)

Here some work (*Gestures left*), there

more work (*Gestures right*),

Everywhere it's work, work.

Times are tough down on the farm,

I know what to do!

    (*Twirls around, curtsies.* OLD MACDONALD *reenters, walking wearily and wiping his brow.*)

OLD MACDONALD: I declare, Maw, there is more work on this farm than one man can handle. I'm all tuckered out! (*Sits on bench*)

MRS. MACDONALD (*Patting his back*): There, there, Paw. I have a good idea. I think you need to advertise for some hired help to watch those sheep and cows. (*Picks up sign leaning against wall*) I made this sign yesterday. Read it and tell me what you think.

OLD MACDONALD (*Reading aloud*): "Help wanted. One hard-working boy to help watch sheep and cows. Good wages. Only dependable person need apply." (*Looks up; brightens*) Say, this just might work! I'll hang the sign over here and see what happens. (*Hangs sign up right*)

OLD MACDONALD *and* MRS. MACDONALD (*Facing audience, singing together*):
We don't want to leave this farm—
Here we want to stay.
If only we could find some help,
Life would be O.K.
With a little help here and a little help there,
Here some help, there some help
Everywhere some help, help.
Times are tough down on the farm,
It's all work, and no play.
(*They dance off left. LITTLE BOY BLUE enters right, blowing horn. He stops, reads sign.*)

LITTLE BOY BLUE (*Facing audience; reciting*):
I'm Little Boy Blue,
I could blow my horn. (*Blows horn*)
Keep the sheep from the meadow
And the cows from the corn.
And maybe sometimes when not watching the sheep,
I'd be under the haystack, catching some sleep!
(*OLD MACDONALD enters left.*)

OLD MACDONALD: Who are you, young fellow?

LITTLE BOY BLUE: My name is Little Boy Blue, and I'd like to apply for the job as sheep and cow watcher. If the sheep or cows tried to get out, I'd just blow my horn—like this. (*Blows horn loudly*)

OLD MACDONALD (*Enthusiastically*): I like a boy with ambition! The job is yours. Besides, I know your dear old mother could use the money. I hear she got laid off from her job at the Cinderella Shoe Factory. (*Points finger*) Now, just remember—keep those sheep out of the meadow and those cows out of the corn. (*Exits. LITTLE BOY BLUE walks up and down stage, blowing horn often, looking off left. He walks more and more slowly, rubbing eyes and yawning, and finally, pauses by hay-stack.)*

LITTLE BOY BLUE (*Wearily*): I didn't know this would be such hard work! Maybe I can just sit down here for a minute and take a little rest. (*Sits by haystack, yawns, then lies down, falls asleep. SHEEP enter left, form line at center, facing audience.*)

SHEEP (*Singing to the tune of "Old MacDonald"*):
This is Old MacDonald's farm,
Baa, baa, baa, baa, baa. (SHEEP *dance, stepping to the left and kicking up their legs.*)
And on this farm he keeps us sheep,
Baa, baa, baa, baa, baa. (SHEEP *step right and kick, as before.*)
With a "don't go here," and a "don't go there."
Here a no, there a no,
Everywhere it's no, no, no.
Let's just run away from here.
Baa, baa, baa, baa, baa.
(SHEEP *dance off right. COWS enter down left, form line at center, and sing to the tune of "Old MacDonald."*)

COWS:
This is Old MacDonald's farm,
Moo, moo, moo, moo, moo. (*All take dance step to left, kick.*)
And on this farm he keeps us cows,
Moo, moo, moo, moo, moo. (*Dance to right, kick*)
With a "don't go here," and a "don't go there."
Here a no, there a no,
Everywhere it's no, no.
Let's just run away from here.
Moo, moo, moo, moo, moo.
(COWS *dance off right.*)

MISTRESS MARY (*Shouting loudly from offstage right*): Get out of my garden! Shoo! Away with all of you! (SHEEP *and* COWS *run in from right and exit left. MISTRESS MARY follows, shouting. She faces audience and recites.*)
I'm Mistress Mary, quite contrary,
How does my garden grow?
Those sheep and cows have

Ruined my plants.

They really have to go!

(*Crosses left and calls loudly*) Mr. MacDonald, I want to talk to you! (OLD MACDONALD *hurries on, followed by* MRS. MACDONALD.)

OLD MACDONALD: What is going on? What's the matter?

MISTRESS MARY: I have told you many times to keep your sheep and cows out of my garden! They've trampled everything, and my garden is completely ruined. (*Cries noisily*) Boo-hoo-hoo!

OLD MACDONALD: Mistress Mary, I am very sad to hear your garden is ruined. Silver bells and cockle shells are very hard to grow.

MISTRESS MARY (*With disgust*): Forget the silver bells and cockle shells, Mr. MacDonald. I'm raising vegetables these days. With grocery prices so high, I've taken up organic gardening this year. Your sheep and cows have spoiled everything. (OLD MACDONALD *runs over to* LITTLE BOY BLUE, *picks up horn and blows it in his ear, then shakes him roughly.*)

OLD MACDONALD (*Angrily*): Wake up! Wake up, I say! (LITTLE BOY BLUE *jumps up, startled.*) Well, Boy Blue, a fine watchman you turned out to be! My sheep and cows have ruined Mistress Mary's garden, and it's all your fault. You're fired.

LITTLE BOY BLUE (*Sniffling*): I really am sorry, sir, but this job was much harder than I thought it would be. I don't think one person can handle all this work. (OLD WOMAN WHO LIVED IN A SHOE *enters right, followed by* EIGHT CHILDREN, *all crying.*)

OLD WOMAN (*Reciting and sobbing loudly at the end of each line*):

I'm the Old Woman Who Lived in a Shoe,

But we've been evicted—what shall we do?

We're all out of butter and all out of bread,

We have nothing left.

Not even a bed!

(CHILDREN *cry noisily, form a line at center.* MRS. MAC-DONALD *goes from one to another, hugging them.*)

CHILDREN (*Reciting*):

We are the Children Who Live in a Shoe,
So what if it's crowded, we like it, we do.
But now we are hungry, we need to be fed,
That's our sad story,
What more can be said?

(*All cry loudly again.*)

MRS. MACDONALD (*Soothingly*): There, there, don't cry! I think I have a plan that will make everyone happy. Paw, I want to talk to you in private. (*Leads* OLD MACDONALD *down left, whispers to him*)

OLD MACDONALD (*After a moment, excitedly*): Maw, that's a fine idea! Let's tell the others.

MRS. MACDONALD (*Crossing to* OLD WOMAN): Paw and I have this big house with lots of room in it. There are only the two of us living here. Why don't all of you move in with us? You children can watch the sheep and cows and keep them where they belong. And we could use the help. Everyone would have a home, and we could all—as they say in fairy tales—live happily ever after.

CHILDREN (*Gathering around* OLD WOMAN; *ad lib*): Say yes! Please say yes! Say we can do it! (*Etc.*)

OLD WOMAN (*With feeling; to* MACDONALDS): Bless your hearts, you dear, kind people! Of course we will come here to stay.

CHILDREN: Hooray! Hooray! (*All line up facing audience, link arms, and sing to the tune of "Old MacDonald."*)

ALL:

We'll live on MacDonald's farm,
Happy we will be.
We'll share the work and share the fun,
One cheerful family.
With a big smile here and a big smile there,
Here a smile, there a smile,
Everywhere a smile, smile. (SHEEP *dance in, form line.*)

SHEEP: With a baa, baa here and a baa, baa there,

Here a baa, there a baa,
Everywhere a baa, baa. (COWS *dance in, form line.*)
COWS: With a moo, moo here and a moo, moo there,
Here a moo, there a moo,
Everywhere a moo, moo.
ALL (*Singing*):
We'll live on MacDonald's farm,
You (*Point to each other*), and you (*Point to each other*) and
me. (*Point to themselves, then dance off right, singing last
song as they exit. Curtain*)

THE END

Production Notes

OLD MACDONALD'S FARMYARD FOLLIES

Characters: 2 male; 3 female; 16 male and female.
Playing Time: 10 minutes.
Costumes: Old MacDonald and Little Boy Blue wear straw hats and overalls.
Sheep and Cows may wear paper masks and tails and jogging suits or
sweatshirts in appropriate colors. Others wear modern dress.
Properties: Rake; handkerchiefs; horn.
Setting: Old MacDonald's farm. Backdrop has large haystack painted on right
side, painting of farmhouse on left. Exits are right and left. Bench is at left.
Sign reading, HELP WANTED, is leaning against wall.
Lighting: No special effects.

Wanted: One Fair Damsel

by Sherrie Dunham

A clever maiden rescues a knight in distress . . . .

Characters

HENRIETTA
GORDON, *her brother*
HORACE HURLEY, *vassal to the King*
DRAGON
SIR KENT, *the knight*
THREE WOMEN

SCENE 1

TIME: *One morning, once upon a time.*
SETTING: *A country road in the kingdom of King Wendell. A tree stands at corner of stage.*
AT RISE: HENRIETTA *and* GORDON *cross stage from left to right, as though walking on road.* HENRIETTA *is reading a large book titled,* HOME CASTLE REPAIR MANUAL, *and lags behind* GORDON.
GORDON (*Annoyed*): Henrietta! Will you get your nose out of that book and hurry up? We'll never reach the castle, at this rate.
HENRIETTA (*Absently*): One more chapter, Gordon.
GORDON (*Mimicking*): One more chapter, Gordon. You said that four chapters and two miles ago. What's so interesting? *The Joy of Jousting? Stringing Your Own Crossbow for Fun and Profit?*

HENRIETTA (*Holding up book*): *The Home Castle Repair Manual.*

GORDON (*Sarcastically*): Oh, splendid! And where will that get you?

HENRIETTA (*Smiling*): Anywhere I want to, Gordon.

GORDON: Take my advice, Henrietta, and . . . (GORDON *is interrupted by sound of pots and pans banging offstage.* THREE WOMEN, *carrying pots, pans, rolling pins, and spoons, enter right and walk rapidly across stage.*)

1ST WOMAN (*Shaking rolling pin*): Enough is enough. I quit!

2ND WOMAN: I'm with you.

3RD WOMAN (*Banging pots together*): Let's take our kettles and get out of here!

GORDON: What happened? Why are you all leaving?

1ST WOMAN (*Shaking rolling pin in* GORDON's *face as she speaks*): Because he's eating us out of house and home—that's why. (GORDON *backs away.*)

HENRIETTA: Who?

2ND WOMAN: The dragon—that greedy, green, over-sized lizard! I've "Yorkshired" my last pudding for him.

1ST WOMAN: I've "creped" my last Suzette.

3RD WOMAN: I've "shished" my last kabob. Come on, let's go. (THREE WOMEN *hike away angrily, exit left.*)

GORDON (*Yelling after them*): But, wait! Wait! (*Turns to* HENRIETTA) Did they say dragon? At this time of year? I thought they'd all gone south for the winter. And what was that about shish kabob?

HENRIETTA (*Shrugging*): I don't know. (HORACE HURLEY, *carrying sign and hammer, enters right and walks over to tree.* HENRIETTA *points to him.*) Maybe he knows something. (HENRIETTA *and* GORDON *approach* HORACE *from behind;* HENRIETTA *taps him on shoulder.*) Excuse me, sir.

HORACE (*Startled; jumping slightly*): Yes, miss? Horace Hurley, vassal to His Majesty, at your service. (*He bows.*)

HENRIETTA: What can you tell us about the dragon?

HORACE (*Holding hand over heart*): The dragon! Good heavens! He invaded King Wendell's castle last week and took Sir Kent prisoner.

GORDON: Who's Sir Kent?

HORACE: Sir Kent is King Wendell's chief knight. The dragon took him to an old tower north of here. King Wendell is most upset. He commanded me to post this sign. (HORACE *turns sign, which reads,* WANTED: ONE FAIR DAMSEL TO RESCUE KNIGHT IN DISTRESS—INQUIRE AT CASTLE ON LEFT.)

HENRIETTA (*Reading*): "Wanted: One Fair Damsel to Rescue Knight in Distress—Inquire at Castle on Left."

GORDON: I don't understand why it asks for a fair damsel. Why not call out your strongest men?

HORACE: Because this is no ordinary dragon. He's a gourmet.

GORDON: A gour-who?

HENRIETTA: A gourmet—someone who loves fine food, Gordon. If you'd read a little more, you'd know that.

HORACE (*Groaning*): Yes, food, food—that's the ransom to be paid for Sir Kent's release, and our women have revolted. They've all tried their best recipes on the dragon—to no avail.

GORDON: So you need a damsel in a hurry.

HORACE: Yes, one who can cook.

GORDON (*To* HENRIETTA): That lets you out, sis. (HENRIETTA *jabs* GORDON *with her elbow.*)

HORACE: The dragon has an enormous appetite. He gobbles up everything we give him, but he won't release Sir Kent.

HENRIETTA (*Matter-of-factly*): Of course not.

HORACE: What do you mean?

HENRIETTA: If everyone keeps feeding him, he'll never let the knight go. This dragon's eating like a king. Hm-m-m. Let's examine the alternatives. There are other ways to rescue Sir Kent, you know.

GORDON: Look out! She has an idea.

HENRIETTA (*To* HORACE): Would you show us the way to the dragon's tower?

HORACE (*Nervously*): Yes, but the dragon guards it by day and sleeps there at night, and I'm allergic to dragons. The smoke makes me sneeze.

HENRIETTA (*In a commanding voice*): Horace, lead us to the dragon! Do it for Sir Kent! For the King! For your kingdom!

HORACE (*Looking meekly at* HENRIETTA): Oh, dear. (*Reluctantly*) O.K., I'll show you the way.
HENRIETTA: Good. Meet us here tonight. We're going dragon hunting! (*Curtain*)

* * * * *

SCENE 2

TIME: *That evening.*
SETTING: *Tower with drawbridge is center. Hidden behind tower is stepladder or stool. To right of tower is jail, which is hidden by a sheet. Key hangs in back of jail. Sir Kent hides behind sheet.*
AT RISE: DRAGON *is sleeping in front of the drawbridge.* HORACE, HENRIETTA, *and* GORDON, *carrying a duffel bag, enter from left.*
GORDON (*Stopping at edge of stage*): Are we almost there? (*Wipes brow*) This bag's heavy.
HORACE: Almost.
GORDON: What's in here, anyway? Rocks?
HENRIETTA: No, just the necessities. I suppose the heaviest thing is the boat anchor.
GORDON: Are you calling a boat anchor a necessity? Where's the boat?
HENRIETTA: You missed the boat, Gordon.
GORDON: Very funny.
HORACE (*Suddenly*): Sh-h-h! There he is. (HORACE *points to* DRAGON.)
GORDON: Good grief! What an ugly beast!
HORACE: Exactly. Now, if you'll excuse me . . . (HORACE *starts to leave, but* GORDON *grabs him and pulls him back.*)
GORDON: Stick around, Horace. The fun's just beginning.
HORACE (*Biting his nails*): Oh, dear.
GORDON: So what's the plan, sis? You can't get in through the drawbridge unless you take Old Fire-and-Smoke in with you. I don't see another way in.

HENRIETTA: According to my manual, most of these old towers have air shafts. All I have to do is climb up to the top, lower a rope, and slide down the rope into the shaft.

GORDON: But how will you get to the top in the first place?

HENRIETTA (*Digging into duffel bag*): With this. (*She brings out cardboard anchor with rope tied to it.*) I'll swing the anchor up to the top of the tower. (*She demonstrates by swinging it over her head a couple of times, lasso style.*) When it catches, I'll climb up the rope.

GORDON (*Pointing to* DRAGON): And I suppose Sleeping Beauty over there will sleep through all the noise you make.

HENRIETTA: Yes, he will, because we're going to plug his ears first.

GORDON: How are we going to do that?

HENRIETTA (*Digging through bag again*): I have a pair of earplugs in here somewhere. Hm-m. I was sure I put them in. (*Annoyed*) I can't find them.

HORACE: That's a shame. Maybe we can't stay here after all. (*Turns to leave, but* GORDON *and* HENRIETTA *pull him back again*) But how can we keep the dragon from waking up if you can't find the earplugs?

HENRIETTA: Someone will just have to hold the dragon's ears while I climb. (HORACE *and* GORDON *look horrified.*)

GORDON: Do you expect me to do that?

HENRIETTA: No, I'll need you to give me a boost up the rope. I thought Horace would do it. (HORACE *is speechless. He points to himself in disbelief and shakes his head "no" vigorously.* HENRIETTA *and* GORDON *answer by giving an exaggerated nod "yes.")*

GORDON: Cheer up, Horace, old boy. After all, if the dragon wakes up, it won't matter who's holding his ears. He'll probably kill us all, anyway.

HORACE: Thanks. That's comforting. (HENRIETTA *and* GORDON *push him toward* DRAGON. HORACE *hesitates.*)

HENRIETTA: For Sir Kent!

HORACE: For the King, I know. I'm going. (HORACE *tiptoes up behind* DRAGON. *Grimacing, he slowly puts his hands up to* DRAGON's *ears. He screws his eyes shut, but* DRAGON *keeps sleeping.*)

GORDON (*To* HENRIETTA): Whew! He made it!

HENRIETTA: Come on. (GORDON *drops bag and follows* HENRIETTA, *who carries rope and anchor. They go to left side of tower and disappear behind it. From behind tower,* HENRIETTA *throws anchor over top of tower, then shouts.*) Give me a boost.

GORDON (*From behind tower*): Ouch! Get off my toe!

HENRIETTA: Get your toe out of the way!

GORDON (*Yelling*): Now you're on my hand!

HENRIETTA: Well, give me a push! (HENRIETTA *climbs up stepladder behind tower, until her head shows above top of tower. She yells to* GORDON.) I made it!

GORDON: Good. Do you see an air shaft?

HENRIETTA (*Looking around*): Yes, yes, there is one. I'll be back in a few minutes if I find Sir Kent. Wait there. (GORDON *remains behind tower, and* HENRIETTA's *head disappears from view as she pretends to climb down rope. In a few seconds she emerges at right of the tower, next to jail. She dusts herself off and calls out.*) Sir Kent! Yoo-hoo! Sir Kent! Where are you?

SIR KENT (*From behind sheet*): I'm in here.

HENRIETTA (*Lifting sheet*): Well, that's a peculiar place to be.

SIR KENT (*Grouchily*): I'll try to be more choosy the next time I'm taken prisoner.

HENRIETTA (*Annoyed*): A little touchy today, aren't you? That's gratitude for you! Perhaps you prefer the dragon's company. (*She starts to exit.*)

SIR KENT: Oh, no! No! Don't go! Look, I'm sorry. Just get me out of here, would you? (*Points behind jail*) I think the keys are back there.

HENRIETTA: Well, all right. (*She unlocks the jail, and* SIR KENT *comes out.*)

SIR KENT: You're not what I'd pictured as a rescue party, but I am pleased to see you. *Very* pleased. (HENRIETTA *beams and fluffs her hair.*) How did you get past the dragon?

HENRIETTA: No time to explain now. We're not safe yet. (HEN-RIETTA *takes* SIR KENT's *hand*.) Come on. (*They go behind the right side of the tower, then pretend to climb down through the air shaft.* HENRIETTA *climbs up and down the ladder first.* SIR KENT *follows her. As soon as* SIR KENT *is out of sight, he unhooks the anchor.* HENRIETTA, GORDON *and* SIR KENT *enter from left side of tower.* HENRIETTA *carries rope and anchor.*)

GORDON: Psst! Horace. We've rescued Sir Kent. Come on, but be careful. (HORACE *nods and carefully removes his hands from the* DRAGON's *ears. But just as the* DRAGON's *ears are uncovered,* HORACE *sneezes.*)

HORACE (*Loudly and with exaggerated motion*): Aah-chew!

DRAGON (*Waking*): Grrrrrrr! (DRAGON *leaps to his feet and starts chasing* HORACE *around the stage, roaring.*)

HORACE (*Holding his back while running*): Ouch! He's burning me! Help! Oh! Ouch!

HENRIETTA (*Shouting*): Quickly, Gordon, take the other end of this rope. (HENRIETTA *and* GORDON *each take one end of rope, then run in circles around* DRAGON, *wrapping rope around him.* HORACE *hides behind* SIR KENT. GORDON *and* HENRIETTA *try to hold* DRAGON, *as he struggles.*)

GORDON: Ouch! Watch out for his flames.

HENRIETTA: Sir Kent! Get the box that's inside my bag over there. (SIR KENT *goes to bag and takes out large box labeled,* BICARBONATE OF SODA *in bold letters, then gives it to* HENRI-ETTA. *She pretends to pour contents of box into* DRAGON's *mouth.* DRAGON *sputters and coughs, then stops struggling.*)

GORDON (*Gleefully*): You've done it! You put out his fire with the bicarbonate of soda.

HENRIETTA (*Casually*): Oh, it was nothing. A little chemistry, a little genius.

HORACE (*Crossing to* DRAGON): Now he's just a harmless windbag. (DRAGON *snaps at* HORACE, *who jumps behind* SIR KENT *again.*)

HENRIETTA: You know, he probably had the worst case of heartburn in history. If you'd eaten everything he ate, you'd be breathing fire, too. (*To* DRAGON) Aren't you ashamed of yourself? (DRAGON *hangs his head.*)

SIR KENT (*To* HENRIETTA): How did you happen to bring along the bicarbonate of soda in the first place?

GORDON: Henrietta burns everything she cooks. We take it with us everywhere for our own survival!

HENRIETTA: Quiet, Gordon.

GORDON: Well, you read all the time. I wish you'd read a cookbook.

SIR KENT: I think she's remarkable—and surely the finest damsel in all the kingdom. (*To* HENRIETTA) You would do me great honor if you'd give me your hand in marriage.

HENRIETTA: Marriage? (*Thinks for a moment*) Can you cook?

SIR KENT: I love to cook.

HENRIETTA: Well, maybe I'll marry you. But we'll have to wait awhile.

SIR KENT: Why?

HENRIETTA: I have a lot of reading to do. This dragon's going to need a good lawyer. (*Quick curtain*)

THE END

Production Notes

WANTED: ONE FAIR DAMSEL

Characters: 3 male; 4 female; 1 male or female.

Playing Time: 15 minutes.

Costumes: Medieval attire. Women wear aprons. Green costume with tail for Dragon.

Properties: Book labeled HOME CASTLE REPAIR MANUAL; pots; pans; spoons; rolling pins; hammer; sign reading WANTED: ONE FAIR DAMSEL TO RESCUE KNIGHT IN DISTRESS INQUIRE AT CASTLE ON LEFT; a small duffel bag; long piece of rope attached to a cardboard cutout of a boat anchor; a large cardboard cutout of a key; a large box labeled BICARBONATE OF SODA.

Setting: Scene 1: A country road in King Wendell's kingdom. Tree stands at one corner of stage. Scene 2: Tower with drawbridge is center. Hidden behind tower is stepladder or stool. To right of tower is jail, which is hidden by a sheet. Key hangs in back of jail.

The Miss Witch Contest

by Val R. Cheatham

"Mirror, mirror, on the wall, who's the meanest of them all?"

Characters

WICKED QUEEN
MIRROR, *life-size looking glass*
WITCH OF THE FOREST
WITCH OF THE WEST
VAMPIRA
DR. JEKYLL
MR. HYDE
SKELETON
HEADLESS HORSEMAN
FRANKENSTEIN'S MONSTER

SCENE 1

SETTING: *Throne room of an old castle. A tattered throne is upstage to one side; a bench stands on opposite side. Simulated coat of arms and pictures of former kings and queens hang crookedly on backdrop. Everything appears dusty and worn.*
AT RISE: MIRROR *is near throne.*
WICKED QUEEN (*Entering; carrying broom*): Home, at last! I'm getting too old to go riding around on this open-air broom. (*To* MIRROR) You're the cause of my misery, Magic Mirror. You and that simple Snow White! (*Primps in front of* MIRROR) Just think . . . at one time I was number one! A queen! Fairest in the land! Now look at me: a Wicked Witch! Oh, well. (*Primps some more*) At least I'm still tops in one category: *Meanest* witch in the land. Isn't that right, Mirror?

MIRROR (*Reciting*):
> To hear the things I have to say,
> You must ask me the proper way.

WICKED QUEEN: Oh, no! You're not still on that ridiculous rhyme bit, are you? Oh, all right . . . . (*Recites*)
> Mirror, mirror on the wall,
> Who's the meanest witch of all?

MIRROR:
> Oh, yes, my queen, you're mean and vile
> And wicked to the core.
> But, meanness seems to be in style
> For many, many more!

WICKED QUEEN (*Shocked*): What? Are there others meaner than I? This cannot be! If I can't be the "fairest in the land," then I must be the meanest. Who are they? Tell me the names of these other amateur meanies.

MIRROR:
> Do you prefer the list to be
> By age or alphabetically?

WICKED QUEEN: Just hold on! There can't be that many witches meaner than I.

MIRROR:
> This flying on your broom at night
> Has kept you out of tune.
> Just watch a TV serial
> Some weekday afternoon.

WICKED QUEEN: By "mean" I'm not talking about poor television, mothers who yell at Little League umpires, or even teachers who keep students in after school. I mean vile, rotten meanness. The kind that goes right down to the bone. (WITCH OF THE FOREST *and* WITCH OF THE WEST *enter.*)

WITCH OF THE FOREST (*Cackling*): You must be talking about me, dearie, the Witch of the Forest. Anybody who has read Hansel and Gretel knows how mean I am.

WITCH OF THE WEST: No, she's talking about me, the Witch of the West. Just ask anybody who has been in Oz—the Scarecrow, the Tinman, or that Cowardly Lion—how mean I am.

WICKED QUEEN: I'm not talking about either of you. I'm just trying to get some straight answers from this moronic Mirror.

WITCH OF THE FOREST: Don't try to kid us, Wicked Queen.

WITCH OF THE WEST: You're on that "Who's the meanest witch of all?" kick again, aren't you?

WITCH OF THE FOREST (*Preening*): Now, if you really want to see a mean witch, take a look at me! My story has been well-known for centuries: I lured Hansel and Gretel into the forest, caged them in my kitchen, and would have served them up for supper if that sneaky little Hansel hadn't crept up on my blind side. You say you think you know mean, eh? Have someone pop *you* into the oven. That makes you meeeeeeeeean!

WITCH OF THE WEST: You call that mean? Ha! You have to *hate* to be mean. I had the perfect life in Oz until that Dorothy blew in from Kansas. I hate all girls named Dorothy . . . and dogs called Toto, too!

VAMPIRA (*Entering, speaking in manner of Dracula*): Good eeeev-en-ing! I am Vampira. My beauty draws others close to me, then I bite them on the neck! (*Shows fangs*) What is meaner than that?

WICKED QUEEN: What is this—an open house? One minute I'm home, alone—tired and exhausted after a long night's romp—and the next minute I have a house full of uninvited, and unwelcome, guests!

WITCH OF THE FOREST: Don't be so uppity, dearie. You may have been a queen once, but you're not one any more.

WITCH OF THE WEST: You were dethroned, remember? And all it took was Snow White and the Seven Shrimps.

WICKED QUEEN: So what if I'm no longer a beautiful queen, fairest in the land? I still have my Magic Mirror. Tell them, Mirror, who is the meanest witch of all?

MIRROR:
To hear the things I have to say,
You must ask the proper way.

WITCH OF THE FOREST (*To* WICKED QUEEN): If you want to find out who really is meanest in the land, don't ask a mirror.

WITCH OF THE WEST: Right. You should have a contest, with judges and everything.

WICKED QUEEN: A contest? A Meanest in the Land Contest? I like the idea! We can have it right here.

WITCH OF THE WEST: Just make sure none of the judges is named Dorothy. I hate all people named Dorothy!

VAMPIRA: Ah ... competition! I love it. I'm always out for blood!

WITCH OF THE FOREST: I know! We can ask Snow White to be the judge. (*Snickers*) After all, she is the "fairest" in the land. (*All laugh, except* WICKED QUEEN.)

WICKED QUEEN: That's not funny! But, go ahead and have your laughs. You'll all be crying when I win!

ALL (*Ad lib*): No! No you won't! Says who? I'm going to win, not you! (*Etc.*)

MIRROR:
Ladies, ladies! All be still!
Quiet! Quiet! Please!
Only monsters of the world
Should judge your destinies.
I'll summon them for twelve tonight
And act as your M.C.
The "meanest" shall be chosen—

WICKED QUEEN: That's me!

WITCH OF THE FOREST: Me!

WITCH OF THE WEST: Me!

VAMPIRA: Me!

WICKED QUEEN: O.K. Twelve, midnight. I don't know about the rest of you, but I have to get ready. (*Moves to exit*)

ALL (*Ad lib*): Let's go! I do, too. Yes, good idea! (*Etc. All exit, except for* WICKED QUEEN.)

WICKED QUEEN (*Moving to* MIRROR *and primping*): Just think! I'll be meanest in the land. A queen again! Tell me, Mirror, how are you going to fix it so I'll win?

MIRROR:
To hear the things I have to say,
You must ask the proper way.
(WICKED QUEEN *groans. Quick curtain*)

* * * * *

SCENE 2

TIME: *Midnight.*

SETTING: *Same as Scene 1.*

AT RISE: MIRROR, *center. On bench are* DR. JEKYLL, MR. HYDE, *and* FRANKENSTEIN'S MONSTER. SKELETON *stands nearby. Galloping noise is heard from offstage, and* HEADLESS HORSEMAN *enters, carrying a prop "head" under one arm.*

HEADLESS HORSEMAN: We can begin. I'm here right on time. This is the right place, isn't it? (FRANKENSTEIN'S MONSTER *stands and lurches forward in threatening manner.* MR. HYDE *snarls, bays, and paws at the air.*)

DR. JEKYLL: Monsters, please. Settle down! All of you! It's just the Headless Horseman.

SKELETON: Yeah, yeah, we know. (*To* HEADLESS HORSEMAN) Hey, Headless Horseman! My mother used to tell me I'd forget my head if it weren't fastened on. What did your mother tell you? (*Snickers*)

HEADLESS HORSEMAN: My mother always told me . . . well, usually she said . . . What was the question again?

SKELETON: Forget it. Just get over here, have a seat and get ready to judge the Meanest Witch in the Land Contest.

MR. HYDE: Tell me, Dr. Jekyll. Why is the contest for witches only? I'm just as mean as any witch—I'd be the winner, for sure.

DR. JEKYLL: You're right, Mr. Hyde. Not many people are as mean as you. Of course, I'm pretty mean myself, probably from having to live with the likes of you.

MR. HYDE: Don't blame me! It's all your fault. If you hadn't been playing doctor with your chemistry set, you wouldn't have me as a problem.

MIRROR:
Gentlemen, gentlemen . . .
If you please! Places, everyone.
The quest for meanest in the land has,
As of now, begun.

(*Witches enter and line up at right.*)
From deep within the forest,
Comes contestant number one . . .
(WITCH OF THE FOREST *parades slowly to center during*
MIRROR's *introduction. This procedure is followed by all
others as they are introduced.*)
She lured small children to her home
With sweets and cinnamon.
WITCH OF THE FOREST (*With mock sweetness*): Any little boy
or girl is welcome in my gingerbread house. Eat as much as
you want—and then come take a tour of my oven! (*Cackles
and moves back to right*)
MIRROR:
The Witch of the West is next in line.
She's wicked, rank, and vile.
She ruled throughout the land of Oz
In surly, brazen style.
WITCH OF THE WEST: Someday I'll fly over the rainbow, and
travel down the yellow brick road, and when I do, I'll get that
sweet, little Dorothy—and her dog, Toto, too!
MIRROR:
Next we have Vampira
With her deadly, biting curse.
Those who spend some time with her,
Will end up in a hearse.
VAMPIRA: Good eeeev-en-ing! I just want to be alone . . . with
you! (*Shows fangs*)
MIRROR:
Now we have the Wicked Queen
Who put Snow White to sleep.
Once the "fairest in the land,"
Now she makes skin creep.
WICKED QUEEN: Is there any Prince Charming who wants to
wake me up with a kiss? (*Puckers lips and looks at judges.
They all look away in disgust.*)
MIRROR:
Now then, Judges, make your choice.

It's time to take a stand.
Step right up and cast your vote
For Meanest in the Land.

(*Judges write votes on slip of paper, then line up facing* MIRROR, *and one by one place slips under* MIRROR *to simulate casting ballot. As each does so, he returns to bench.*)

WICKED QUEEN: Come on, Witches, we should get to vote, too. After all, we know better than anybody what "mean" is. (*Witches line up, also, and simulate voting.*) Now, Mirror, tell us who won.

MIRROR:
To hear the things I have to say,
You must ask the proper way—

ALL (*Ad lib*): Come on! Give us a break! Let's hear it. (*Etc.*)

MIRROR:
All right, all right. Here it is.
Get ready for a cry.
The contest for the meanest
Has ended in a tie.
Each cast a vote. Each won a vote.
It's simple as can be.
It doesn't take a genius
To figure it out for me.

WITCH OF THE FOREST (*Incredulous*): What? Do you mean each of us voted for ourselves?

WITCH OF THE WEST: All of us?

VAMPIRA: Even the judges?

MIRROR: That's true.

WICKED QUEEN: What a mean thing to do. (*Chuckles*) But, what can we expect?

WITCH OF THE FOREST (*Nodding*): Yes, we're despicable.

WITCH OF THE WEST (*Laughing*): Not to mention detestable.

WICKED QUEEN (*Chuckling*): Let's try it again next year! (*Curtain*)

THE END

Production Notes

THE MISS WITCH CONTEST

Characters: 5 male; 4 female; 1 male or female for Mirror.

Playing Time: 15 minutes.

Costumes: Witches wear traditional black outfits with peaked hats, and carry brooms. Vampira wears black cape with high collar, has ashen face, and long, straight black hair with widow's peak. Skeleton, black body suit with white skull and bones sewn onto it. Frankenstein's Monster, oversize suit (to make arms appear longer, hold sticks with gloves on them extending out of sleeves), clogs (or other thick-soled shoes that add height), and elongated head (created by cutting the bottom off a large plastic jug, adding hair and scars to it, and slipping it on top of actor's head). Dr. Jekyll, formal attire, with top hat. Mr. Hyde, ordinary suit, face covered with hair. Headless Horseman, suit extending over head, and extra "head" that he carries (a jack-o'-lantern, or manikin's head). Mirror, large box covering actor from head to knees, with an oval section in the front covered with foil or painted to resemble mirror.

Properties: Brooms, ballots (slips of paper).

Setting: Castle interior (throne room), with throne upstage at one side, bench, at opposite side. Furniture appears dusty, worn, and tattered. Simulated coat of arms and portraits hang crookedly on backdrop.

Lighting: No special effects.

A Tree Grows in Hollywood

by Steven Pricone

"For the best movie about trees, the winner is . . ."

Characters
ANNOUNCER, *offstage voice*

Hosts:
ROBIN WILLOW
GOLDIE ASPEN

Nominees:
CHARLES OAKTREE
ROBERT REDWOOD
MARLEE MAPLE
JOHNNY APPLE
CHERRY SEINFELD
JOE BANANA
WILLOW MAYS
BARBARA WALNUT
SPRUCE WILLIS
ELM TREE FUDD
FOREST STUMP
ASH LEE

Presenters:
MICK JUNIPER
ROSEANNE BARK
WINONA CEDAR
CLINT BEECHWOOD
SYCAMORE STALLONE
JOANNE WOOD

RAIN FOREST, *two actors*
SPRUCE SPRINGSTEEN, *poet*

Film actors:
TILLY
TED
NILA
PATTI

Rap Artists:
SNOOP DOGWOOD
ICE TREE
QUEEN LA LEAFA

TIME: *The present.*
SETTING: *"Tree Academy Awards" ceremony in Hollywood. Podiums with microphones are down right and left. Backdrop depicts large golden tree trophy, above which reads:* TENTH

ANNUAL TREE ACADEMY AWARDS. *Actual tree trophies are stored behind both podiums.*

AT RISE: *Stage is dimly lit.*

ANNOUNCER (*From microphone offstage*): Ladies and gentlemen! Welcome to the Earth's Tenth Annual Tree Academy Awards! And now, the hosts of tonight's telecast: Robin Willow and Goldie Aspen! (*Lights come up on ROBIN WILLOW, entering left, and GOLDIE ASPEN, entering right. Stagehands may wave signs reading APPLAUSE at this point, and throughout ceremony, as needed. WILLOW and ASPEN walk center, join hands, bow, then go to podium, right.*)

WILLOW (*Jovially*): Thank you! (*Peering at audience*) It's good to see so many tree lovers out there. I'm sure there are even more watching at home, Goldie

ASPEN (*In a perky voice*): Trees do so much for us, Robin. Which is why we're here to honor those great "woody perennial plants," (*Giggles*) or, *trees*, that we love so well.

WILLOW: Did you say *trees?* Why, that's the title of our first big musical number! (*At that, music swells as nominees, dressed as various trees, enter from either side of stage. They stand in rows, center, or dance about while singing a song about trees [see Production Notes]. Nominees then bow and exit.*)

ASPEN (*Gushing*): How beautiful! What's next, Robin?

WILLOW: It's time for the Tallest Tree Award. Let's give a big hand to our presenters, Roseanne Bark and Mick Juniper! (*They applaud as ROSEANNE BARK, holding envelope, and MICK JUNIPER enter and walk to podium, left.*)

BARK (*To JUNIPER*): Mick, I want to say how honored I am to be here. Trees are so special.

JUNIPER: Absolutely, Roseanne. And I'm happy to announce the nominees in the category of Tallest Tree. They are: (*As nominees' names are called throughout play, each enters and walks center.*) Charles Oaktree . . . Robert Redwood . . . and Marlee Maple. (*Nominees join hands.*)

BARK (*Fumbling with envelope*): And the winner is . . .

JUNIPER: I'm so nervous, Roseanne!

BARK (*Reading, excitedly*): Robert Redwood! (OAKTREE *and* MAPLE *hug* REDWOOD, *then exit as* REDWOOD *goes to left podium.* JUNIPER *takes trophy from behind podium, hands it to* REDWOOD.)

REDWOOD (*Emotionally*): I'd like to thank the soil, the sun, and tall trees everywhere. Redwoods, also called sequoias, are native to Oregon and California. We grow to be very tall, and may reach over 300 feet and live to be over 2,000 years old. My relative, the giant sequoia, can live over 4,000 years. Only the bristle cone pine tree lives longer than that! (*Holds up trophy; triumphantly*) Thank you for *this!* (*He exits with* BARK *and* JUNIPER.)

ASPEN: And now, nominated for Best Movie About Trees, a clip from *The Rain Forest.* (*Lights dim, then come up on* TILLY *and* TED, *as they stumble on left, dressed in hiking gear.* TED *holds a map.*)

TILLY (*Breathlessly*): What a hike! (*Looking about*) Well, the rain forest should be around here someplace.

TED (*Consulting map*): According to our map, it should be right about—(*Pointing right*) there! (*At that,* RAIN FOREST, *carrying opened umbrellas, enters right.*)

TILLY (*Crestfallen*): Two trees? Is that all there is to the rain forest?

1ST TREE (*Wistfully*): We used to be tropical forests that covered most of the equator.

2ND TREE: Great, deep forests that gave the earth twenty percent of its oxygen and provided shelter for millions of animals.

1ST TREE: Rain forests house a treasure of plant life, some that can be used as medicine.

TED (*Nodding*): But we've cut and burned millions of acres of rain forest, all in the name of greed. Now, many of the animals that once lived in these forests are threatened with extinction.

TILLY (*Dramatically; to audience*): Oh, no! How could we? (*Lights dim as* TED, TILLY, *and* RAIN FOREST *exit. Lights up on* WILLOW *and* ASPEN *down right.*)

ASPEN (*Applauding*): Wow!

WILLOW: And now, a special treat. A poem about trees, read by the winner of last year's Tree of the Year: Spruce Springsteen!

(*Lights up center as* SPRUCE SPRINGSTEEN *enters, poses dramatically, and recites appropriate poem, such as Joyce Kilmer's "Trees." Afterwards, lights dim as* SPRUCE *exits.*)

ASPEN: Wasn't that moving, Robin? (WILLOW *nods enthusiastically.*) I am pleased to introduce the presenters for Best Fruit Tree: Winona Cedar and Clint Beechwood! (*All clap as* WINONA CEDAR, *carrying envelope, and* CLINT BEECHWOOD *enter, go to podium left.*)

CEDAR (*Peering out into audience*): There are so many trees out there I can't see the forest.

BEECHWOOD (*Chuckles*): Nominees for Best Fruit Tree are Johnny Apple . . . Cherry Seinfeld . . . Joe Banana.

CEDAR (*Tearing open envelope and reading*): And the winner for Best Fruit Tree is Johnny Apple! (*All applaud as* CHERRY *and* BANANA *congratulate* APPLE, *then exit while* APPLE *goes down left, accepts award, and steps up to microphone.*)

APPLE (*Visibly moved*): When I think of all the delicious fruit trees in the world and realize that the Academy selected me— (*Emotionally, holding trophy aloft*) You like trees . . . you *really* like trees! (*Struggles for control*) I want to thank my producer (*Looks up, pauses*), the bees and butterflies for pollinating my blossoms, the birds for eating those pesky caterpillars, the rain, and of course, the sun. Thank you so much! (*He exits.*)

ASPEN (*Sincerely*): And I like apples. . . . I *really* like apples.

WILLOW: And now, a scene from another film nominated for Best Movie About Trees: *Interview with a Tree*, starring Willow Mays. (*Lights up center on* WILLOW MAYS, *who looks out at audience, then begins to weep. After a pause,* NILA *enters and goes to him.*)

NILA (*With concern*): Why are you weeping, Willow?

WILLOW MAYS (*Sobbing*): I can't help it. It's in my genes.

NILA: Don't cry. Be proud! You give shade, you shelter small animals, and you prevent topsoil erosion. (*Tenderly*) And you're beautiful.

WILLOW MAYS (*Suddenly cheerful*): You're right, Nila. I *am* special.

NILA (*Nodding*): In fact, I'm so proud to know you, I think I'll carve my initials into your bark (*Pointing to his trunk*) right here.

WILLOW MAYS (*Screeching*): No! Stop! (*Shuddering*) When you cut into my bark, germs and bugs can get in and make me sick. It could even kill me!

NILA (*Recoiling*): Oh! I'm sorry! (*Upset*) I didn't realize! (*Hysterically*) How was I to know? (*Suddenly rushes off, right, with* WILLOW MAYS *following quickly behind her. Lights dim, then come up right.*)

WILLOW: What a scene! That really hit home, didn't it, Goldie?

ASPEN (*Emphatically*): Incredible! Our next presenters are for the category of Nicest Bark. Allow me to introduce Joanne Wood and Sycamore Stallone. (JOANNE WOOD *and* SYCAMORE STALLONE, *carrying envelope, enter and stand behind podium, left.*)

SYCAMORE: We all know that bark protects the tree and also serves as home for insects, who in turn, provide food for a variety of animals.

WOOD: Nominated in the category of Nicest Bark, we have Barbara Walnut . . . Spruce Willis . . . Elm Tree Fudd.

SYCAMORE (*Opening envelope; reading*): And the winner is Barbara Walnut! (SPRUCE WILLIS *and* ELM TREE FUDD *hug* BARBARA WALNUT, *then exit as she goes to receive award. She gives dazzling smile to audience, then pulls reading glasses, note from pocket.*)

WALNUT (*Putting on glasses; reading*): My thank-you list is so long: carbon dioxide, my cambium layer, xylem, phloem. (*Sighs, looks up from list, takes off glasses*) But I'd like especially to thank all you people out there who respect trees and care for them. (*Waving trophy*) Thank you! (*She exits.*)

ASPEN: And now, a rap number from the movie, *Trees in the Hood.*

WILLOW: To perform it, who better than . . . Snoop Dogwood, Ice Tree, and Queen La Leafa. (*They applaud. Lights come up center as rappers enter and strike a pose. Rap may be accompanied by taped music, or sung a cappella. Rappers dance as they sing.*)

SNOOP DOGWOOD:
  All over this earth we stand so tall,
  We give you food and that ain't all!
ICE TREE:
  We give you air so you can breathe,
  We give you shade beneath our leaves!
RAPPERS (*Together*): Trees!
QUEEN LA LEAFA:
  Our roots keep dirt from washing away,
  We clean your air every single day.
  Our arms hold nests for tiny birds.
DOGWOOD:
  Did we say who does this?
ICE TREE:
  Did we tell you the word?
RAPPERS (*Together*): Trees! (*Sriking pose*) Peace! (*Music stops abruptly. Lights dim as* RAPPERS *exit.*)
WILLOW (*Clapping*): Wow! Who said they don't write songs like they used to?
ASPEN: Why, I think you just did, Robin. (*Giggles*) Now, for our final clip, nominated for Best Movie About Trees, a scene from *Forest Stump.* (*Lights come up center on* FOREST STUMP, *holding a small box, and* ASH LEE. *They stand, facing each other.*)
FOREST (*Slowly*): Momma always said, "Life is like a box of termites—you have to get rid of those little things that eat away at you."
ASH: I know what you mean, Forest. What bothers me is the way people waste paper: newspaper, homework paper, test paper, computer paper. (*Exasperated*) Don't they know paper comes from trees? (PATTI *enters left, carrying recycling bin.*)
PATTI: I know that paper comes from you both, so I respect that. I try not to waste paper *and* I recycle it.
FOREST *and* ASH (*Ad lib, excitedly*): You do? Finally, someone who understands! (*Etc. Lights dim.* PATTI, FOREST, *and* ASH *exit.*)
ASPEN (*Taking envelope from behind podium*): Ladies and gentlemen. The moment we've all been waiting for.

WILLOW (*Excitedly*): The award for the Best Movie About Trees?

ASPEN: That's right, Robin! (*Tears at envelope*) And the winner is . . . (*Reading*) *The Rain Forest!* (ASPEN *and* WILLOW *applaud wildly as* RAIN FOREST, TILLY, *and* TED *enter and join them at podium.* WILLOW *reaches behind podium for trophy and hands it to* RAIN FOREST.)

RAIN FOREST (*Together*): In honor of trees everywhere, we accept this award. Thank you! (ASPEN *and* WILLOW *step up to microphone.*)

ASPEN *and* WILLOW (*Waving to audience; together*): Thank you and good night! (*Lights may come up center as all reenter and sing reprise of first musical number. Curtain*)

THE END

Production Notes

A TREE GROWS IN HOLLYWOOD

Characters: 17 male; 11 female; 3 male or female for Rainforest and Announcer.

Playing Time: 25 minutes.

Costumes: Trees wear hats, brown leotards and tights with leaves attached. Tilly and Ted wear hiking gear; Nila and Patti, casual dress.

Properties: Cards inside envelopes; two umbrellas; note; reading glasses; small box; recycling bin; four golden tree-shaped trophies.

Setting: The stage of the Tree Academy Awards. Painted backdrop of large golden tree trophy, over which reads TENTH ANNUAL TREE ACADEMY AWARDS. Hosts' podium and microphone are down right; stored behind it are trophy and envelope with card. Presenters' podium and microphone are down left; stored behind it are three trophies.

Lighting: Spotlights down right and left, if desired. Lights, center, come up and dim as noted in text.

Sound: Song about trees or spoof of popular song (i.e., "We Are the World, We Are the Trees"); taped rap music to accompany lyrics used in text.